The Quran With Tafsir Ibn Kathir Part 5 of 30: An Nisaa 024 To An Nisaa 147

The Quran With Tafsir Ibn Kathir
Part 5 of 30:
An Nisaa 024 To An Nisaa 147

With
Arabic Script, Transliteration of Arabic, Meaning in English
and Ibn Kathir's Abridged Tafsir (Explanation)

Muhammad Saed Abdul-Rahman
BSc, DipHE

© Muhammad Saed Abdul-Rahman, 2012
ISBN 978-1-86179-840-4

All Rights reserved

British Library Cataloguing in Publication Data. A Catalogue record for this book is available from the British Library

Designed, Typeset and produced by:
MSA Publication Limited, 4 Bello Close, Herne Hill,
London SE24 9BW
United Kingdom

Cover design: Houriyah Abdul-Rahman

TABLE OF CONTENTS

TABLE OF CONTENTS V

PRELUDE XI
   OPENING SERMAN XI
   OUR MISSION XII
   BIOGRAPHY OF HAFIZ IBN KATHIR (701 H - 774 H) XII
      Ibn Kathir's Teachers xii
      Ibn Kathir's Students xiii
      Ibn Kathir's Books xiii
      Ibn Kathir's Death xiv

PREFACE XV
   ABOUT THIS BOOK XV
   PERFORMING PROSTRATION WHILE READING THE QUR'AN XV

PART 5 FULL ARABIC TEXT 1

INTRODUCTION TO CHAPTER (SURAH) 4: AN-NISAA (THE WOMEN) 12
   IBN KATHIR'S INTRODUCTION 12
      Virtues of Surat An-Nisa, A Madinan Surah 12

CHAPTER (SURAH) 4: AN-NISAA (THE WOMEN), VERSES 024-147 13
   Surah: 4 Ayah: 24 13
      Tafsir Ibn Kathir 13
         Forbidding Women Already Married, Except for Female Slaves 13
         The Permission to Marry All Other Women 14
         Prohibiting the Mut`ah of Marriage 14
   Surah: 4 Ayah: 25 15
      Tafsir Ibn Kathir 16
         Marrying a Female Slave, if One Cannot Marry a Free Woman 16
         The Slave Girl's Punishment for Adultery is Half that of a Free Unmarried Woman 17
   Surah: 4 Ayah: 26, Ayah: 27 & Ayah: 28 18
      Tafsir Ibn Kathir 18
   Surah: 4 Ayah: 29, Ayah: 30 & Ayah: 31 19
      Tafsir Ibn Kathir 19
         Prohibiting Unlawfully Earned Money 19
         The Option to Buy or Sell Before Parting, is Part of `Mutual Consent' in Trading 20
         Forbidding Murder and Suicide 20
         Minor Sins Will be Pardoned if One Refrains from Major Sins 22
         The Seven Destructive Sins 22
   Surah: 4 Ayah: 32 25
      Tafsir Ibn Kathir 25
         Do Not Wish for the Things Which Allah has Made Some Others to Excel In 25

Surah: 4 Ayah: 33 26
   Tafsir Ibn Kathir 26
Surah: 4 Ayah: 34 27
   Tafsir Ibn Kathir 28
      Qualities of the Righteous Wife 28
      Dealing with the Wife's Ill-Conduct 29
      When the Wife Obeys Her Husband, Means of Annoyance Against Her are Prohibited ... 31
Surah: 4 Ayah: 35 31
   Tafsir Ibn Kathir 31
      Appointing Two Arbitrators When the Possibility of Estrangement Between Husband and Wife Occurs 31
Surah: 4 Ayah: 36 32
   Tafsir Ibn Kathir 32
      The Order to Worship Allah Alone and to Be Dutiful to Parents 32
      The Right of the Neighbor 33
      Being Kind to Slaves and Servants 35
      Allah Does Not Like the Arrogant 37
Surah: 4 Ayah: 37, Ayah: 38 & Ayah: 39 37
   Tafsir Ibn Kathir 38
      The Censure of Stingy Behavior 38
Surah: 4 Ayah: 40, Ayah: 41 & Ayah: 42 40
   Tafsir Ibn Kathir 41
      Allah Wrongs Not Even the Weight of a Speck of Dust 41
      Will Punishment be Diminished for the Disbelievers 41
      What Does `Great Reward' Mean 42
      Our Prophet will be a Witness Against, or For his Ummah on the Day of Resurrection, When the Disbelievers Will Wish for Death 43
Surah: 4 Ayah: 43 44
   Tafsir Ibn Kathir 44
      The Prohibition of Approaching Prayer When Drunk or Junub 44
      Causes of Its Revelation 45
      Description of Tayammum 47
      The Reason behind allowing Tayammum 50
Surah: 4 Ayah: 44, Ayah: 45 & Ayah: 46 50
   Tafsir Ibn Kathir 51
      Chastising the Jews for Choosing Misguidance, Altering Allah's Words, and Mocking Islam 51
Surah: 4 Ayah: 47 & Ayah: 48 52
   Tafsir Ibn Kathir 53
      Calling the People of the Book to Embrace the Faith, Warning them Against Doing Otherwise 53
      Ka`b Al-Ahbar Embraces Islam Upon Hearing this Ayah [4:47] 53
      Allah Does not Forgive Shirk, Except After Repenting From it 54
Surah: 4 Ayah: 49, Ayah: 50, Ayah: 51 & Ayah: 52 55
   Tafsir Ibn Kathir 56

Table of Contents

      Chastising and Cursing the Jews for Claiming Purity for Themselves and Believing in Jibt and Taghut..56
      Disbelievers Are not Better Guided Than Believers..57
Surah: 4 Ayah: 53, Ayah: 54 & Ayah: 55... 58
   Tafsir Ibn Kathir 58
      The Envy and Miserly Conduct of the Jews 58
Surah: 4 Ayah: 56 & Ayah: 57.. 59
   Tafsir Ibn Kathir 60
      The Punishment of Those Who Disbelieve in Allah's Books and Messengers 60
      The Wealth of the Righteous; Paradise and its Joy..60
Surah: 4 Ayah: 58 61
   Tafsir Ibn Kathir 61
      The Command to Return the Trusts to Whomever They Are Due......................................61
      The Order to Be Just 62
Surah: 4 Ayah: 59 63
   Tafsir Ibn Kathir 63
      The Necessity of Obeying the Rulers in Obedience to Allah..63
      The Necessity of Referring to the Qur'an and Sunnah for Judgment 65
Surah: 4 Ayah: 60, Ayah: 61, Ayah: 62 & Ayah: 63... 66
   Kathir's Tafsir..67
      Referring to Other than the Qur'an and Sunnah for Judgment is Characteristic of Non-Muslims 67
      Chastising the Hypocrites 67
Surah: 4 Ayah: 64 & Ayah: 65.. 68
   Tafsir Ibn Kathir 69
      The Necessity of Obeying the Messenger 69
      One Does not Become a Believer Unless He Refers to the Messenger for Judgment and Submits to his Decisions 69
Surah: 4 Ayah: 66, Ayah: 67, Ayah: 68, Ayah: 69 & Ayah: 70... 71
   Tafsir Ibn Kathir 72
      Most People Disobey What They Are Ordered...72
      Whoever Obeys Allah and His Messenger Will Be Honored by Allah 72
      The Reason Behind Revealing this Honorable Ayah 73
Surah: 4 Ayah: 71, Ayah: 72, Ayah: 73 & Ayah: 74.. 74
   Tafsir Ibn Kathir 75
      The Necessity of Taking Necessary Precautions Against the Enemy 75
      Refraining from Joining Jihad is a Sign of Hypocrites..75
      The Encouragement to Participation in Jihad 76
Surah: 4 Ayah: 75 & Ayah: 76.. 77
   Tafsir Ibn Kathir 77
      Encouraging Jihad to Defend the Oppressed...77
Surah: 4 Ayah: 77, Ayah: 78 & Ayah: 79... 78
   Tafsir Ibn Kathir 79
      The Wish that the Order for Jihad be Delayed 79
      There is No Escaping Death 80

The Hypocrites Sense a Bad Omen Because of the Prophet! 80
Surah: 4 Ayah: 80 & Ayah: 81.. 81
    Tafsir Ibn Kathir 82
        Obeying the Messenger is Obeying Allah 82
        The Foolishness of the Hypocrites 83
Surah: 4 Ayah: 82 & Ayah: 83... 83
    Tafsir Ibn Kathir 84
        The Qur'an is True 84
        The Prohibition of Disclosing Unreliable and Uninvestigated News 85
Surah: 4 Ayah: 84, Ayah: 85, Ayah: 86 & Ayah: 87... 86
    Tafsir Ibn Kathir 87
        Allah Commands His Messenger to Perform Jihad 87
        Inciting the Believers to Fight 87
        Interceding for a Good or an Evil Cause 89
        Returning the Salam, With a Better Salam 90
Surah: 4 Ayah: 88, Ayah: 89, Ayah: 90 & Ayah: 91... 91
    Tafsir Ibn Kathir 93
        Censuring the Companions for Disagreeing over the Hypocrites who Returned to Al-Madinah Before Uhud 93
        Combatants and Noncombatants 94
Surah: 4 Ayah: 92 & Ayah: 93... 95
    Tafsir Ibn Kathir 96
        The Ruling Concerning Killing a Believer by Mistake 96
        Warning Against Intentional Murder 99
        Will the Repentance of those who Commit Intentional Murder be Accepted 100
Surah: 4 Ayah: 94 101
    Tafsir Ibn Kathir 101
        Greeting with the Salam is a Sign of Islam 101
Surah: 4 Ayah: 95 & Ayah: 96... 103
    Tafsir Ibn Kathir 104
        The Mujahid and those Who Do not Join Jihad are Not the Same, [and Jihad is Fard Kifayah] 104
Surah: 4 Ayah: 97, Ayah: 98, Ayah: 99 & Ayah: 100... 106
    Tafsir Ibn Kathir 107
        The Prohibition of Residing Among the Disbelievers While Able to Emigrate 107
Surah: 4 Ayah: 101 110
    Tafsir Ibn Kathir 110
        Salat Al-Qasr, Shortening the Prayer 110
Surah: 4 Ayah: 102 111
    Tafsir Ibn Kathir 112
        The Description of The Fear Prayer 112
        The Reason behind Revealing this Ayah 112
Surah: 4 Ayah: 103 & Ayah: 104... 114
    Tafsir Ibn Kathir 114
        The Order for Ample Remembrance After the Fear Prayer 114

Table of Contents

    The Encouragement to Pursue the Enemy Despite Injuries 115
Surah: 4 Ayah: 105, Ayah: 106, Ayah: 107, Ayah: 108 & Ayah: 109 115
    Tafsir Ibn Kathir 116
        The Necessity of Referring to What Allah has Revealed for Judgement 116
Surah: 4 Ayah: 110, Ayah: 111, Ayah: 112 & Ayah: 113 118
    Tafsir Ibn Kathir 119
        The Encouragement to Seek Allah's Forgiveness, and Warning those who Falsely Accuse Innocent People 119
Surah: 4 Ayah: 114 & Ayah: 115 120
    Tafsir Ibn Kathir 120
        Righteous Najwa, Secret Talk 120
        The Punishment for Contradicting and Opposing the Messenger and Following a Path Other than That of the Believers 121
Surah: 4 Ayah: 116, Ayah: 117, Ayah: 118, Ayah: 119, Ayah: 120, Ayah: 121 & Ayah: 122 122
    Tafsir Ibn Kathir 124
        Shirk Shall not be Forgiven, in Reality the Idolators Worship Shaytan 124
        The Reward of Righteous Believers 126
Surah: 4 Ayah: 123, Ayah: 124, Ayah: 125 & Ayah: 126 126
    Tafsir Ibn Kathir 127
        Success is Only Achieved by Performing Righteous Deeds, not Wishful Thinking 127
        Ibrahim is Allah's Khalil 130
Surah: 4 Ayah: 127 131
    Tafsir Ibn Kathir 131
        The Ruling Concerning Female Orphans 131
Surah: 4 Ayah: 128, Ayah: 129 & Ayah: 130 133
    Tafsir Ibn Kathir 133
        The Ruling Concerning Desertion on the Part of the Husband 133
        Meaning of "Making Peace is Better 134
Surah: 4 Ayah: 131, Ayah: 132, Ayah: 133 & Ayah: 134 136
    Tafsir Ibn Kathir 137
        The Necessity of Taqwa of Allah 137
Surah: 4 Ayah: 135 138
    Tafsir Ibn Kathir 138
        Commanding Justice and Conveying the Witness for Allah 138
Surah: 4 Ayah: 136 139
    Tafsir Ibn Kathir 140
        The Order to Have Faith after Believing 140
Surah: 4 Ayah: 137, Ayah: 138, Ayah: 139 & Ayah: 140 140
    Tafsir Ibn Kathir 141
        Characteristics of the Hypocrites and Their Destination 141
Surah: 4 Ayah: 141 143
    Tafsir Ibn Kathir 143
        Hypocrites Wait and Watch what Happens to Muslims 143

Surah: 4 Ayah: 142 & Ayah: 143 .... *144*
    Tafsir Ibn Kathir 145
        The Hypocrites Try to Deceive Allah and Sway Between Believers and Disbelievers 145
Surah: 4 Ayah: 144, Ayah: 145, Ayah: 146 & Ayah: 147 .... *147*
    Tafsir Ibn Kathir 148
        The Prohibition of Wilayah with the Disbelievers 148
        The Hypocrites and the Friends of Disbelievers are in the Lowest Depth of the Fire, Unless they Repent 149

PRELUDE

Opening Serman

Indeed, all praise is due to Allah. We praise Him and seek His help and forgiveness. We seek refuge with Allah from our soul's evil and our wrong doings. He whom Allah guides, no one can misguide; and he whom He misguides, no one can guide

I bear witness that there is no (true) god except Allah – alone without a partner, and I bear witness that Muhammad (peace and blessings of Allah be upon him) is His 'abd (servant) and messenger.

يَٰٓأَيُّهَا ٱلَّذِينَ ءَامَنُوا۟ ٱتَّقُوا۟ ٱللَّهَ حَقَّ تُقَاتِهِۦ وَلَا تَمُوتُنَّ إِلَّا وَأَنتُم مُّسْلِمُونَ ﴿١٠٢﴾

O you who believe! Fear Allâh (by doing all that He has ordered and by abstaining from all that He has forbidden) as He should be feared. (Obey Him, be thankful to Him, and remember Him always), and die not except in a state of Islâm (as Muslims (with complete submission to Allâh)).

يَٰٓأَيُّهَا ٱلنَّاسُ ٱتَّقُوا۟ رَبَّكُمُ ٱلَّذِى خَلَقَكُم مِّن نَّفْسٍ وَٰحِدَةٍ وَخَلَقَ مِنْهَا زَوْجَهَا وَبَثَّ مِنْهُمَا رِجَالًا كَثِيرًا وَنِسَآءً ۚ وَٱتَّقُوا۟ ٱللَّهَ ٱلَّذِى تَسَآءَلُونَ بِهِۦ وَٱلْأَرْحَامَ ۚ إِنَّ ٱللَّهَ كَانَ عَلَيْكُمْ رَقِيبًا ﴿١﴾

O mankind! Be dutiful to your Lord, Who created you from a single person (Adam), and from him (Adam) He created his wife (Hawwâ (Eve)) and from them both He created many men and women; and fear Allâh through Whom you demand (your mutual rights), and (do not cut the relations of) the wombs (kinship). Surely, Allâh is Ever an All-Watcher over you.

يُصْلِحْ لَكُمْ أَعْمَٰلَكُمْ وَيَغْفِرْ لَكُمْ ذُنُوبَكُمْ ۗ وَمَن يُطِعِ ٱللَّهَ وَرَسُولَهُۥ فَقَدْ فَازَ فَوْزًا عَظِيمًا ﴿٧١﴾

He will direct you to do righteous good deeds and will forgive you your sins. And whosoever obeys Allâh and His Messenger (peace be upon him), he has indeed achieved a great achievement (i.e. he will be saved from the Hell-fire and will be admitted to Paradise).

Indeed, the best speech is Allah's Book and the best guidance is Muhammad's () guidance. The worst affairs (of religion) are those innovated (by people), for every such innovation is an act of misguidance leading to the Fire

Our Mission

Our mission is to gather in one place, for the English-speaking public, all relevant information needed to make the Qur'an more understandable and easier to study. This book tries to do this by providing the following:

1. The Arabic Text for those who are able to read Arabic
2. Transliteration of the Arabic text for those who are unable to read the Arabic script. This will give them a sample of the sound of the Qur'an, which they could not otherwise comprehend from reading the English meaning.
3. The meaning of the qur'an (translated by Dr. Muhammad Taqi-ud-Din Al-Hilali, Ph.D. and Dr. Muhammad Muhsin Khan)
4. Explanation (abridged Tafsir) by Ibn Kathir (translated by Safi-ur-Rahman al-Mubarakpuri)

We hope that by doing this an ordinary English-speaker will be able to pick up a copy of this book and study and comprehend The Glorious Qur'an in a way that is acceptable to the understanding of the Rightly-guided Muslim Ummah (Community).

Biography of Hafiz Ibn Kathir (701 H - 774 H)

By the Honored Shaykh `Abdul-Qadir Al-Arna'ut, may Allah protect him.

He is the respected Imam, Abu Al-Fida', `Imad Ad-Din Isma il bin 'Umar bin Kathir Al-Qurashi Al-Busrawi - Busraian in origin; Dimashqi in training, learning and residence.

Ibn Kathir was born in the city of Busra in 701 H. His father was the Friday speaker of the village, but he died while Ibn Kathir was only four years old. Ibn Kathir's brother, Shaykh Abdul-Wahhab, reared him and taught him until he moved to Damascus in 706 H., when he was five years old.

Ibn Kathir's Teachers

Ibn Kathir studied Fiqh - Islamic jurisprudence - with Burhan Ad-Din, Ibrahim bin `Abdur-Rahman Al-Fizari, known as Ibn Al-Firkah (who died in 729 H). Ibn Kathir heard Hadiths from `Isa bin Al-Mutim, Ahmad bin Abi Talib, (Ibn Ash-Shahnah) (who died in 730 H), Ibn Al-Hajjar, (who died in 730 H), and the Hadith narrator of Ash-Sham (modern day Syria and surrounding areas); Baha Ad-Din Al-Qasim bin Muzaffar bin `Asakir (who died in 723 H), and Ibn Ash-Shirdzi, Ishaq bin Yahya Al-Ammuddi, also known as `Afif Ad-Din, the Zahiriyyah Shaykh who died in 725 H, and Muhammad bin Zarrad. He remained with Jamal Ad-Din, Yusuf bin Az-Zaki AlMizzi who died in 724 H, he benefited from his knowledge and also married his daughter. He also read with Shaykh Al-Islam, Taqi Ad-Din Ahmad bin `Abdul-Halim bin `Abdus-Salam bin Taymiyyah who died in 728 H. He also read with the Imam Hafiz and historian Shams Ad-Din, Muhammad bin Ahmad bin Uthman bin Qaymaz Adh-Dhahabi, who died in 748 H. Also, Abu Musa Al-Qarafai, Abu Al-Fath Ad-Dabbusi and

'Ali bin `Umar As-Suwani and others who gave him permission to transmit the knowledge he learned with them in Egypt.

In his book, Al-Mu jam Al-Mukhtas, Al-Hafiz Adh-Dhaliabi wrote that Ibn Kathir was, "The Imam, scholar of jurisprudence, skillful scholar of Hadith, renowned Fagih and scholar of Tafsir who wrote several beneficial books."

Further, in Ad-Durar Al-Kdminah, Al-Hafiz Ibn Hajar AlAsqalani said, "Ibn Kathir worked on the subject of the Hadith in the areas of texts and chains of narrators. He had a good memory, his books became popular during his lifetime, and people benefited from them after his death."

Also, the renowned historian Abu Al-Mahasin, Jamal Ad-Din Yusuf bin Sayf Ad-Din (Ibn Taghri Bardi), said in his book, AlManhal As-Safi, "He is the Shaykh, the Imam, the great scholar `Imad Ad-Din Abu Al-Fida'. He learned extensively and was very active in collecting knowledge and writing. He was excellent in the areas of Fiqh, Tafsfr and Hadith. He collected knowledge, authored (books), taught, narrated Hadith and wrote. He had immense knowledge in the fields of Hadith, Tafsir, Fiqh, the Arabic language, and so forth. He gave Fatawa (religious verdicts) and taught until he died, may Allah grant him mercy. He was known for his precision and vast knowledge, and as a scholar of history, Hadith and Tafsir."

Ibn Kathir's Students

Ibn Hajji was one of Ibn Kathir's students, and he described Ibn Kathir: "He had the best memory of the Hadith texts. He also had the most knowledge concerning the narrators and authenticity, his contemporaries and teachers admitted to these qualities. Every time I met him I gained some benefit from him."

Also, Ibn Al-`Imad Al-Hanbali said in his book, Shadhardt Adh-Dhahab, "He is the renowned Hafiz `Imad Ad-Din, whose memory was excellent, whose forgetfulness was miniscule, whose understanding was adequate, and who had good knowledge in the Arabic language." Also, Ibn Habib said about Ibn Kathir, "He heard knowledge and collected it and wrote various books. He brought comfort to the ears with his Fatwas and narrated Hadith and brought benefit to other people. The papers that contained his Fatwas were transmitted to the various (Islamic) provinces. Further, he was known for his precision and encompassing knowledge."

Ibn Kathir's Books

1 - One of the greatest books that Ibn Kathir wrote was his Tafsir of the Noble Qur'an, which is one of the best Tafsir that rely on narrations [of Ahadith, the Tafsir of the Companions, etc.]. The Tafsir by Ibn Kathir was printed many times and several scholars have summarized it.

2- The History Collection known as Al-Biddyah, which was printed in 14 volumes under the name Al-Bidayah wanNihdyah, and contained the stories of the Prophets and previous nations, the Prophet's Seerah (life story) and Islamic history until his time. He also added a book Al-Fitan, about the Signs of the Last Hour.

3- At-Takmil ft Ma`rifat Ath-Thiqat wa Ad-Du'afa wal Majdhil which Ibn Kathir collected from the books of his two Shaykhs Al-Mizzi and Adh-Dhahabi; Al-Kdmal and Mizan Al-Ftiddl. He added several benefits regarding the subject of Al-Jarh and AtT'adil.

4- Al-Hadi was-Sunan ft Ahadith Al-Masdnfd was-Sunan which is also known by, Jami` Al-Masdnfd. In this book, Ibn Kathir collected the narrations of Imams Ahmad bin Hanbal, Al-Bazzar, Abu Ya`la Al-Mawsili, Ibn Abi Shaybah and from the six collections of Hadith: the Two Sahihs [Al-Bukhari and Muslim] and the Four Sunan [Abu Dawud, At-Tirmidhi, AnNasa and Ibn Majah]. Ibn Kathir divided this book according to areas of Fiqh.

5-Tabaqat Ash-Shaf iyah which also contains the virtues of Imam Ash-Shafi.

6- Ibn Kathir wrote references for the Ahadith of Adillat AtTanbfh, from the Shafi school of Fiqh.

7- Ibn Kathir began an explanation of Sahih Al-Bukhari, but he did not finish it.

8- He started writing a large volume on the Ahkam (Laws), but finished only up to the Hajj rituals.

9- He summarized Al-Bayhaqi's 'Al-Madkhal. Many of these books were not printed.

10- He summarized `Ulum Al-Hadith, by Abu `Amr bin AsSalah and called it Mukhtasar `Ulum Al-Hadith. Shaykh Ahmad Shakir, the Egyptian Muhaddith, printed this book along with his commentary on it and called it Al-Ba'th Al-Hathfth fi Sharh Mukhtasar `Ulum Al-Hadith.

11- As-Sfrah An-Nabawiyyah, which is contained in his book Al-Biddyah, and both of these books are in print.

12- A research on Jihad called Al-Ijtihad ft Talabi Al-Jihad, which was printed several times.

Ibn Kathir's Death

Al-Hafiz Ibn Hajar Al-Asgalani said, "Ibn Kathir lost his sight just before his life ended. He died in Damascus in 774 H." May Allah grant mercy upon Ibn Kathir and make him among the residents of His Paradise.

… Preface

PREFACE

In the name of Allah, Most Gracious, Most Merciful.

About this book

The previous publication of this book included some background information to the chapters of the Qur'an by an Islamic scholar known as Abul Ala Maududi. This information was used to shed more light on the chapters by giving a summery of why each chapter was given its name, It's period of revelation and the circumstances surrounding its revelatiom. However, some Muslims objected to the inclusion of the contributions of Maududi.

In this new publication of Tafsir Ibn Kathir, we have removed all traces of the contribution of Abul Ala Maududi. Personally, I do not know the reasons for the objections to Maududi, but this work concerns only the tafsir of Ibn Kathir, so we have not included anything from Maududi in it. We have also corrected all the typing and formatting errors found in the previous publication. We have not alter the structure of the book. The reader is still able to read the full Arabic Text of the thirty Parts of the Qur'an and follow its meanings in the English language. The transliteration of the Arabic text should also give the reader a taste of the sound of the original Arabic.

May Almighty Allah accept this effort from us, and make it a source of blessings for us in this world and in the next. I bear witness that there is none worthy of worship but Allah and I bear witness that Muhammad (may the peace and blessings of Allah be upon him) is the slave and messenger of Allah.

Performing Prostration While Reading the Qur'an

Question:

Could you please give a list of the Qur'anic verses when a prostration is recommended? What happens if we read these verses and not perform a prostration?

A. Jalil

Answer:

There are 15 verses in the Qur'an that mention prostration before God Almighty as a good action by God-fearing believers. Therefore, it is strongly recommended to perform such a prostration when we read or listen to any of these verses, whether during prayer or in any situation.

Some scholars are of the view that even if one has not performed ablution, one should prostrate oneself. These verses are given here, starting with the Arabic title of the surah which is followed by two numbers, the first indicating the surah, and the second indicating the verse,: Al-Araf 7: 206; Al-Raad 13: 15; Al-Nahl 16: 50; Al-Isra 17: 109; Maryam 19: 58; Al-Hajj 22: 18 & 22: 77; Al-Furqan 25: 60; Al-Naml 27: 26;

Al-Sajdah 32: 15; Saad 38: 25; Fussilat 41: 38; Al-Najm 53: 62; Al-Inshiqaq 84: 21 and Al-Alaq 96: 19.

If you do not perform a prostration when you read or listen to any of these verses, you have done badly because you miss out on the reward of performing a prostration for God. You incur no sin and violate no divine order.

Reference:
http://archive.arabnews.com/?page=5&section=0&article=97811&d=1&m=7&y=2007

The Glorious Qur'an Juz' 5 (Part 5):
Chapter (Surah) 4: An-Nisaa (The Women) 024
To Chapter (Surah) 4: An-Nisaa (The Women) 147

PART 5 FULL ARABIC TEXT

Chapter (Surah) 4: An-Nisaa 024-147

۞ وَٱلْمُحْصَنَٰتُ مِنَ ٱلنِّسَآءِ إِلَّا مَا مَلَكَتْ أَيْمَٰنُكُمْ ۖ كِتَٰبَ ٱللَّهِ عَلَيْكُمْ ۚ وَأُحِلَّ لَكُم مَّا وَرَآءَ ذَٰلِكُمْ أَن تَبْتَغُوا۟ بِأَمْوَٰلِكُم مُّحْصِنِينَ غَيْرَ مُسَٰفِحِينَ ۚ فَمَا ٱسْتَمْتَعْتُم بِهِۦ مِنْهُنَّ فَـَٔاتُوهُنَّ أُجُورَهُنَّ فَرِيضَةً ۚ وَلَا جُنَاحَ عَلَيْكُمْ فِيمَا تَرَٰضَيْتُم بِهِۦ مِنۢ بَعْدِ ٱلْفَرِيضَةِ ۚ إِنَّ ٱللَّهَ كَانَ عَلِيمًا حَكِيمًا ﴿٢٤﴾ وَمَن لَّمْ يَسْتَطِعْ مِنكُمْ طَوْلًا أَن يَنكِحَ ٱلْمُحْصَنَٰتِ ٱلْمُؤْمِنَٰتِ فَمِن مَّا مَلَكَتْ أَيْمَٰنُكُم مِّن فَتَيَٰتِكُمُ ٱلْمُؤْمِنَٰتِ ۚ وَٱللَّهُ أَعْلَمُ بِإِيمَٰنِكُم ۚ بَعْضُكُم مِّنۢ بَعْضٍ ۚ فَٱنكِحُوهُنَّ بِإِذْنِ أَهْلِهِنَّ وَءَاتُوهُنَّ أُجُورَهُنَّ بِٱلْمَعْرُوفِ مُحْصَنَٰتٍ غَيْرَ مُسَٰفِحَٰتٍ وَلَا مُتَّخِذَٰتِ أَخْدَانٍ ۚ فَإِذَآ أُحْصِنَّ فَإِنْ أَتَيْنَ بِفَٰحِشَةٍ فَعَلَيْهِنَّ نِصْفُ مَا عَلَى ٱلْمُحْصَنَٰتِ مِنَ ٱلْعَذَابِ ۚ ذَٰلِكَ لِمَنْ خَشِىَ ٱلْعَنَتَ مِنكُمْ ۚ وَأَن تَصْبِرُوا۟ خَيْرٌ لَّكُمْ ۗ وَٱللَّهُ غَفُورٌ رَّحِيمٌ ﴿٢٥﴾ يُرِيدُ ٱللَّهُ لِيُبَيِّنَ لَكُمْ وَيَهْدِيَكُمْ سُنَنَ ٱلَّذِينَ مِن قَبْلِكُمْ وَيَتُوبَ عَلَيْكُمْ ۗ وَٱللَّهُ عَلِيمٌ حَكِيمٌ ﴿٢٦﴾ وَٱللَّهُ يُرِيدُ أَن يَتُوبَ عَلَيْكُمْ وَيُرِيدُ ٱلَّذِينَ يَتَّبِعُونَ ٱلشَّهَوَٰتِ أَن تَمِيلُوا۟ مَيْلًا عَظِيمًا ﴿٢٧﴾ يُرِيدُ ٱللَّهُ أَن يُخَفِّفَ عَنكُمْ ۚ وَخُلِقَ ٱلْإِنسَٰنُ ضَعِيفًا ﴿٢٨﴾ يَٰٓأَيُّهَا ٱلَّذِينَ ءَامَنُوا۟ لَا تَأْكُلُوٓا۟ أَمْوَٰلَكُم بَيْنَكُم بِٱلْبَٰطِلِ إِلَّآ أَن تَكُونَ تِجَٰرَةً عَن تَرَاضٍ مِّنكُمْ ۚ وَلَا تَقْتُلُوٓا۟ أَنفُسَكُمْ ۚ إِنَّ ٱللَّهَ كَانَ بِكُمْ

رَحِيمًا ۝ وَمَن يَفْعَلْ ذَٰلِكَ عُدْوَٰنًا وَظُلْمًا فَسَوْفَ نُصْلِيهِ نَارًا ۚ وَكَانَ ذَٰلِكَ عَلَى ٱللَّهِ يَسِيرًا ۝ إِن تَجْتَنِبُوا۟ كَبَآئِرَ مَا تُنْهَوْنَ عَنْهُ نُكَفِّرْ عَنكُمْ سَيِّـَٔاتِكُمْ وَنُدْخِلْكُم مُّدْخَلًا كَرِيمًا ۝ وَلَا تَتَمَنَّوْا۟ مَا فَضَّلَ ٱللَّهُ بِهِ بَعْضَكُمْ عَلَىٰ بَعْضٍ ۚ لِّلرِّجَالِ نَصِيبٌ مِّمَّا ٱكْتَسَبُوا۟ ۖ وَلِلنِّسَآءِ نَصِيبٌ مِّمَّا ٱكْتَسَبْنَ ۚ وَسْـَٔلُوا۟ ٱللَّهَ مِن فَضْلِهِۦٓ ۗ إِنَّ ٱللَّهَ كَانَ بِكُلِّ شَىْءٍ عَلِيمًا ۝ وَلِكُلٍّ جَعَلْنَا مَوَٰلِىَ مِمَّا تَرَكَ ٱلْوَٰلِدَانِ وَٱلْأَقْرَبُونَ ۚ وَٱلَّذِينَ عَقَدَتْ أَيْمَٰنُكُمْ فَـَٔاتُوهُمْ نَصِيبَهُمْ ۚ إِنَّ ٱللَّهَ كَانَ عَلَىٰ كُلِّ شَىْءٍ شَهِيدًا ۝ ٱلرِّجَالُ قَوَّٰمُونَ عَلَى ٱلنِّسَآءِ بِمَا فَضَّلَ ٱللَّهُ بَعْضَهُمْ عَلَىٰ بَعْضٍ وَبِمَآ أَنفَقُوا۟ مِنْ أَمْوَٰلِهِمْ ۚ فَٱلصَّٰلِحَٰتُ قَٰنِتَٰتٌ حَٰفِظَٰتٌ لِّلْغَيْبِ بِمَا حَفِظَ ٱللَّهُ ۚ وَٱلَّٰتِى تَخَافُونَ نُشُوزَهُنَّ فَعِظُوهُنَّ وَٱهْجُرُوهُنَّ فِى ٱلْمَضَاجِعِ وَٱضْرِبُوهُنَّ ۖ فَإِنْ أَطَعْنَكُمْ فَلَا تَبْغُوا۟ عَلَيْهِنَّ سَبِيلًا ۗ إِنَّ ٱللَّهَ كَانَ عَلِيًّا كَبِيرًا ۝ وَإِنْ خِفْتُمْ شِقَاقَ بَيْنِهِمَا فَٱبْعَثُوا۟ حَكَمًا مِّنْ أَهْلِهِۦ وَحَكَمًا مِّنْ أَهْلِهَآ إِن يُرِيدَآ إِصْلَٰحًا يُوَفِّقِ ٱللَّهُ بَيْنَهُمَآ ۗ إِنَّ ٱللَّهَ كَانَ عَلِيمًا خَبِيرًا ۝ وَٱعْبُدُوا۟ ٱللَّهَ وَلَا تُشْرِكُوا۟ بِهِۦ شَيْـًٔا ۖ وَبِٱلْوَٰلِدَيْنِ إِحْسَٰنًا وَبِذِى ٱلْقُرْبَىٰ وَٱلْيَتَٰمَىٰ وَٱلْمَسَٰكِينِ وَٱلْجَارِ ذِى ٱلْقُرْبَىٰ وَٱلْجَارِ ٱلْجُنُبِ وَٱلصَّاحِبِ بِٱلْجَنۢبِ وَٱبْنِ ٱلسَّبِيلِ وَمَا مَلَكَتْ أَيْمَٰنُكُمْ ۗ إِنَّ ٱللَّهَ لَا يُحِبُّ مَن كَانَ مُخْتَالًا فَخُورًا ۝ ٱلَّذِينَ يَبْخَلُونَ وَيَأْمُرُونَ ٱلنَّاسَ بِٱلْبُخْلِ وَيَكْتُمُونَ مَآ ءَاتَىٰهُمُ ٱللَّهُ مِن فَضْلِهِۦ ۗ وَأَعْتَدْنَا لِلْكَٰفِرِينَ عَذَابًا مُّهِينًا ۝ وَٱلَّذِينَ يُنفِقُونَ أَمْوَٰلَهُمْ رِئَآءَ ٱلنَّاسِ وَلَا يُؤْمِنُونَ بِٱللَّهِ وَلَا بِٱلْيَوْمِ ٱلْءَاخِرِ ۗ وَمَن يَكُنِ ٱلشَّيْطَٰنُ لَهُۥ قَرِينًا فَسَآءَ قَرِينًا ۝ وَمَاذَا عَلَيْهِمْ لَوْ ءَامَنُوا۟ بِٱللَّهِ وَٱلْيَوْمِ ٱلْءَاخِرِ وَأَنفَقُوا۟ مِمَّا رَزَقَهُمُ ٱللَّهُ ۚ وَكَانَ ٱللَّهُ بِهِمْ عَلِيمًا ۝ إِنَّ ٱللَّهَ لَا يَظْلِمُ

مِثْقَالَ ذَرَّةٍ ۖ وَإِن تَكُ حَسَنَةً يُضَاعِفْهَا وَيُؤْتِ مِن لَّدُنْهُ أَجْرًا عَظِيمًا ۝ فَكَيْفَ إِذَا جِئْنَا مِن كُلِّ أُمَّةٍ بِشَهِيدٍ وَجِئْنَا بِكَ عَلَىٰ هَٰٓؤُلَآءِ شَهِيدًا ۝ يَوْمَئِذٍ يَوَدُّ ٱلَّذِينَ كَفَرُوا۟ وَعَصَوُا۟ ٱلرَّسُولَ لَوْ تُسَوَّىٰ بِهِمُ ٱلْأَرْضُ وَلَا يَكْتُمُونَ ٱللَّهَ حَدِيثًا ۝ يَٰٓأَيُّهَا ٱلَّذِينَ ءَامَنُوا۟ لَا تَقْرَبُوا۟ ٱلصَّلَوٰةَ وَأَنتُمْ سُكَٰرَىٰ حَتَّىٰ تَعْلَمُوا۟ مَا تَقُولُونَ وَلَا جُنُبًا إِلَّا عَابِرِى سَبِيلٍ حَتَّىٰ تَغْتَسِلُوا۟ ۚ وَإِن كُنتُم مَّرْضَىٰٓ أَوْ عَلَىٰ سَفَرٍ أَوْ جَآءَ أَحَدٌ مِّنكُم مِّنَ ٱلْغَآئِطِ أَوْ لَٰمَسْتُمُ ٱلنِّسَآءَ فَلَمْ تَجِدُوا۟ مَآءً فَتَيَمَّمُوا۟ صَعِيدًا طَيِّبًا فَٱمْسَحُوا۟ بِوُجُوهِكُمْ وَأَيْدِيكُمْ ۗ إِنَّ ٱللَّهَ كَانَ عَفُوًّا غَفُورًا ۝ أَلَمْ تَرَ إِلَى ٱلَّذِينَ أُوتُوا۟ نَصِيبًا مِّنَ ٱلْكِتَٰبِ يَشْتَرُونَ ٱلضَّلَٰلَةَ وَيُرِيدُونَ أَن تَضِلُّوا۟ ٱلسَّبِيلَ ۝ وَٱللَّهُ أَعْلَمُ بِأَعْدَآئِكُمْ ۚ وَكَفَىٰ بِٱللَّهِ وَلِيًّا وَكَفَىٰ بِٱللَّهِ نَصِيرًا ۝ مِّنَ ٱلَّذِينَ هَادُوا۟ يُحَرِّفُونَ ٱلْكَلِمَ عَن مَّوَاضِعِهِۦ وَيَقُولُونَ سَمِعْنَا وَعَصَيْنَا وَٱسْمَعْ غَيْرَ مُسْمَعٍ وَرَٰعِنَا لَيًّۢا بِأَلْسِنَتِهِمْ وَطَعْنًا فِى ٱلدِّينِ ۚ وَلَوْ أَنَّهُمْ قَالُوا۟ سَمِعْنَا وَأَطَعْنَا وَٱسْمَعْ وَٱنظُرْنَا لَكَانَ خَيْرًا لَّهُمْ وَأَقْوَمَ وَلَٰكِن لَّعَنَهُمُ ٱللَّهُ بِكُفْرِهِمْ فَلَا يُؤْمِنُونَ إِلَّا قَلِيلًا ۝ يَٰٓأَيُّهَا ٱلَّذِينَ أُوتُوا۟ ٱلْكِتَٰبَ ءَامِنُوا۟ بِمَا نَزَّلْنَا مُصَدِّقًا لِّمَا مَعَكُم مِّن قَبْلِ أَن نَّطْمِسَ وُجُوهًا فَنَرُدَّهَا عَلَىٰٓ أَدْبَارِهَآ أَوْ نَلْعَنَهُمْ كَمَا لَعَنَّآ أَصْحَٰبَ ٱلسَّبْتِ ۚ وَكَانَ أَمْرُ ٱللَّهِ مَفْعُولًا ۝ إِنَّ ٱللَّهَ لَا يَغْفِرُ أَن يُشْرَكَ بِهِۦ وَيَغْفِرُ مَا دُونَ ذَٰلِكَ لِمَن يَشَآءُ ۚ وَمَن يُشْرِكْ بِٱللَّهِ فَقَدِ ٱفْتَرَىٰٓ إِثْمًا عَظِيمًا ۝ أَلَمْ تَرَ إِلَى ٱلَّذِينَ يُزَكُّونَ أَنفُسَهُم ۚ بَلِ ٱللَّهُ يُزَكِّى مَن يَشَآءُ وَلَا يُظْلَمُونَ فَتِيلًا ۝ ٱنظُرْ كَيْفَ يَفْتَرُونَ عَلَى ٱللَّهِ ٱلْكَذِبَ ۖ وَكَفَىٰ بِهِۦٓ إِثْمًا مُّبِينًا ۝ أَلَمْ تَرَ إِلَى ٱلَّذِينَ أُوتُوا۟ نَصِيبًا مِّنَ ٱلْكِتَٰبِ يُؤْمِنُونَ بِٱلْجِبْتِ وَٱلطَّٰغُوتِ وَيَقُولُونَ لِلَّذِينَ كَفَرُوا۟ هَٰٓؤُلَآءِ أَهْدَىٰ مِنَ ٱلَّذِينَ ءَامَنُوا۟ سَبِيلًا ۝ أُو۟لَٰٓئِكَ ٱلَّذِينَ لَعَنَهُمُ ٱللَّهُ ۖ وَمَن يَلْعَنِ ٱللَّهُ

فَلَن تَجِدَ لَهُ نَصِيرًا ۝ أَمْ لَهُمْ نَصِيبٌ مِّنَ ٱلْمُلْكِ فَإِذًا لَّا يُؤْتُونَ ٱلنَّاسَ نَقِيرًا ۝ أَمْ يَحْسُدُونَ ٱلنَّاسَ عَلَىٰ مَآ ءَاتَىٰهُمُ ٱللَّهُ مِن فَضْلِهِۦ ۖ فَقَدْ ءَاتَيْنَآ ءَالَ إِبْرَٰهِيمَ ٱلْكِتَٰبَ وَٱلْحِكْمَةَ وَءَاتَيْنَٰهُم مُّلْكًا عَظِيمًا ۝ فَمِنْهُم مَّنْ ءَامَنَ بِهِۦ وَمِنْهُم مَّن صَدَّ عَنْهُ ۚ وَكَفَىٰ بِجَهَنَّمَ سَعِيرًا ۝ إِنَّ ٱلَّذِينَ كَفَرُوا۟ بِـَٔايَٰتِنَا سَوْفَ نُصْلِيهِمْ نَارًا كُلَّمَا نَضِجَتْ جُلُودُهُم بَدَّلْنَٰهُمْ جُلُودًا غَيْرَهَا لِيَذُوقُوا۟ ٱلْعَذَابَ ۗ إِنَّ ٱللَّهَ كَانَ عَزِيزًا حَكِيمًا ۝ وَٱلَّذِينَ ءَامَنُوا۟ وَعَمِلُوا۟ ٱلصَّٰلِحَٰتِ سَنُدْخِلُهُمْ جَنَّٰتٍ تَجْرِى مِن تَحْتِهَا ٱلْأَنْهَٰرُ خَٰلِدِينَ فِيهَآ أَبَدًا ۖ لَّهُمْ فِيهَآ أَزْوَٰجٌ مُّطَهَّرَةٌ ۖ وَنُدْخِلُهُمْ ظِلًّا ظَلِيلًا ۝ إِنَّ ٱللَّهَ يَأْمُرُكُمْ أَن تُؤَدُّوا۟ ٱلْأَمَٰنَٰتِ إِلَىٰٓ أَهْلِهَا وَإِذَا حَكَمْتُم بَيْنَ ٱلنَّاسِ أَن تَحْكُمُوا۟ بِٱلْعَدْلِ ۚ إِنَّ ٱللَّهَ نِعِمَّا يَعِظُكُم بِهِۦٓ ۗ إِنَّ ٱللَّهَ كَانَ سَمِيعًۢا بَصِيرًا ۝ يَٰٓأَيُّهَا ٱلَّذِينَ ءَامَنُوٓا۟ أَطِيعُوا۟ ٱللَّهَ وَأَطِيعُوا۟ ٱلرَّسُولَ وَأُو۟لِى ٱلْأَمْرِ مِنكُمْ ۖ فَإِن تَنَٰزَعْتُمْ فِى شَىْءٍ فَرُدُّوهُ إِلَى ٱللَّهِ وَٱلرَّسُولِ إِن كُنتُمْ تُؤْمِنُونَ بِٱللَّهِ وَٱلْيَوْمِ ٱلْءَاخِرِ ۚ ذَٰلِكَ خَيْرٌ وَأَحْسَنُ تَأْوِيلًا ۝ أَلَمْ تَرَ إِلَى ٱلَّذِينَ يَزْعُمُونَ أَنَّهُمْ ءَامَنُوا۟ بِمَآ أُنزِلَ إِلَيْكَ وَمَآ أُنزِلَ مِن قَبْلِكَ يُرِيدُونَ أَن يَتَحَاكَمُوٓا۟ إِلَى ٱلطَّٰغُوتِ وَقَدْ أُمِرُوٓا۟ أَن يَكْفُرُوا۟ بِهِۦ وَيُرِيدُ ٱلشَّيْطَٰنُ أَن يُضِلَّهُمْ ضَلَٰلًۢا بَعِيدًا ۝ وَإِذَا قِيلَ لَهُمْ تَعَالَوْا۟ إِلَىٰ مَآ أَنزَلَ ٱللَّهُ وَإِلَى ٱلرَّسُولِ رَأَيْتَ ٱلْمُنَٰفِقِينَ يَصُدُّونَ عَنكَ صُدُودًا ۝ فَكَيْفَ إِذَآ أَصَٰبَتْهُم مُّصِيبَةٌۢ بِمَا قَدَّمَتْ أَيْدِيهِمْ ثُمَّ جَآءُوكَ يَحْلِفُونَ بِٱللَّهِ إِنْ أَرَدْنَآ إِلَّآ إِحْسَٰنًا وَتَوْفِيقًا ۝ أُو۟لَٰٓئِكَ ٱلَّذِينَ يَعْلَمُ ٱللَّهُ مَا فِى قُلُوبِهِمْ فَأَعْرِضْ عَنْهُمْ وَعِظْهُمْ وَقُل لَّهُمْ فِىٓ أَنفُسِهِمْ قَوْلًۢا بَلِيغًا ۝ وَمَآ أَرْسَلْنَا مِن رَّسُولٍ إِلَّا لِيُطَاعَ بِإِذْنِ ٱللَّهِ ۚ وَلَوْ أَنَّهُمْ إِذ ظَّلَمُوٓا۟ أَنفُسَهُمْ جَآءُوكَ فَٱسْتَغْفَرُوا۟ ٱللَّهَ وَٱسْتَغْفَرَ لَهُمُ ٱلرَّسُولُ لَوَجَدُوا۟ ٱللَّهَ تَوَّابًا رَّحِيمًا ۝ فَلَا وَرَبِّكَ لَا

يُؤْمِنُونَ حَتَّىٰ يُحَكِّمُوكَ فِيمَا شَجَرَ بَيْنَهُمْ ثُمَّ لَا يَجِدُوا۟ فِىٓ أَنفُسِهِمْ حَرَجًۭا مِّمَّا قَضَيْتَ وَيُسَلِّمُوا۟ تَسْلِيمًۭا ۝٦٥ وَلَوْ أَنَّا كَتَبْنَا عَلَيْهِمْ أَنِ ٱقْتُلُوٓا۟ أَنفُسَكُمْ أَوِ ٱخْرُجُوا۟ مِن دِيَـٰرِكُم مَّا فَعَلُوهُ إِلَّا قَلِيلٌۭ مِّنْهُمْ ۖ وَلَوْ أَنَّهُمْ فَعَلُوا۟ مَا يُوعَظُونَ بِهِۦ لَكَانَ خَيْرًۭا لَّهُمْ وَأَشَدَّ تَثْبِيتًۭا ۝٦٦ وَإِذًۭا لَّـَٔاتَيْنَـٰهُم مِّن لَّدُنَّآ أَجْرًا عَظِيمًۭا ۝٦٧ وَلَهَدَيْنَـٰهُمْ صِرَٰطًۭا مُّسْتَقِيمًۭا ۝٦٨ وَمَن يُطِعِ ٱللَّهَ وَٱلرَّسُولَ فَأُو۟لَـٰٓئِكَ مَعَ ٱلَّذِينَ أَنْعَمَ ٱللَّهُ عَلَيْهِم مِّنَ ٱلنَّبِيِّـۧنَ وَٱلصِّدِّيقِينَ وَٱلشُّهَدَآءِ وَٱلصَّـٰلِحِينَ ۚ وَحَسُنَ أُو۟لَـٰٓئِكَ رَفِيقًۭا ۝٦٩ ذَٰلِكَ ٱلْفَضْلُ مِنَ ٱللَّهِ ۚ وَكَفَىٰ بِٱللَّهِ عَلِيمًۭا ۝٧٠ يَـٰٓأَيُّهَا ٱلَّذِينَ ءَامَنُوا۟ خُذُوا۟ حِذْرَكُمْ فَٱنفِرُوا۟ ثُبَاتٍ أَوِ ٱنفِرُوا۟ جَمِيعًۭا ۝٧١ وَإِنَّ مِنكُمْ لَمَن لَّيُبَطِّئَنَّ فَإِنْ أَصَـٰبَتْكُم مُّصِيبَةٌۭ قَالَ قَدْ أَنْعَمَ ٱللَّهُ عَلَىَّ إِذْ لَمْ أَكُن مَّعَهُمْ شَهِيدًۭا ۝٧٢ وَلَئِنْ أَصَـٰبَكُمْ فَضْلٌۭ مِّنَ ٱللَّهِ لَيَقُولَنَّ كَأَن لَّمْ تَكُنۢ بَيْنَكُمْ وَبَيْنَهُۥ مَوَدَّةٌۭ يَـٰلَيْتَنِى كُنتُ مَعَهُمْ فَأَفُوزَ فَوْزًا عَظِيمًۭا ۝٧٣ ۞ فَلْيُقَـٰتِلْ فِى سَبِيلِ ٱللَّهِ ٱلَّذِينَ يَشْرُونَ ٱلْحَيَوٰةَ ٱلدُّنْيَا بِٱلْـَٔاخِرَةِ ۚ وَمَن يُقَـٰتِلْ فِى سَبِيلِ ٱللَّهِ فَيُقْتَلْ أَوْ يَغْلِبْ فَسَوْفَ نُؤْتِيهِ أَجْرًا عَظِيمًۭا ۝٧٤ وَمَا لَكُمْ لَا تُقَـٰتِلُونَ فِى سَبِيلِ ٱللَّهِ وَٱلْمُسْتَضْعَفِينَ مِنَ ٱلرِّجَالِ وَٱلنِّسَآءِ وَٱلْوِلْدَٰنِ ٱلَّذِينَ يَقُولُونَ رَبَّنَآ أَخْرِجْنَا مِنْ هَـٰذِهِ ٱلْقَرْيَةِ ٱلظَّالِمِ أَهْلُهَا وَٱجْعَل لَّنَا مِن لَّدُنكَ وَلِيًّۭا وَٱجْعَل لَّنَا مِن لَّدُنكَ نَصِيرًا ۝٧٥ ٱلَّذِينَ ءَامَنُوا۟ يُقَـٰتِلُونَ فِى سَبِيلِ ٱللَّهِ ۖ وَٱلَّذِينَ كَفَرُوا۟ يُقَـٰتِلُونَ فِى سَبِيلِ ٱلطَّـٰغُوتِ فَقَـٰتِلُوٓا۟ أَوْلِيَآءَ ٱلشَّيْطَـٰنِ ۖ إِنَّ كَيْدَ ٱلشَّيْطَـٰنِ كَانَ ضَعِيفًا ۝٧٦ أَلَمْ تَرَ إِلَى ٱلَّذِينَ قِيلَ لَهُمْ كُفُّوٓا۟ أَيْدِيَكُمْ وَأَقِيمُوا۟ ٱلصَّلَوٰةَ وَءَاتُوا۟ ٱلزَّكَوٰةَ فَلَمَّا كُتِبَ عَلَيْهِمُ ٱلْقِتَالُ إِذَا فَرِيقٌۭ مِّنْهُمْ يَخْشَوْنَ ٱلنَّاسَ كَخَشْيَةِ ٱللَّهِ أَوْ أَشَدَّ خَشْيَةًۭ ۚ وَقَالُوا۟ رَبَّنَا لِمَ كَتَبْتَ عَلَيْنَا ٱلْقِتَالَ لَوْلَآ أَخَّرْتَنَآ إِلَىٰٓ أَجَلٍۢ قَرِيبٍۢ ۗ قُلْ مَتَـٰعُ ٱلدُّنْيَا قَلِيلٌۭ وَٱلْـَٔاخِرَةُ خَيْرٌۭ لِّمَنِ ٱتَّقَىٰ وَلَا تُظْلَمُونَ

فَتِيلاً ۞ أَيْنَمَا تَكُونُوا۟ يُدْرِككُّمُ ٱلْمَوْتُ وَلَوْ كُنتُمْ فِى بُرُوجٍ مُّشَيَّدَةٍ ۗ وَإِن تُصِبْهُمْ حَسَنَةٌ يَقُولُوا۟ هَـٰذِهِۦ مِنْ عِندِ ٱللَّهِ ۖ وَإِن تُصِبْهُمْ سَيِّئَةٌ يَقُولُوا۟ هَـٰذِهِۦ مِنْ عِندِكَ ۚ قُلْ كُلٌّ مِّنْ عِندِ ٱللَّهِ ۖ فَمَالِ هَـٰٓؤُلَآءِ ٱلْقَوْمِ لَا يَكَادُونَ يَفْقَهُونَ حَدِيثًا ۞ مَّآ أَصَابَكَ مِنْ حَسَنَةٍ فَمِنَ ٱللَّهِ ۖ وَمَآ أَصَابَكَ مِن سَيِّئَةٍ فَمِن نَّفْسِكَ ۚ وَأَرْسَلْنَـٰكَ لِلنَّاسِ رَسُولاً ۚ وَكَفَىٰ بِٱللَّهِ شَهِيدًا ۞ مَّن يُطِعِ ٱلرَّسُولَ فَقَدْ أَطَاعَ ٱللَّهَ ۖ وَمَن تَوَلَّىٰ فَمَآ أَرْسَلْنَـٰكَ عَلَيْهِمْ حَفِيظًا ۞ وَيَقُولُونَ طَاعَةٌ فَإِذَا بَرَزُوا۟ مِنْ عِندِكَ بَيَّتَ طَآئِفَةٌ مِّنْهُمْ غَيْرَ ٱلَّذِى تَقُولُ ۖ وَٱللَّهُ يَكْتُبُ مَا يُبَيِّتُونَ ۖ فَأَعْرِضْ عَنْهُمْ وَتَوَكَّلْ عَلَى ٱللَّهِ ۚ وَكَفَىٰ بِٱللَّهِ وَكِيلاً ۞ أَفَلَا يَتَدَبَّرُونَ ٱلْقُرْءَانَ ۚ وَلَوْ كَانَ مِنْ عِندِ غَيْرِ ٱللَّهِ لَوَجَدُوا۟ فِيهِ ٱخْتِلَـٰفًا كَثِيرًا ۞ وَإِذَا جَآءَهُمْ أَمْرٌ مِّنَ ٱلْأَمْنِ أَوِ ٱلْخَوْفِ أَذَاعُوا۟ بِهِۦ ۖ وَلَوْ رَدُّوهُ إِلَى ٱلرَّسُولِ وَإِلَىٰٓ أُو۟لِى ٱلْأَمْرِ مِنْهُمْ لَعَلِمَهُ ٱلَّذِينَ يَسْتَنۢبِطُونَهُۥ مِنْهُمْ ۗ وَلَوْلَا فَضْلُ ٱللَّهِ عَلَيْكُمْ وَرَحْمَتُهُۥ لَٱتَّبَعْتُمُ ٱلشَّيْطَـٰنَ إِلَّا قَلِيلاً ۞ فَقَـٰتِلْ فِى سَبِيلِ ٱللَّهِ لَا تُكَلَّفُ إِلَّا نَفْسَكَ ۚ وَحَرِّضِ ٱلْمُؤْمِنِينَ ۖ عَسَى ٱللَّهُ أَن يَكُفَّ بَأْسَ ٱلَّذِينَ كَفَرُوا۟ ۚ وَٱللَّهُ أَشَدُّ بَأْسًا وَأَشَدُّ تَنكِيلاً ۞ مَّن يَشْفَعْ شَفَـٰعَةً حَسَنَةً يَكُن لَّهُۥ نَصِيبٌ مِّنْهَا ۖ وَمَن يَشْفَعْ شَفَـٰعَةً سَيِّئَةً يَكُن لَّهُۥ كِفْلٌ مِّنْهَا ۗ وَكَانَ ٱللَّهُ عَلَىٰ كُلِّ شَىْءٍ مُّقِيتًا ۞ وَإِذَا حُيِّيتُم بِتَحِيَّةٍ فَحَيُّوا۟ بِأَحْسَنَ مِنْهَآ أَوْ رُدُّوهَآ ۗ إِنَّ ٱللَّهَ كَانَ عَلَىٰ كُلِّ شَىْءٍ حَسِيبًا ۞ ٱللَّهُ لَآ إِلَـٰهَ إِلَّا هُوَ ۚ لَيَجْمَعَنَّكُمْ إِلَىٰ يَوْمِ ٱلْقِيَـٰمَةِ لَا رَيْبَ فِيهِ ۗ وَمَنْ أَصْدَقُ مِنَ ٱللَّهِ حَدِيثًا ۞ ۞ فَمَا لَكُمْ فِى ٱلْمُنَـٰفِقِينَ فِئَتَيْنِ وَٱللَّهُ أَرْكَسَهُم بِمَا كَسَبُوٓا۟ ۚ أَتُرِيدُونَ أَن تَهْدُوا۟ مَنْ أَضَلَّ ٱللَّهُ ۖ وَمَن يُضْلِلِ ٱللَّهُ فَلَن تَجِدَ لَهُۥ سَبِيلاً ۞ وَدُّوا۟ لَوْ تَكْفُرُونَ كَمَا كَفَرُوا۟ فَتَكُونُونَ سَوَآءً ۖ فَلَا تَتَّخِذُوا۟ مِنْهُمْ أَوْلِيَآءَ حَتَّىٰ يُهَاجِرُوا۟ فِى سَبِيلِ ٱللَّهِ ۚ فَإِن

تَوَلَّوْا۟ فَخُذُوهُمْ وَٱقْتُلُوهُمْ حَيْثُ وَجَدتُّمُوهُمْ ۚ وَلَا تَتَّخِذُوا۟ مِنْهُمْ وَلِيًّا وَلَا نَصِيرًا ۝ إِلَّا ٱلَّذِينَ يَصِلُونَ إِلَىٰ قَوْمٍۭ بَيْنَكُمْ وَبَيْنَهُم مِّيثَـٰقٌ أَوْ جَآءُوكُمْ حَصِرَتْ صُدُورُهُمْ أَن يُقَـٰتِلُوكُمْ أَوْ يُقَـٰتِلُوا۟ قَوْمَهُمْ ۚ وَلَوْ شَآءَ ٱللَّهُ لَسَلَّطَهُمْ عَلَيْكُمْ فَلَقَـٰتَلُوكُمْ ۚ فَإِنِ ٱعْتَزَلُوكُمْ فَلَمْ يُقَـٰتِلُوكُمْ وَأَلْقَوْا۟ إِلَيْكُمُ ٱلسَّلَمَ فَمَا جَعَلَ ٱللَّهُ لَكُمْ عَلَيْهِمْ سَبِيلًا ۝ سَتَجِدُونَ ءَاخَرِينَ يُرِيدُونَ أَن يَأْمَنُوكُمْ وَيَأْمَنُوا۟ قَوْمَهُمْ كُلَّ مَا رُدُّوٓا۟ إِلَى ٱلْفِتْنَةِ أُرْكِسُوا۟ فِيهَا ۚ فَإِن لَّمْ يَعْتَزِلُوكُمْ وَيُلْقُوٓا۟ إِلَيْكُمُ ٱلسَّلَمَ وَيَكُفُّوٓا۟ أَيْدِيَهُمْ فَخُذُوهُمْ وَٱقْتُلُوهُمْ حَيْثُ ثَقِفْتُمُوهُمْ ۚ وَأُو۟لَـٰٓئِكُمْ جَعَلْنَا لَكُمْ عَلَيْهِمْ سُلْطَـٰنًا مُّبِينًا ۝ وَمَا كَانَ لِمُؤْمِنٍ أَن يَقْتُلَ مُؤْمِنًا إِلَّا خَطَـًٔا ۚ وَمَن قَتَلَ مُؤْمِنًا خَطَـًٔا فَتَحْرِيرُ رَقَبَةٍ مُّؤْمِنَةٍ وَدِيَةٌ مُّسَلَّمَةٌ إِلَىٰٓ أَهْلِهِۦٓ إِلَّآ أَن يَصَّدَّقُوا۟ ۚ فَإِن كَانَ مِن قَوْمٍ عَدُوٍّ لَّكُمْ وَهُوَ مُؤْمِنٌ فَتَحْرِيرُ رَقَبَةٍ مُّؤْمِنَةٍ ۖ وَإِن كَانَ مِن قَوْمٍۭ بَيْنَكُمْ وَبَيْنَهُم مِّيثَـٰقٌ فَدِيَةٌ مُّسَلَّمَةٌ إِلَىٰٓ أَهْلِهِۦ وَتَحْرِيرُ رَقَبَةٍ مُّؤْمِنَةٍ ۖ فَمَن لَّمْ يَجِدْ فَصِيَامُ شَهْرَيْنِ مُتَتَابِعَيْنِ تَوْبَةً مِّنَ ٱللَّهِ ۗ وَكَانَ ٱللَّهُ عَلِيمًا حَكِيمًا ۝ وَمَن يَقْتُلْ مُؤْمِنًا مُّتَعَمِّدًا فَجَزَآؤُهُۥ جَهَنَّمُ خَـٰلِدًا فِيهَا وَغَضِبَ ٱللَّهُ عَلَيْهِ وَلَعَنَهُۥ وَأَعَدَّ لَهُۥ عَذَابًا عَظِيمًا ۝ يَـٰٓأَيُّهَا ٱلَّذِينَ ءَامَنُوٓا۟ إِذَا ضَرَبْتُمْ فِى سَبِيلِ ٱللَّهِ فَتَبَيَّنُوا۟ وَلَا تَقُولُوا۟ لِمَنْ أَلْقَىٰٓ إِلَيْكُمُ ٱلسَّلَـٰمَ لَسْتَ مُؤْمِنًا تَبْتَغُونَ عَرَضَ ٱلْحَيَوٰةِ ٱلدُّنْيَا فَعِندَ ٱللَّهِ مَغَانِمُ كَثِيرَةٌ ۚ كَذَٰلِكَ كُنتُم مِّن قَبْلُ فَمَنَّ ٱللَّهُ عَلَيْكُمْ فَتَبَيَّنُوٓا۟ ۚ إِنَّ ٱللَّهَ كَانَ بِمَا تَعْمَلُونَ خَبِيرًا ۝ لَّا يَسْتَوِى ٱلْقَـٰعِدُونَ مِنَ ٱلْمُؤْمِنِينَ غَيْرُ أُو۟لِى ٱلضَّرَرِ وَٱلْمُجَـٰهِدُونَ فِى سَبِيلِ ٱللَّهِ بِأَمْوَٰلِهِمْ وَأَنفُسِهِمْ ۚ فَضَّلَ ٱللَّهُ ٱلْمُجَـٰهِدِينَ بِأَمْوَٰلِهِمْ وَأَنفُسِهِمْ عَلَى ٱلْقَـٰعِدِينَ دَرَجَةً ۚ وَكُلًّا وَعَدَ ٱللَّهُ ٱلْحُسْنَىٰ ۚ وَفَضَّلَ ٱللَّهُ ٱلْمُجَـٰهِدِينَ عَلَى ٱلْقَـٰعِدِينَ أَجْرًا عَظِيمًا

۹۵ دَرَجَـٰتٍ مِّنْهُ وَمَغْفِرَةً وَرَحْمَةً ۚ وَكَانَ ٱللَّهُ غَفُورًا رَّحِيمًا ۞ إِنَّ ٱلَّذِينَ تَوَفَّىٰهُمُ ٱلْمَلَـٰٓئِكَةُ ظَالِمِىٓ أَنفُسِهِمْ قَالُوا۟ فِيمَ كُنتُمْ ۖ قَالُوا۟ كُنَّا مُسْتَضْعَفِينَ فِى ٱلْأَرْضِ ۚ قَالُوٓا۟ أَلَمْ تَكُنْ أَرْضُ ٱللَّهِ وَٰسِعَةً فَتُهَاجِرُوا۟ فِيهَا ۚ فَأُو۟لَـٰٓئِكَ مَأْوَىٰهُمْ جَهَنَّمُ ۖ وَسَآءَتْ مَصِيرًا ۞ إِلَّا ٱلْمُسْتَضْعَفِينَ مِنَ ٱلرِّجَالِ وَٱلنِّسَآءِ وَٱلْوِلْدَٰنِ لَا يَسْتَطِيعُونَ حِيلَةً وَلَا يَهْتَدُونَ سَبِيلًا ۞ فَأُو۟لَـٰٓئِكَ عَسَى ٱللَّهُ أَن يَعْفُوَ عَنْهُمْ ۚ وَكَانَ ٱللَّهُ عَفُوًّا غَفُورًا ۞ ۞ وَمَن يُهَاجِرْ فِى سَبِيلِ ٱللَّهِ يَجِدْ فِى ٱلْأَرْضِ مُرَٰغَمًا كَثِيرًا وَسَعَةً ۚ وَمَن يَخْرُجْ مِنۢ بَيْتِهِۦ مُهَاجِرًا إِلَى ٱللَّهِ وَرَسُولِهِۦ ثُمَّ يُدْرِكْهُ ٱلْمَوْتُ فَقَدْ وَقَعَ أَجْرُهُۥ عَلَى ٱللَّهِ ۗ وَكَانَ ٱللَّهُ غَفُورًا رَّحِيمًا ۞ وَإِذَا ضَرَبْتُمْ فِى ٱلْأَرْضِ فَلَيْسَ عَلَيْكُمْ جُنَاحٌ أَن تَقْصُرُوا۟ مِنَ ٱلصَّلَوٰةِ إِنْ خِفْتُمْ أَن يَفْتِنَكُمُ ٱلَّذِينَ كَفَرُوٓا۟ ۚ إِنَّ ٱلْكَـٰفِرِينَ كَانُوا۟ لَكُمْ عَدُوًّا مُّبِينًا ۞ وَإِذَا كُنتَ فِيهِمْ فَأَقَمْتَ لَهُمُ ٱلصَّلَوٰةَ فَلْتَقُمْ طَآئِفَةٌ مِّنْهُم مَّعَكَ وَلْيَأْخُذُوٓا۟ أَسْلِحَتَهُمْ فَإِذَا سَجَدُوا۟ فَلْيَكُونُوا۟ مِن وَرَآئِكُمْ وَلْتَأْتِ طَآئِفَةٌ أُخْرَىٰ لَمْ يُصَلُّوا۟ فَلْيُصَلُّوا۟ مَعَكَ وَلْيَأْخُذُوا۟ حِذْرَهُمْ وَأَسْلِحَتَهُمْ ۗ وَدَّ ٱلَّذِينَ كَفَرُوا۟ لَوْ تَغْفُلُونَ عَنْ أَسْلِحَتِكُمْ وَأَمْتِعَتِكُمْ فَيَمِيلُونَ عَلَيْكُم مَّيْلَةً وَٰحِدَةً ۚ وَلَا جُنَاحَ عَلَيْكُمْ إِن كَانَ بِكُمْ أَذًى مِّن مَّطَرٍ أَوْ كُنتُم مَّرْضَىٰٓ أَن تَضَعُوٓا۟ أَسْلِحَتَكُمْ ۖ وَخُذُوا۟ حِذْرَكُمْ ۗ إِنَّ ٱللَّهَ أَعَدَّ لِلْكَـٰفِرِينَ عَذَابًا مُّهِينًا ۞ فَإِذَا قَضَيْتُمُ ٱلصَّلَوٰةَ فَٱذْكُرُوا۟ ٱللَّهَ قِيَـٰمًا وَقُعُودًا وَعَلَىٰ جُنُوبِكُمْ ۚ فَإِذَا ٱطْمَأْنَنتُمْ فَأَقِيمُوا۟ ٱلصَّلَوٰةَ ۚ إِنَّ ٱلصَّلَوٰةَ كَانَتْ عَلَى ٱلْمُؤْمِنِينَ كِتَـٰبًا مَّوْقُوتًا ۞ وَلَا تَهِنُوا۟ فِى ٱبْتِغَآءِ ٱلْقَوْمِ ۖ إِن تَكُونُوا۟ تَأْلَمُونَ فَإِنَّهُمْ يَأْلَمُونَ كَمَا تَأْلَمُونَ ۖ وَتَرْجُونَ مِنَ ٱللَّهِ مَا لَا يَرْجُونَ ۗ وَكَانَ ٱللَّهُ عَلِيمًا حَكِيمًا ۞ إِنَّآ أَنزَلْنَآ إِلَيْكَ ٱلْكِتَـٰبَ بِٱلْحَقِّ لِتَحْكُمَ بَيْنَ ٱلنَّاسِ بِمَآ أَرَىٰكَ ٱللَّهُ ۚ وَلَا تَكُن

لِّلْخَآئِنِينَ خَصِيمًا ۝ وَٱسْتَغْفِرِ ٱللَّهَ ۖ إِنَّ ٱللَّهَ كَانَ غَفُورًا رَّحِيمًا ۝ وَلَا تُجَٰدِلْ عَنِ ٱلَّذِينَ يَخْتَانُونَ أَنفُسَهُمْ ۚ إِنَّ ٱللَّهَ لَا يُحِبُّ مَن كَانَ خَوَّانًا أَثِيمًا ۝ يَسْتَخْفُونَ مِنَ ٱلنَّاسِ وَلَا يَسْتَخْفُونَ مِنَ ٱللَّهِ وَهُوَ مَعَهُمْ إِذْ يُبَيِّتُونَ مَا لَا يَرْضَىٰ مِنَ ٱلْقَوْلِ ۚ وَكَانَ ٱللَّهُ بِمَا يَعْمَلُونَ مُحِيطًا ۝ هَـٰٓأَنتُمْ هَـٰٓؤُلَآءِ جَٰدَلْتُمْ عَنْهُمْ فِى ٱلْحَيَوٰةِ ٱلدُّنْيَا فَمَن يُجَٰدِلُ ٱللَّهَ عَنْهُمْ يَوْمَ ٱلْقِيَٰمَةِ أَم مَّن يَكُونُ عَلَيْهِمْ وَكِيلًا ۝ وَمَن يَعْمَلْ سُوٓءًا أَوْ يَظْلِمْ نَفْسَهُۥ ثُمَّ يَسْتَغْفِرِ ٱللَّهَ يَجِدِ ٱللَّهَ غَفُورًا رَّحِيمًا ۝ وَمَن يَكْسِبْ إِثْمًا فَإِنَّمَا يَكْسِبُهُۥ عَلَىٰ نَفْسِهِۦ ۚ وَكَانَ ٱللَّهُ عَلِيمًا حَكِيمًا ۝ وَمَن يَكْسِبْ خَطِيٓـَٔةً أَوْ إِثْمًا ثُمَّ يَرْمِ بِهِۦ بَرِيٓـًٔا فَقَدِ ٱحْتَمَلَ بُهْتَٰنًا وَإِثْمًا مُّبِينًا ۝ وَلَوْلَا فَضْلُ ٱللَّهِ عَلَيْكَ وَرَحْمَتُهُۥ لَهَمَّت طَّآئِفَةٌ مِّنْهُمْ أَن يُضِلُّوكَ وَمَا يُضِلُّونَ إِلَّآ أَنفُسَهُمْ ۖ وَمَا يَضُرُّونَكَ مِن شَىْءٍ ۚ وَأَنزَلَ ٱللَّهُ عَلَيْكَ ٱلْكِتَٰبَ وَٱلْحِكْمَةَ وَعَلَّمَكَ مَا لَمْ تَكُن تَعْلَمُ ۚ وَكَانَ فَضْلُ ٱللَّهِ عَلَيْكَ عَظِيمًا ۝ ۞ لَّا خَيْرَ فِى كَثِيرٍ مِّن نَّجْوَىٰهُمْ إِلَّا مَنْ أَمَرَ بِصَدَقَةٍ أَوْ مَعْرُوفٍ أَوْ إِصْلَٰحٍۭ بَيْنَ ٱلنَّاسِ ۚ وَمَن يَفْعَلْ ذَٰلِكَ ٱبْتِغَآءَ مَرْضَاتِ ٱللَّهِ فَسَوْفَ نُؤْتِيهِ أَجْرًا عَظِيمًا ۝ وَمَن يُشَاقِقِ ٱلرَّسُولَ مِنۢ بَعْدِ مَا تَبَيَّنَ لَهُ ٱلْهُدَىٰ وَيَتَّبِعْ غَيْرَ سَبِيلِ ٱلْمُؤْمِنِينَ نُوَلِّهِۦ مَا تَوَلَّىٰ وَنُصْلِهِۦ جَهَنَّمَ ۖ وَسَآءَتْ مَصِيرًا ۝ إِنَّ ٱللَّهَ لَا يَغْفِرُ أَن يُشْرَكَ بِهِۦ وَيَغْفِرُ مَا دُونَ ذَٰلِكَ لِمَن يَشَآءُ ۚ وَمَن يُشْرِكْ بِٱللَّهِ فَقَدْ ضَلَّ ضَلَٰلًۢا بَعِيدًا ۝ إِن يَدْعُونَ مِن دُونِهِۦٓ إِلَّآ إِنَٰثًا وَإِن يَدْعُونَ إِلَّا شَيْطَٰنًا مَّرِيدًا ۝ لَّعَنَهُ ٱللَّهُ ۘ وَقَالَ لَأَتَّخِذَنَّ مِنْ عِبَادِكَ نَصِيبًا مَّفْرُوضًا ۝ وَلَأُضِلَّنَّهُمْ وَلَأُمَنِّيَنَّهُمْ وَلَءَامُرَنَّهُمْ فَلَيُبَتِّكُنَّ ءَاذَانَ ٱلْأَنْعَٰمِ وَلَءَامُرَنَّهُمْ فَلَيُغَيِّرُنَّ خَلْقَ ٱللَّهِ ۚ وَمَن يَتَّخِذِ ٱلشَّيْطَٰنَ وَلِيًّا مِّن دُونِ ٱللَّهِ فَقَدْ خَسِرَ خُسْرَانًا مُّبِينًا ۝

يَعِدُهُمْ وَيُمَنِّيهِمْ ۖ وَمَا يَعِدُهُمُ ٱلشَّيْطَـٰنُ إِلَّا غُرُورًا ۝ أُو۟لَـٰٓئِكَ مَأْوَىٰهُمْ جَهَنَّمُ وَلَا يَجِدُونَ عَنْهَا مَحِيصًا ۝ وَٱلَّذِينَ ءَامَنُوا۟ وَعَمِلُوا۟ ٱلصَّـٰلِحَـٰتِ سَنُدْخِلُهُمْ جَنَّـٰتٍ تَجْرِى مِن تَحْتِهَا ٱلْأَنْهَـٰرُ خَـٰلِدِينَ فِيهَآ أَبَدًا ۖ وَعْدَ ٱللَّهِ حَقًّا ۚ وَمَنْ أَصْدَقُ مِنَ ٱللَّهِ قِيلًا ۝ لَّيْسَ بِأَمَانِيِّكُمْ وَلَآ أَمَانِىِّ أَهْلِ ٱلْكِتَـٰبِ ۗ مَن يَعْمَلْ سُوٓءًا يُجْزَ بِهِۦ وَلَا يَجِدْ لَهُۥ مِن دُونِ ٱللَّهِ وَلِيًّا وَلَا نَصِيرًا ۝ وَمَن يَعْمَلْ مِنَ ٱلصَّـٰلِحَـٰتِ مِن ذَكَرٍ أَوْ أُنثَىٰ وَهُوَ مُؤْمِنٌ فَأُو۟لَـٰٓئِكَ يَدْخُلُونَ ٱلْجَنَّةَ وَلَا يُظْلَمُونَ نَقِيرًا ۝ وَمَنْ أَحْسَنُ دِينًا مِّمَّنْ أَسْلَمَ وَجْهَهُۥ لِلَّهِ وَهُوَ مُحْسِنٌ وَٱتَّبَعَ مِلَّةَ إِبْرَٰهِيمَ حَنِيفًا ۗ وَٱتَّخَذَ ٱللَّهُ إِبْرَٰهِيمَ خَلِيلًا ۝ وَلِلَّهِ مَا فِى ٱلسَّمَـٰوَٰتِ وَمَا فِى ٱلْأَرْضِ ۚ وَكَانَ ٱللَّهُ بِكُلِّ شَىْءٍ مُّحِيطًا ۝ وَيَسْتَفْتُونَكَ فِى ٱلنِّسَآءِ ۖ قُلِ ٱللَّهُ يُفْتِيكُمْ فِيهِنَّ وَمَا يُتْلَىٰ عَلَيْكُمْ فِى ٱلْكِتَـٰبِ فِى يَتَـٰمَى ٱلنِّسَآءِ ٱلَّـٰتِى لَا تُؤْتُونَهُنَّ مَا كُتِبَ لَهُنَّ وَتَرْغَبُونَ أَن تَنكِحُوهُنَّ وَٱلْمُسْتَضْعَفِينَ مِنَ ٱلْوِلْدَٰنِ وَأَن تَقُومُوا۟ لِلْيَتَـٰمَىٰ بِٱلْقِسْطِ ۚ وَمَا تَفْعَلُوا۟ مِنْ خَيْرٍ فَإِنَّ ٱللَّهَ كَانَ بِهِۦ عَلِيمًا ۝ وَإِنِ ٱمْرَأَةٌ خَافَتْ مِنۢ بَعْلِهَا نُشُوزًا أَوْ إِعْرَاضًا فَلَا جُنَاحَ عَلَيْهِمَآ أَن يُصْلِحَا بَيْنَهُمَا صُلْحًا ۚ وَٱلصُّلْحُ خَيْرٌ ۗ وَأُحْضِرَتِ ٱلْأَنفُسُ ٱلشُّحَّ ۚ وَإِن تُحْسِنُوا۟ وَتَتَّقُوا۟ فَإِنَّ ٱللَّهَ كَانَ بِمَا تَعْمَلُونَ خَبِيرًا ۝ وَلَن تَسْتَطِيعُوٓا۟ أَن تَعْدِلُوا۟ بَيْنَ ٱلنِّسَآءِ وَلَوْ حَرَصْتُمْ ۖ فَلَا تَمِيلُوا۟ كُلَّ ٱلْمَيْلِ فَتَذَرُوهَا كَٱلْمُعَلَّقَةِ ۚ وَإِن تُصْلِحُوا۟ وَتَتَّقُوا۟ فَإِنَّ ٱللَّهَ كَانَ غَفُورًا رَّحِيمًا ۝ وَإِن يَتَفَرَّقَا يُغْنِ ٱللَّهُ كُلًّا مِّن سَعَتِهِۦ ۚ وَكَانَ ٱللَّهُ وَٰسِعًا حَكِيمًا ۝ وَلِلَّهِ مَا فِى ٱلسَّمَـٰوَٰتِ وَمَا فِى ٱلْأَرْضِ ۗ وَلَقَدْ وَصَّيْنَا ٱلَّذِينَ أُوتُوا۟ ٱلْكِتَـٰبَ مِن قَبْلِكُمْ وَإِيَّاكُمْ أَنِ ٱتَّقُوا۟ ٱللَّهَ ۚ وَإِن تَكْفُرُوا۟ فَإِنَّ لِلَّهِ مَا فِى ٱلسَّمَـٰوَٰتِ وَمَا فِى ٱلْأَرْضِ ۚ وَكَانَ ٱللَّهُ غَنِيًّا حَمِيدًا ۝ وَلِلَّهِ مَا

فِي ٱلسَّمَٰوَٰتِ وَمَا فِي ٱلْأَرْضِ ۚ وَكَفَىٰ بِٱللَّهِ وَكِيلًا ۞ إِن يَشَأْ يُذْهِبْكُمْ أَيُّهَا ٱلنَّاسُ وَيَأْتِ بِـَٔاخَرِينَ ۚ وَكَانَ ٱللَّهُ عَلَىٰ ذَٰلِكَ قَدِيرًا ۞ مَّن كَانَ يُرِيدُ ثَوَابَ ٱلدُّنْيَا فَعِندَ ٱللَّهِ ثَوَابُ ٱلدُّنْيَا وَٱلْـَٔاخِرَةِ ۚ وَكَانَ ٱللَّهُ سَمِيعًۢا بَصِيرًا ۞ ۞ يَـٰٓأَيُّهَا ٱلَّذِينَ ءَامَنُوا۟ كُونُوا۟ قَوَّٰمِينَ بِٱلْقِسْطِ شُهَدَآءَ لِلَّهِ وَلَوْ عَلَىٰٓ أَنفُسِكُمْ أَوِ ٱلْوَٰلِدَيْنِ وَٱلْأَقْرَبِينَ ۚ إِن يَكُنْ غَنِيًّا أَوْ فَقِيرًا فَٱللَّهُ أَوْلَىٰ بِهِمَا ۖ فَلَا تَتَّبِعُوا۟ ٱلْهَوَىٰٓ أَن تَعْدِلُوا۟ ۚ وَإِن تَلْوُۥٓا۟ أَوْ تُعْرِضُوا۟ فَإِنَّ ٱللَّهَ كَانَ بِمَا تَعْمَلُونَ خَبِيرًا ۞ يَـٰٓأَيُّهَا ٱلَّذِينَ ءَامَنُوٓا۟ ءَامِنُوا۟ بِٱللَّهِ وَرَسُولِهِۦ وَٱلْكِتَٰبِ ٱلَّذِى نَزَّلَ عَلَىٰ رَسُولِهِۦ وَٱلْكِتَٰبِ ٱلَّذِىٓ أَنزَلَ مِن قَبْلُ ۚ وَمَن يَكْفُرْ بِٱللَّهِ وَمَلَـٰٓئِكَتِهِۦ وَكُتُبِهِۦ وَرُسُلِهِۦ وَٱلْيَوْمِ ٱلْـَٔاخِرِ فَقَدْ ضَلَّ ضَلَـٰلًۢا بَعِيدًا ۞ إِنَّ ٱلَّذِينَ ءَامَنُوا۟ ثُمَّ كَفَرُوا۟ ثُمَّ ءَامَنُوا۟ ثُمَّ كَفَرُوا۟ ثُمَّ ٱزْدَادُوا۟ كُفْرًا لَّمْ يَكُنِ ٱللَّهُ لِيَغْفِرَ لَهُمْ وَلَا لِيَهْدِيَهُمْ سَبِيلًۢا ۞ بَشِّرِ ٱلْمُنَٰفِقِينَ بِأَنَّ لَهُمْ عَذَابًا أَلِيمًا ۞ ٱلَّذِينَ يَتَّخِذُونَ ٱلْكَٰفِرِينَ أَوْلِيَآءَ مِن دُونِ ٱلْمُؤْمِنِينَ ۚ أَيَبْتَغُونَ عِندَهُمُ ٱلْعِزَّةَ فَإِنَّ ٱلْعِزَّةَ لِلَّهِ جَمِيعًا ۞ وَقَدْ نَزَّلَ عَلَيْكُمْ فِى ٱلْكِتَٰبِ أَنْ إِذَا سَمِعْتُمْ ءَايَٰتِ ٱللَّهِ يُكْفَرُ بِهَا وَيُسْتَهْزَأُ بِهَا فَلَا تَقْعُدُوا۟ مَعَهُمْ حَتَّىٰ يَخُوضُوا۟ فِى حَدِيثٍ غَيْرِهِۦٓ ۚ إِنَّكُمْ إِذًا مِّثْلُهُمْ ۗ إِنَّ ٱللَّهَ جَامِعُ ٱلْمُنَٰفِقِينَ وَٱلْكَٰفِرِينَ فِى جَهَنَّمَ جَمِيعًا ۞ ٱلَّذِينَ يَتَرَبَّصُونَ بِكُمْ فَإِن كَانَ لَكُمْ فَتْحٌ مِّنَ ٱللَّهِ قَالُوٓا۟ أَلَمْ نَكُن مَّعَكُمْ وَإِن كَانَ لِلْكَٰفِرِينَ نَصِيبٌ قَالُوٓا۟ أَلَمْ نَسْتَحْوِذْ عَلَيْكُمْ وَنَمْنَعْكُم مِّنَ ٱلْمُؤْمِنِينَ ۚ فَٱللَّهُ يَحْكُمُ بَيْنَكُمْ يَوْمَ ٱلْقِيَٰمَةِ ۗ وَلَن يَجْعَلَ ٱللَّهُ لِلْكَٰفِرِينَ عَلَى ٱلْمُؤْمِنِينَ سَبِيلًا ۞ إِنَّ ٱلْمُنَٰفِقِينَ يُخَٰدِعُونَ ٱللَّهَ وَهُوَ خَٰدِعُهُمْ وَإِذَا قَامُوٓا۟ إِلَى ٱلصَّلَوٰةِ قَامُوا۟ كُسَالَىٰ يُرَآءُونَ ٱلنَّاسَ وَلَا يَذْكُرُونَ ٱللَّهَ إِلَّا قَلِيلًا ۞ مُّذَبْذَبِينَ بَيْنَ ذَٰلِكَ لَآ إِلَىٰ هَـٰٓؤُلَآءِ وَلَآ إِلَىٰ هَـٰٓؤُلَآءِ ۚ وَمَن يُضْلِلِ ٱللَّهُ فَلَن تَجِدَ

$$\text{لَهُ سَبِيلًا ۞ يَٰٓأَيُّهَا ٱلَّذِينَ ءَامَنُوا۟ لَا تَتَّخِذُوا۟ ٱلْكَٰفِرِينَ أَوْلِيَآءَ مِن دُونِ ٱلْمُؤْمِنِينَ ۚ أَتُرِيدُونَ أَن تَجْعَلُوا۟ لِلَّهِ عَلَيْكُمْ سُلْطَٰنًا مُّبِينًا ۞ إِنَّ ٱلْمُنَٰفِقِينَ فِى ٱلدَّرْكِ ٱلْأَسْفَلِ مِنَ ٱلنَّارِ وَلَن تَجِدَ لَهُمْ نَصِيرًا ۞ إِلَّا ٱلَّذِينَ تَابُوا۟ وَأَصْلَحُوا۟ وَٱعْتَصَمُوا۟ بِٱللَّهِ وَأَخْلَصُوا۟ دِينَهُمْ لِلَّهِ فَأُو۟لَٰٓئِكَ مَعَ ٱلْمُؤْمِنِينَ ۖ وَسَوْفَ يُؤْتِ ٱللَّهُ ٱلْمُؤْمِنِينَ أَجْرًا عَظِيمًا ۞ مَّا يَفْعَلُ ٱللَّهُ بِعَذَابِكُمْ إِن شَكَرْتُمْ وَءَامَنتُمْ ۚ وَكَانَ ٱللَّهُ شَاكِرًا عَلِيمًا ۞}$$

(An-Nisaa 024-147)

INTRODUCTION TO CHAPTER (SURAH) 4: AN-NISAA (THE WOMEN)

Ibn Kathir's Introduction

Virtues of Surat An-Nisa, A Madinan Surah

Al-`Awfi reported that Ibn `Abbas said that Surat An-Nisa' was revealed in Al-Madinah. Ibn Marduwyah recorded similar statements from `Abdullah bin Az-Zubayr and Zayd bin Thabit. In his Mustadrak, Al-Hakim recorded that `Abdullah bin Mas`ud said, "There are five Ayat in Surat An-Nisa' that I would prefer to the life of this world and all that is in it,

(Surely, Allah wrongs not even the weight of an atom,) (4:40),

(If you avoid the great sins which you are forbidden to do) (4:31),

(Verily, Allah forgives not that partners should be set up with Him (in worship), but He forgives except that (anything else) to whom He wills) (4:48),

(If they (hypocrites), when they had been unjust to themselves, had come to you) (4:64), and,

(And whoever does evil or wrongs himself, but afterwards seeks Allah's forgiveness, he will find Allah Oft-Forgiving, Most Merciful) (4:110)." Al-Hakim recorded that Ibn `Abbas said, "Ask me about Surat An-Nisa', for I learned the Qur'an when I was still young." Al-Hakim said, "This Hadith is Sahih according to the criteria of the Two Sahihs, and they did not collect it."

CHAPTER (SURAH) 4: AN-NISAA (THE WOMEN), VERSES 024-147

Surah: 4 Ayah: 24

﴿ ۞ وَٱلْمُحْصَنَٰتُ مِنَ ٱلنِّسَآءِ إِلَّا مَا مَلَكَتْ أَيْمَٰنُكُمْ ۖ كِتَٰبَ ٱللَّهِ عَلَيْكُمْ ۚ وَأُحِلَّ لَكُم مَّا وَرَآءَ ذَٰلِكُمْ أَن تَبْتَغُوا۟ بِأَمْوَٰلِكُم مُّحْصِنِينَ غَيْرَ مُسَٰفِحِينَ ۚ فَمَا ٱسْتَمْتَعْتُم بِهِۦ مِنْهُنَّ فَـَٔاتُوهُنَّ أُجُورَهُنَّ فَرِيضَةً ۚ وَلَا جُنَاحَ عَلَيْكُمْ فِيمَا تَرَٰضَيْتُم بِهِۦ مِنۢ بَعْدِ ٱلْفَرِيضَةِ ۚ إِنَّ ٱللَّهَ كَانَ عَلِيمًا حَكِيمًا ﴾

24. Also (forbidden are) women already married, except those (slaves) whom your right hands possess. Thus has Allâh ordained for you. All others are lawful, provided you seek (them in marriage) with Mahr (bridal money given by the husband to his wife at the time of marriage) from your property, desiring chastity, not committing illegal sexual intercourse, so with those of whom you have enjoyed sexual relations, give them their Mahr as prescribed; but if after a Mahr is prescribed, you agree mutually (to give more), there is no sin on you. Surely, Allâh is Ever All-Knowing, All-Wise.

Transliteration

24. Waalmuhsanatu mina alnnisa-i illa ma malakat aymanukum kitaba Allahi AAalaykum waohilla lakum ma waraa thalikum an tabtaghoo bi-amwalikum muhsineena ghayra musafiheena fama istamtaAAtum bihi minhunna faatoohunna ojoorahunna fareedatan wala junaha AAalaykum feema taradaytum bihi min baAAdi alfareedati inna Allaha kana AAaleeman hakeeman

Tafsir Ibn Kathir

Forbidding Women Already Married, Except for Female Slaves

Allah said,

(Also (forbidden are) women already married, except those whom your right hands possess.) The Ayah means, you are prohibited from marrying women who are already married,

(except those whom your right hands possess) except those whom you acquire through war, for you are allowed such women after making sure they are not pregnant. Imam Ahmad recorded that Abu Sa`id Al-Khudri said, "We captured some women from the area of Awtas who were already married, and we disliked having sexual relations with them because they already had husbands. So, we asked the Prophet about this matter, and this Ayah was revealed,

(Also (forbidden are) women already married, except those whom your right hands possess). Consequently, we had sexual relations with these women." This is the wording collected by At-Tirmidhi An-Nasa'i, Ibn Jarir and Muslim in his Sahih. Allah's statement,

(Thus has Allah ordained for you) means, this prohibition was ordained for you by Allah. Therefore, adhere to Allah's Book, do not transgress His set limits, and adhere to His legislation and decrees.

The Permission to Marry All Other Women

Allah said,

(All others are lawful) meaning, you are allowed to marry women other than the prohibited types mentioned here, as `Ata' and others have stated. Allah's statement,

(provided you seek them (with a dowry) from your property, desiring chastity, not fornication,) meaning, you are allowed to use your money to marry up to four wives and for (the purchase of) as many female slaves as you like, all through legal means,

((desiring) chastity, not fornication.) Allah's statement,

(So with those among them whom you have enjoyed, give them their required due,) means, to enjoy them sexually, surrender to them their rightful dowry as compensation. In other Ayat, Allah said,

(And how could you take it (back) while you have gone in unto each other),

(And give to the women (whom you marry) their dowry with a good heart), and,

(And it is not lawful for you (men) to take back (from your wives) any of what (dowry) you gave them)

Prohibiting the Mut`ah of Marriage

Mujahid stated that,

(So with those among them whom you have enjoyed, give them their required due,) was revealed about the Mut`ah marriage. A Mut`ah marriage is a marriage that ends upon a predeterminied date. In the Two Sahihs, it is recorded that the Leader of the Faithful `Ali bin Abi Talib said, "The Messenger of Allah prohibited Mut`ah marriage and eating the meat of domesticated donkeys on the day of Khaybar (battle)." In addition, in his Sahih, Muslim recorded that Ar-Rabi` bin Sabrah bin Ma`bad Al-Juhani said that his father said that he accompanied the Messenger of Allah during the conquest of Makkah, and that the Prophet said,

Chapter 4: An-Nisaa (The Women), Verses 024-147

»يَا أَيُّهَا النَّاسُ إِنِّي كُنْتُ أَذِنْتُ لَكُمْ فِي الاسْتِمْتَاعِ مِنَ النِّسَاءِ، وَإِنَّ اللهَ قَدْ حَرَّمَ ذَلِكَ إِلَى يَوْمِ الْقِيَامَةِ، فَمَنْ كَانَ عِنْدَهُ مِنْهُنَّ شَيْءٌ فَلْيُخَلِّ سَبِيلَهُ، وَلَا تَأْخُذُوا مِمَّا آتَيْتُمُوهُنَّ شَيْئًا«

(O people! I allowed you the Mut`ah marriage with women before. Now, Allah has prohibited it until the Day of Resurrection. Therefore, anyone who has any women in Mut`ah, let him let them go, and do not take anything from what you have given them.) Allah's statement,

(but if you agree mutually (to give more) after the requirement (has been determined), there is no sin on you.) is similar to His other statement,

(And give to the women their dowry with a good heart). The meaning of these Ayat is: If you have stipulated a dowry for her, and she later forfeits it, either totally or partially, then this bears no harm on you or her in this case. Ibn Jarir said, "Al-Hadrami said that some men would designate a certain dowry, but then fall into financial difficulties. Therefore, Allah said that there is no harm on you, O people, concerning your mutual agreement after the requirement (has been determined)." meaning, if she gives up part of the dowry, then you men are allowed to accept that. Allah's statement,

(Surely, Allah is Ever All-Knowing, All-Wise.) is suitable here, after Allah mentioned these prohibitions.

Surah: 4 Ayah: 25

﴿ وَمَن لَّمْ يَسْتَطِعْ مِنكُمْ طَوْلاً أَن يَنكِحَ ٱلْمُحْصَنَٰتِ ٱلْمُؤْمِنَٰتِ فَمِن مَّا مَلَكَتْ أَيْمَٰنُكُم مِّن فَتَيَٰتِكُمُ ٱلْمُؤْمِنَٰتِ وَٱللَّهُ أَعْلَمُ بِإِيمَٰنِكُم بَعْضُكُم مِّنْ بَعْضٍ فَٱنكِحُوهُنَّ بِإِذْنِ أَهْلِهِنَّ وَءَاتُوهُنَّ أُجُورَهُنَّ بِٱلْمَعْرُوفِ مُحْصَنَٰتٍ غَيْرَ مُسَٰفِحَٰتٍ وَلَا مُتَّخِذَٰتِ أَخْدَانٍ فَإِذَا أُحْصِنَّ فَإِنْ أَتَيْنَ بِفَٰحِشَةٍ فَعَلَيْهِنَّ نِصْفُ مَا عَلَى ٱلْمُحْصَنَٰتِ مِنَ ٱلْعَذَابِ ذَٰلِكَ لِمَنْ خَشِيَ ٱلْعَنَتَ مِنكُمْ وَأَن تَصْبِرُواْ خَيْرٌ لَّكُمْ وَٱللَّهُ غَفُورٌ رَّحِيمٌ ﴿٢٥﴾

25. And whoever of you has not the means wherewith to wed free, believing women, they may wed believing girls from among those (slaves) whom your right hands possess, and Allâh has full knowledge about your Faith; you are one from another. Wed them with the permission of their own folk (guardians, Auliyâ' or masters) and give them their Mahr according to what is reasonable; they (the

above said captive and slave-girls) should be chaste, not adulterous, nor taking boy-friends. And after they have been taken in wedlock, if they commit illegal sexual intercourse, their punishment is half that for free (unmarried) women. This is for him among you who is afraid of being harmed in his religion or in his body; but it is better for you that you practice self-restraint, and Allâh is Oft-Forgiving, Most Merciful.

Transliteration

25. Waman lam yastatiAA minkum tawlan an yankiha almuhsanati almu/minati famin ma malakat aymanukum min fatayatikumu almu/minati waAllahu aAAlamu bi-eemanikum baAAdukum min baAAdin fainkihoohunna bi-ithni ahlihinna waatoohunna ojoorahunna bialmaAAroofi muhsanatin ghayra masafihatin wala muttakhithati akhdanin fa-itha ohsinna fa-in atayna bifahishatin faAAalayhinna nisfu ma AAala almuhsanati mina alAAathabi thalika liman khashiya alAAanata minkum waan tasbiroo khayrun lakum waAllahu ghafoorun raheemun

Tafsir Ibn Kathir

Marrying a Female Slave, if One Cannot Marry a Free Woman

Allah said, those who do not have,

(the means), financial capability,

(Wherewith to wed free believing women) meaning, free faithful, chaste women.

(They may wed believing girls from among those whom your right hands possess,) meaning, they are allowed to wed believing slave girls owned by the believers.

(and Allah has full knowledge about your faith; you are one from another.) Allah knows the true reality and secrets of all things, but you people know only the apparent things. Allah then said,

(Wed them with the permission of their own folk) indicating that the owner is responsible for the slave girl, and consequently, she cannot marry without his permission. The owner is also responsible for his male slave and they cannot wed without his permission. A Hadith states,

»أَيُّمَا عَبْدٍ تَزَوَّجَ بِغَيْرِ إِذْنِ مَوَالِيهِ، فَهُوَ عَاهِر«

(Any male slave who marries without permission from his master, is a fornicator.) When the owner of the female slave is a female, those who are allowed to give away the free woman in marriage, with her permission, become responsible for giving away her female slave in marriage, as well. A Hadith states that

»لَا تُزَوِّجِ الْمَرْأَةُ الْمَرْأَةَ، وَلَا الْمَرْأَةُ نَفْسَهَا، فَإِنَّ الزَّانِيَةَ هِيَ الَّتِي تُزَوِّجُ نَفْسَهَا«

Chapter 4: An-Nisaa (The Women), Verses 024-147

(The woman does not give away another woman, or herself in marriage, for only the adulteress gives herself away in marriage.) Allah's statement,

(And give them their due in a good manner;) meaning, pay them their dowry with a good heart, and do not keep any of it, belittling the matter due to the fact that they are owned slaves. Allah's statement,

(they should be chaste) means, they are honorable women who do not commit adultery, and this is why Allah said,

(not fornicators) referring to dishonorable women, who do not refrain from illicit sexual relations with those who ask. Ibn `Abbas said that the fornicating women are the whores, who do not object to having relations with whomever seeks it, while,

(nor promiscuous.) refers to taking boyfriends. Similar was said by Abu Hurayrah, Mujahid, Ash-Sha`bi, Ad-Dahhak, `Ata' Al-Khurasani, Yahya bin Abi Kathir, Muqatil bin Hayyan and As-Suddi.

The Slave Girl's Punishment for Adultery is Half that of a Free Unmarried Woman

Allah said,

(And after they have been taken in wedlock, if they commit Fahishah, their punishment is half of that for free (unmarried) women.) this is about the slave women who got married, as indicated by the Ayah;

(And whoever of you have not the means wherewith to wed free believing women, they may wed believing girls from among those whom your right hands possess,) Therefore, since the honorable Ayah is about believing slave girls, then,

(And after they have been taken in wedlock,) refers to when they (believing slave girls) get married, as Ibn `Abbas and others have said. Allah's statement,

(their punishment is half of that for free (unmarried) women.) indicates that the type of punishment prescribed here is the one that can be reduced to half, lashes in this case, not stoning to death, and Allah knows best. Allah's statement,

(This is for him among you who is afraid of being harmed in his religion or in his body;) indicates that marrying slave girls, providing one satisfies the required conditions, is for those who fear for their chastity and find it hard to be patient and refrain from sex. In this difficult circumstance, one is allowed to marry a slave girl. However, it is better to refrain from marrying slave girls and to observe patience, for otherwise, the offspring will become slaves to the girl's master. Allah said,

(but it is better for you that you practice self-restraint, and Allah is Oft-Forgiving, Most Merciful.)

Surah: 4 Ayah: 26, Ayah: 27 & Ayah: 28

﴿ يُرِيدُ ٱللَّهُ لِيُبَيِّنَ لَكُمْ وَيَهْدِيَكُمْ سُنَنَ ٱلَّذِينَ مِن قَبْلِكُمْ وَيَتُوبَ عَلَيْكُمْ ۗ وَٱللَّهُ عَلِيمٌ حَكِيمٌ ﴾

26. Allâh wishes to make clear (what is lawful and what is unlawful) to you, and to show you the ways of those before you, and accept your repentance, and Allâh is All-Knower, All-Wise.

﴿ وَٱللَّهُ يُرِيدُ أَن يَتُوبَ عَلَيْكُمْ وَيُرِيدُ ٱلَّذِينَ يَتَّبِعُونَ ٱلشَّهَوَاتِ أَن تَمِيلُوا۟ مَيْلًا عَظِيمًا ﴾

27. Allâh wishes to accept your repentance, but those who follow their lusts, wish that you (believers) should deviate tremendously away (from the Right Path).

﴿ يُرِيدُ ٱللَّهُ أَن يُخَفِّفَ عَنكُمْ ۚ وَخُلِقَ ٱلْإِنسَٰنُ ضَعِيفًا ﴾

28. Allâh wishes to lighten (the burden) for you; and man was created weak (cannot be patient to leave sexual intercourse with woman).

Transliteration

26. Yureedu Allahu liyubayyina lakum wayahdiyakum sunana allatheena min qablikum wayatooba AAalaykum waAllahu AAaleemun hakeemun 27. WaAllahu yureedu an yatooba AAalaykum wayureedu allatheena yattabiAAoona alshshahawati an tameeloo maylan AAatheeman 28. Yureedu Allahu an yukhaffifa AAankum wakhuliqa al-insanu daAAeefan

Tafsir Ibn Kathir

Allah explains to the believers what He has allowed and prohibited for them in this and other Surahs,

(And to show you the ways of those before you,) meaning their righteous ways and how to adhere to the commandments that He likes and is pleased with.

(and accept your repentance) from sin and error,

(and Allah is All-Knower, All-Wise.) in His commands, decrees, actions and statements. Allah's statement,

(but those who follow their lusts, wish that you (believers) should deviate tremendously away from the right path)) indicates that the followers of Shaytan among the Jews, Christians and the adulterous, wish that you would take the horrendous path of falsehood instead of the truth.

(Allah wishes to lighten (the burden) for you") His legislation, orders, what He prohibits and what He decrees for you. This is why Allah has allowed free men to marry slave girls under certain conditions, as Mujahid and others have stated.

(and man was created weak.) and this is why it is suitable in his case that the commands are made easy for him, because of his weakness and feebleness. Ibn Abi Hatim recorded that Tawus said that,

(and man was created weak), "Concerning women". Waki` said, "Man's mind leaves when women are involved."

Surah: 4 Ayah: 29, Ayah: 30 & Ayah: 31

﴿ يَٰٓأَيُّهَا ٱلَّذِينَ ءَامَنُوا۟ لَا تَأْكُلُوٓا۟ أَمْوَٰلَكُم بَيْنَكُم بِٱلْبَٰطِلِ إِلَّآ أَن تَكُونَ تِجَٰرَةً عَن تَرَاضٍ مِّنكُمْ وَلَا تَقْتُلُوٓا۟ أَنفُسَكُمْ إِنَّ ٱللَّهَ كَانَ بِكُمْ رَحِيمًا ﴾

29. O you who believe! Eat not up your property among yourselves unjustly except it be a trade amongst you, by mutual consent. And do not kill yourselves (nor kill one another). Surely, Allâh is Most Merciful to you.

﴿ وَمَن يَفْعَلْ ذَٰلِكَ عُدْوَٰنًا وَظُلْمًا فَسَوْفَ نُصْلِيهِ نَارًا وَكَانَ ذَٰلِكَ عَلَى ٱللَّهِ يَسِيرًا ﴾

30. And whoever commits that through aggression and injustice, We shall cast him into the Fire, and that is easy for Allâh.

﴿ إِن تَجْتَنِبُوا۟ كَبَآئِرَ مَا تُنْهَوْنَ عَنْهُ نُكَفِّرْ عَنكُمْ سَيِّـَٔاتِكُمْ وَنُدْخِلْكُم مُّدْخَلًا كَرِيمًا ﴾

31. If you avoid the great sins which you are forbidden to do, We shall expiate from you your (small) sins, and admit you to a Noble Entrance (i.e. Paradise).

Transliteration

29. Ya ayyuha allatheena amanoo la ta/kuloo amwalakum baynakum bialbatili illa an takoona tijaratan AAan taradin minkum wala taqtuloo anfusakum inna Allaha kana bikum raheeman 30. Waman yafAAal thalika AAudwanan wathulman fasawfa nusleehi naran wakana thalika AAala Allahi yaseeran 31. In tajtaniboo kaba-ira ma tunhawna AAanhu nukaffir AAankum sayyi-atikum wanudkhilkum mudkhalan kareeman

Tafsir Ibn Kathir

Prohibiting Unlawfully Earned Money

Allah, the Exalted and Most Honored, prohibits His believing servants from illegally acquiring each other's property using various dishonest methods such as Riba, gambling and other wicked methods that appear to be legal, but Allah knows that, in reality, those involved seek to deal in interest. Ibn Jarir recorded that Ibn `Abbas commented on a man who buys a garment, saying that if he likes it he will keep it, or he will return it along with an extra Dirham, "This is what Allah meant, when He said,

(Eat not up your property among yourselves unjustly.") `Ali bin Abi Talhah reported that Ibn `Abbas said, "When Allah sent down,

(O you who believe! Eat not up your property among yourselves unjustly) some Muslims said, `Allah has forbidden us from eating up each other's property unjustly, and food is our best property. Therefore, none among us is allowed to eat from anyone else's food.' After that Allah sent down,

(There is no restriction on the blind) (until the end of the Ayah). (24:61).'" Qatadah said similarly. Allah's statement,

(except it be a trade amongst you, by mutual consent.) means, do not revert to illegal ways and means to acquire money. However, there is no harm in commercial transactions that transpire between the buyer and the seller with mutual consent, so that money is legally earned from these transactions. Mujahid said that,

(except it be a trade amongst you, by mutual consent.) means, "By selling and buying, or giving someone a gift." Ibn Jarir recorded this statement.

The Option to Buy or Sell Before Parting, is Part of `Mutual Consent' in Trading

Mutual agreement in various transactions is attained when both parties have the right to uphold or dissolve the agreement before they part. In the Two Sahihs, it is recorded that the Messenger of Allah said,

«الْبَيِّعَانِ بِالْخِيَارِ مَا لَمْ يَتَفَرَّقَا»

(The seller and the buyer retain the (right to change their mind) as long as they have not parted.) Al-Bukhari's wording for this Hadith reads,

«إِذَا تَبَايَعَ الرَّجُلَانِ فَكُلُّ وَاحِدٍ مِنْهُمَا بِالْخِيَارِ، مَا لَمْ يَتَفَرَّقَا»

(When two men conduct a transaction, they retain their (right to change their mind) as long as they have not parted.)

Forbidding Murder and Suicide

Allah said,

(And do not kill yourselves.) by committing Allah's prohibitions, falling into sin and eating up each other's property unjustly,

(Surely, Allah is Most Merciful to you.) in what He commanded you and prohibited you from. Imam Ahmad recorded that `Amr bin Al-`As said that when the Prophet sent him for the battle of Dhat As-Salasil, "I had a wet dream during a very cold night and feared that if I bathed, I would die. So I performed Tayammum (with pure earth) and led my company in the Dawn prayer. When I went back to the Messenger of Allah, I mentioned what had happened to me and he said,

«يَا عَمْرُو صَلَّيْتَ بِأَصْحَابِكَ وَأَنْتَ جُنُب»

(O `Amr! Have you led your people in prayer while you were in a state of sexual impurity) I said, 'O Messenger of Allah! I had a wet dream on a very cold night and feared that if I bathed I would perish, and I remembered Allah's statement,

(And do not kill yourselves. Surely, Allah is Most Merciful to you). So I performed Tayammum and prayed.' The Messenger of Allah smiled and did not say anything." This is the narration reported by Abu Dawud. Ibn Marduwyah mentioned this honorable Ayah and then reported that Abu Hurayrah said that the Messenger of Allah said,

«مَنْ قَتَلَ نَفْسَهُ بِحَدِيدَةٍ، فَحَدِيدَتُهُ فِي يَدِهِ، يَجَأُ بِهَا بَطْنَهُ يَوْمَ الْقِيَامَةِ فِي نَارِ جَهَنَّمَ، خَالِدًا مُخَلَّدًا فِيهَا أَبَدًا، وَمَنْ قَتَلَ نَفْسَهُ بِسُمٍّ فَسُمُّهُ فِي يَدِهِ، يَتَحَسَّاهُ فِي نَارِ جَهَنَّمَ، خَالِدًا مُخَلَّدًا فِيهَا أَبَدًا، وَمَنْ تَرَدَّى مِنْ جَبَلٍ فَقَتَلَ نَفْسَهُ، فَهُوَ مُتَرَدٍّ فِي نَارِ جَهَنَّمَ، خَالِدًا مُخَلَّدًا فِيهَا أَبَدًا»

(Whoever kills himself with an iron tool, then his tool will be in his hand and he will keep stabbing himself with it in the Fire of Jahannam, forever and ever. Whoever kills himself with poison, then his poison will be in his hand and he will keep taking it in the Fire of Jahannam forever and ever. Whoever kills himself by throwing himself from a mountain, will keep falling in the Fire of Jahannam forever and ever.) This Hadith was also collected in the Two Sahihs. Abu Qilabah said that Thabit bin Ad-Dahhak said that the Messenger of Allah said,

«مَنْ قَتَلَ نَفْسَهُ بِشَيْءٍ، عُذِّبَ بِهِ يَوْمَ الْقِيَامَةِ»

(Whoever kills himself with an instrument, will be punished with it on the Day of Resurrection.) This Hadith was collected by the Group. This is why Allah said,

(And whoever commits that through aggression and injustice,) meaning, whoever commits what Allah has forbidden for him transgression and injustice - while knowing that it is forbidden for him, yet he still dares to commit it,

(We shall cast him into the Fire,). This Ayah carries a stern warning and a truthful promise. Therefore, every sane person should beware of it, those who hear the speech with full comprehension.

Minor Sins Will be Pardoned if One Refrains from Major Sins

Allah said,

(If you avoid the great sins which you are forbidden to do, We shall remit from you your (small) sins,) meaning, if you avoid the major evil deeds that you were prohibited We will forgive you the minor evil deeds and will admit you into Paradise. This is why Allah said,

(and admit you to a Noble Entrance (i.e. Paradise).) There are several Hadiths on the subject of this honorable Ayah. Imam Ahmad recorded that Salman Al-Farisi said, "The Prophet said to me, `Do you know what the day of Al-Jumu`ah is' I said, `It is the day during which Allah brought together the creation of your father (Adam).' He said,

«لكِنْ أَدْرِي مَا يَوْمُ الْجُمُعَةِ، لَا يَتَطَهَّرُ الرَّجُلُ فَيُحْسِنُ طُهُورَهُ، ثُمَّ يَأْتِي الْجُمُعَةَ فَيُنْصِتُ حَتَّى يَقْضِيَ الْإِمَامُ صَلَاتَهُ، إِلَّا كَانَ كَفَّارَةً لَهُ مَا بَيْنَهُ وَبَيْنَ الْجُمُعَةِ الْمُقْبِلَةِ، مَا اجْتُنِبَتِ الْمَقْتَلَة»

(I know what the day of Jumu`ah is. Anyone who takes a bath and cleans himself as much as he can and then proceeds for the Friday prayer and remains quiet until the Imam finishes the prayer, all his sins in between the present and the next Friday will be forgiven, as long as major sins were avoided.)" Al-Bukhari recorded similar wording from Salman Al-Farisi.

The Seven Destructive Sins

What are the Seven Destructive Sins In the Two Sahihs, it is recorded that Abu Hurayrah said that the Messenger of Allah said,

«اجْتَنِبُوا السَّبْعَ الْمُوبِقَات»

(Avoid the seven great destructive sins.) The people inquired, 'O Allah's Messenger! What are they' He said,

«الشِّرْكُ بِاللهِ، وَقَتْلُ النَّفْسِ الَّتِي حَرَّمَ اللهُ إِلَّا بِالْحَقِّ، وَالسِّحْرُ، وَأَكْلُ الرِّبَا، وَأَكْلُ مَالِ الْيَتِيمِ، وَالتَّوَلِّي يَوْمَ الزَّحْفِ، وَقَذْفُ الْمُحْصَنَاتِ الْمُؤْمِنَاتِ الْغَافِلَاتِ»

(To join others in worship along with Allah, to kill the life which Allah has forbidden except for a just cause, magic, to consume Riba, to consume an orphan's wealth, to turn away from the enemy and flee from the battlefield when the battle begins, and to accuse chaste women, who never even think of anything that would tarnish their chastity and are good believers.) Another Hadith that mentions False Witness Imam Ahmad recorded that Anas bin Malik said, "The Messenger of Allah mentioned the major sins, or was asked about the major sins. He said,

«الشِّرْكُ بِاللهِ، وَقَتْلُ النَّفْسِ، وَعُقُوقُ الْوَالِدَيْنِ»

(Associating others with Allah in worship, killing the life, and being undutiful to the parents.) He then said,

«أَلَا أُنَبِّئُكُمْ بِأَكْبَرِ الْكَبَائِرِ؟»

(Should I tell you about the biggest of the major sins)

He said:

«قَوْلُ الزُّورِ أَوْ شَهَادَةُ الزُّورِ»

(The false statement - or the false testimony.)" Shu`bah - one of the narrators of the Hadith - said, "Most likely, in my opinion, he said, `False testimony.'" The Two Sahihs recorded this Hadith from Shu`bah from Anas. Another Hadith In the Two Sahihs, it is recorded that `Abdur-Rahman bin Abi Bakrah said that his father said, "The Prophet said,

«أَلَا أُنَبِّئُكُمْ بِأَكْبَرِ الْكَبَائِرِ؟»

(Should I inform you about the greatest of the great sins) We said, `Yes, O Allah's Messenger !' He said,

«الْإِشْرَاكُ بِاللهِ، وَعُقُوقُ الْوَالِدَيْنِ»

(To join others in worship with Allah and to be undutiful to one's parents.) He was reclining, then he sat up and said;

«أَلَا وَشَهَادَةُ الزُّورِ، أَلَا وَقَوْلُ الزُّورِ»

(And I warn you against false testimony and false speech.) and he continued repeating it until we wished that he would stop." Another Hadith that mentions killing the Offspring In the Two Sahihs, it is recorded that `Abdullah bin Mas`ud said, "I asked, `O Allah's Messenger! What is the greatest sin' ((in one narration) the biggest sin)' He said,

«أَنْ تَجْعَلَ لِلَّهِ نِدًّا وَهُوَ خَلَقَكَ»

(To make a rival for Allah while He Alone created you.) I said, `Then' He said,

«أَنْ تَقْتُلَ وَلَدَكَ خَشْيَةَ أَنْ يَطْعَمَ مَعَكَ»

(To kill your offspring for fear that he might share your food with you.) I said, `Then' He said,

«أَنْ تُزَانِيَ حَلِيلَةَ جَارِكَ»

(To commit adultery with your neighbor's wife.) He then recited,

(And those who invoke not any other god along with Allah), until,

(Except those who repent)." Another Hadith from `Abdullah bin `Amr Imam Ahmad recorded that `Abdullah bin `Amr said that the Prophet said,

«أَكْبَرُ الْكَبَائِرِ: الْإِشْرَاكُ بِاللَّهِ، وَعُقُوقُ الْوَالِدَيْنِ أَوْ قَتْلُ النَّفْسِ شعبة الشاك وَالْيَمِينُ الْغَمُوسُ»

(The greatest sins are: To join others in worship with Allah, to be undutiful to one's parents - or to take a life) Shu`bah was uncertain of which one - (and the false oath). Recorded by Al-Bukhari, At-Tirmidhi, and An-Nasai. Another Hadith by `Abdullah bin `Amr about Causing one's Parents to be Cursed `Abdullah bin `Amr said that the Messenger of Allah said,

«إِنَّ مِنْ أَكْبَرِ الْكَبَائِرِ أَنْ يَلْعَنَ الرَّجُلُ وَالِدَيْهِ»

(Among the worst of the major sins is for a man to curse his own parents.) They said, "How can one curse his own parents" He said,

«يَسُبُّ الرَّجُلُ أَبَا الرَّجُلِ، فَيَسُبُّ أَبَاهُ، وَيَسُبُّ أُمَّهُ فَيَسُبُّ أُمَّهُ»

(One curses another man's father, and that man curses his father in retaliation, or he curses someone's mother and that man curses his mother.) This is the wording of Muslim. At-Tirmidhi said, "Sahih." It is recorded in the Sahih that the Messenger of Allah said,

«سِبَابُ الْمُسْلِمِ فُسُوقٌ، وَقِتَالُهُ كُفْرٌ»

(Cursing a Muslim is a sin and fighting him is Kufr.)

Surah: 4 Ayah: 32

﴿ وَلَا تَتَمَنَّوْا مَا فَضَّلَ ٱللَّهُ بِهِ بَعْضَكُمْ عَلَىٰ بَعْضٍ ۚ لِلرِّجَالِ نَصِيبٌ مِّمَّا ٱكْتَسَبُوا ۖ وَلِلنِّسَاءِ نَصِيبٌ مِّمَّا ٱكْتَسَبْنَ ۚ وَسْـَٔلُوا ٱللَّهَ مِن فَضْلِهِۦٓ ۗ إِنَّ ٱللَّهَ كَانَ بِكُلِّ شَىْءٍ عَلِيمًا ﴾

32. And wish not for the things in which Allâh has made some of you to excel others. For men there is reward for what they have earned, (and likewise) for women there is reward for what they have earned, and ask Allâh of His Bounty. Surely, Allâh is Ever All-Knower of everything.

Transliteration

32. Wala tatamannaw ma faddala Allahu bihi baAAdakum AAala baAAdin lilrrijali naseebun mimma iktasaboo walilnnisa-i naseebun mimma iktasabna wais-aloo Allaha min fadlihi inna Allaha kana bikulli shay-in AAaleeman

Tafsir Ibn Kathir

Do Not Wish for the Things Which Allah has Made Some Others to Excel In

Imam Ahmad recorded that Umm Salamah said, "O Messenger of Allah! Men go to battle, but we do not go to battle, and we earn one-half of the inheritance (that men get)." Allah sent down,

(And wish not for the things in which Allah has made some of you to excel others). At-Tirmidhi also recorded this Hadith. Allah's statement,

(For men there is reward for what they have earned, (and likewise) for women there is reward for what they have earned,) indicates, according to Ibn Jarir, that each person will earn his wages for his works, a reward if his deeds are good, and punishment if his deeds are evil. It was also reported that this Ayah is talking about inheritance, indicating the fact that each person will get his due share of the inheritance, as Al-Walibi reported from Ibn `Abbas. Allah then directed the servants to what benefits them,

(and ask Allah of His Bounty.)Therefore, the Ayah states, "Do not wish for what other people were endowed with over you, for this is a decision that will come to pass, and wishing does not change its decree. However, ask Me of My favor and I will grant it to you, for I Am Most Generous and Most Giving." Allah then said,

(Surely, Allah is Ever All-Knower of everything.) meaning, Allah knows who deserves this life, and so He gives him riches, and whoever deserves poverty, He makes him poor. He also knows who deserves the Hereafter, and He directs him to perform the deeds that will help him to be sucessful in it, and whoever deserves failure, He prevents him from achieving righteousness and what leads to it. Hence, Allah said,

(Surely, Allah is Ever All-Knower of everything).

Surah: 4 Ayah: 33

﴿ وَلِكُلٍّ جَعَلْنَا مَوَالِيَ مِمَّا تَرَكَ ٱلْوَٰلِدَانِ وَٱلْأَقْرَبُونَ ۚ وَٱلَّذِينَ عَقَدَتْ أَيْمَٰنُكُمْ فَـَٔاتُوهُمْ نَصِيبَهُمْ ۚ إِنَّ ٱللَّهَ كَانَ عَلَىٰ كُلِّ شَىْءٍ شَهِيدًا ﴾

33. And to everyone, We have appointed heirs of that (property) left by parents and relatives. To those also with whom you have made a pledge (brotherhood), give them their due portion (by Wasiyya - wills). Truly, Allâh is Ever a Witness over all things.

Transliteration

33. Walikullin jaAAalna mawaliya mimma taraka alwalidani waal-aqraboona waallatheena AAaqadat aymanukum faatoohum naseebahum inna Allaha kana AAala kulli shay-in shaheedan

Tafsir Ibn Kathir

Ibn `Abbas, Mujahid, Sa`id bin Jubayr, Abu Salih, Qatadah, Zayd bin Aslam, As-Suddi, Ad-Dahhak, Muqatil bin Hayyan, and others said that Allah's statement,

(And to everyone, We have appointed Mawali) means, "Heirs." Ibn `Abbas was also reported to have said that Mawali refers to relatives. Ibn Jarir commented, "The Arabs call the cousin a Mawla." Ibn Jarir continued, "Allah's statement,

(of that (property) left by parents and relatives.) means, from what he inherited from his parents and family members. Therefore, the meaning of the Ayah becomes: `To all of you, O people, We appointed relatives (such as children) who will later inherit what you inherited from your own parents and relatives." Allah's statement,

Chapter 4: An-Nisaa (The Women), Verses 024-147

(To those also with whom you have made a pledge (brotherhood), give them their due portion.) means, "Those with whom you have a pledge of brotherhood, give them their share of inheritance, thus fulfilling the ratified pledges that you gave them. Allah has witnessed all of you when you gave these pledges and promises." This practice was followed in the beginning of Islam, but was later on abrogated when Muslims were commanded to fulfill the pledges (brotherhood) they had already given, but to refrain from making any new pledges after that. Al-Bukhari recorded that Ibn `Abbas said,

(And to everyone, We have appointed Mawali) "meaning, heirs;

(To those also with whom you have made a pledge (brotherhood)) When the emigrants came to Al-Madinah, the emigrant would inherit from the Ansari, while the latter's relatives would not inherit from him because of the bond of brotherhood which the Prophet established between them (the emigrants and the Ansar). When the verse,

(And to everyone We have appointed Mawali) was revealed, it cancelled (the pledge of brotherhood regarding inheritance)." Then he said, "The verse,

(To those also with whom you have made a pledge (brotherhood), give them their due portion.) remained valid for cases of co-operation and mutual advice, while the matter of inheritance was excluded and it became permissible to assign something in one's will to the person who had the right of inheriting before."

Surah: 4 Ayah: 34

﴿ ٱلرِّجَالُ قَوَّٰمُونَ عَلَى ٱلنِّسَآءِ بِمَا فَضَّلَ ٱللَّهُ بَعْضَهُمْ عَلَىٰ بَعْضٍ وَبِمَآ أَنفَقُوا۟ مِنْ أَمْوَٰلِهِمْ ۚ فَٱلصَّٰلِحَٰتُ قَٰنِتَٰتٌ حَٰفِظَٰتٌ لِّلْغَيْبِ بِمَا حَفِظَ ٱللَّهُ ۚ وَٱلَّٰتِى تَخَافُونَ نُشُوزَهُنَّ فَعِظُوهُنَّ وَٱهْجُرُوهُنَّ فِى ٱلْمَضَاجِعِ وَٱضْرِبُوهُنَّ ۖ فَإِنْ أَطَعْنَكُمْ فَلَا تَبْغُوا۟ عَلَيْهِنَّ سَبِيلًا ۗ إِنَّ ٱللَّهَ كَانَ عَلِيًّا كَبِيرًا ﴾

34. Men are the protectors and maintainers of women, because Allâh has made one of them to excel the other, and because they spend (to support them) from their means. Therefore the righteous women are devoutly obedient (to Allâh and to their husbands), and guard in the husband's absence what Allâh orders them to guard (e.g. their chastity, their husband's property). As to those women on whose part you see ill-conduct, admonish them (first), (next), refuse to share their beds, (and last) beat them (lightly, if it is useful); but if they return to obedience, seek not against them means (of annoyance). Surely, Allâh is Ever Most High, Most Great.

Transliteration

34. Alrrijalu qawwamoona AAala alnnisa-i bima faddala Allahu baAAdahum AAala baAAdin wabima anfaqoo min amwalihim faalssalihatu qanitatun hafithatun lilghaybi

bima hafitha Allahu waallatee takhafoona nushoozahunna faAAithoohunna waohjuroohunna fee almadajiAAi waidriboohunna fa-in ataAAnakum fala tabghoo AAalayhinna sabeelan inna Allaha kana AAaliyyan kabeeran

Tafsir Ibn Kathir

Allah said,

(Men are the protectors and maintainers of women,) meaning, the man is responsible for the woman, and he is her maintainer, caretaker and leader who disciplines her if she deviates.

(because Allah has made one of them to excel the other,) meaning, because men excel over women and are better than them for certain tasks. This is why prophethood was exclusive of men, as well as other important positions of leadership. The Prophet said,

«لَنْ يُفْلِحَ قَوْمٌ وَلَّوْا أَمْرَهُمُ امْرَأَةً»

(People who appoint a woman to be their leader, will never achieve success.) Al-Bukhari recorded this Hadith. Such is the case with appointing women as judges or on other positions of leadership.

(and because they spend from their means.) meaning the dowry, expenditures and various expenses that Allah ordained in His Book and the Sunnah of His Messenger for men to spend on women. For these reasons it is suitable that he is appointed her maintainer, just as Allah said,

(But men have a degree (of responsibility) over them).

Qualities of the Righteous Wife

Allah said,

(Therefore, the righteous) women,

(are Qanitat), obedient to their husbands, as Ibn `Abbas and others stated.

(and guard in the husband's absence) As-Suddi and others said that it means she protects her honor and her husband's property when he is absent, and Allah's statement,

(what Allah orders them to guard.) means, the protected (husband) is the one whom Allah protects. Ibn Jarir recorded that Abu Hurayrah said that the Messenger of Allah said,

Chapter 4: An-Nisaa (The Women), Verses 024-147

»خَيْرُ النِّسَاءِ امْرَأَةٌ إِذَا نَظَرْتَ إِلَيْهَا سَرَّتْكَ، وَإِذَا أَمَرْتَهَا أَطَاعَتْكَ، وَإِذَا غِبْتَ عَنْهَا حَفِظَتْكَ فِي نَفْسِهَا وَمَالِكِ«

(The best women is she who when you look at her, she pleases you, when you command her she obeys you, and when you are absent, she protects her honor and your property.) Then, the Messenger of Allah recited the Ayah,

(Men are the protectors and maintainers of women,) until its end. Imam Ahmad recorded that `Abdur-Rahman bin 'Awf said that the Messenger of Allah said,

»إِذَا صَلَّتِ الْمَرْأَةُ خَمْسَهَا، وَصَامَتْ شَهْرَهَا، وَحَفِظَتْ فَرْجَهَا، وَأَطَاعَتْ زَوْجَهَا، قِيلَ لَهَا: ادْخُلِي الْجَنَّةَ مِنْ أَيِّ الْأَبْوَابِ شِئْتِ«

(If the woman prayed her five daily prayers, fasted her month, protected her chastity and obeyed her husband, she will be told, 'Enter Paradise from any of its doors you wish.')

Dealing with the Wife's Ill-Conduct

Allah said,

(As to those women on whose part you see ill conduct,) meaning, the woman from whom you see ill conduct with her husband, such as when she acts as if she is above her husband, disobeys him, ignores him, dislikes him, and so forth. When these signs appear in a woman, her husband should advise her and remind her of Allah's torment if she disobeys him. Indeed, Allah ordered the wife to obey her husband and prohibited her from disobeying him, because of the enormity of his rights and all that he does for her. The Messenger of Allah said,

»لَوْ كُنْتُ آمِرًا أَحَدًا أَنْ يَسْجُدَ لِأَحَدٍ، لَأَمَرْتُ الْمَرْأَةَ أَنْ تَسْجُدَ لِزَوْجِهَا، مِنْ عِظَمِ حَقِّهِ عَلَيْهَا«

(If I were to command anyone to prostrate before anyone, I would have commanded the wife to prostrate before her husband, because of the enormity of his right upon her.) Al-Bukhari recorded that Abu Hurayrah said that the Messenger of Allah said,

»إِذَا دَعَا الرَّجُلُ امْرَأَتَهُ إِلَى فِرَاشِهِ فَأَبَتْ عَلَيْهِ، لَعَنَتْهَا الْمَلَائِكَةُ حَتَّى تُصْبِحَ«

(If the man asks his wife to come to his bed and she declines, the angels will keep cursing her until the morning.) Muslim recorded it with the wording,

«إِذَا بَاتَتِ الْمَرْأَةُ هَاجِرَةً فِرَاشَ زَوْجِهَا، لَعَنَتْهَا الْمَلَائِكَةُ حَتَّى تُصْبِحَ»

(If the wife goes to sleep while ignoring her husband's bed, the angels will keep cursing her until the morning.) This is why Allah said,

(As to those women on whose part you see ill conduct, admonish them (first)). Allah's statement,

(abandon them in their beds,) `Ali bin Abi Talhah reported that Ibn `Abbas said "The abandonment refers to not having intercourse with her, to lie on her bed with his back to her." Several others said similarly. As-Suddi, Ad-Dahhak, `Ikrimah, and Ibn `Abbas, in another narration, added, "Not to speak with her or talk to her." The Sunan and Musnad compilers recorded that Mu`awiyah bin Haydah Al-Qushayri said, "O Allah's Messenger! What is the right that the wife of one of us has on him" The Prophet said,

«أَنْ تُطْعِمَهَا إِذَا طَعِمْتَ، وَتَكْسُوَهَا إِذَا اكْتَسَيْتَ، وَلَا تَضْرِبِ الْوَجْهَ، وَلَا تُقَبِّحْ، وَلَا تَهْجُرْ إِلَّا فِي الْبَيْتِ»

(To feed her when you eat, cloth her when you buy clothes for yourself, refrain from striking her face or cursing her, and to not abandon her, except in the house.) Allah's statement,

(beat them) means, if advice and ignoring her in the bed do not produce the desired results, you are allowed to discipline the wife, without severe beating. Muslim recorded that Jabir said that during the Farewell Hajj, the Prophet said;

«وَاتَّقُوا اللهَ فِي النِّسَاءِ، فَإِنَّهُنَّ عِنْدَكُمْ عَوَانٍ، وَلَكُمْ عَلَيْهِنَّ أَنْ لَا يُوطِئْنَ فُرُشَكُمْ أَحَدًا تَكْرَهُونَهُ، فَإِنْ فَعَلْنَ ذَلِكَ فَاضْرِبُوهُنَّ ضَرْبًا غَيْرَ مُبَرِّحٍ، وَلَهُنَّ عَلَيْكُمْ رِزْقُهُنَّ وَكِسْوَتُهُنَّ بِالْمَعْرُوفِ»

(Fear Allah regarding women, for they are your assistants. You have the right on them that they do not allow any person whom you dislike to step on your mat. However, if they do that, you are allowed to discipline them lightly. They have a right on you that you provide them with their provision and clothes, in a reasonable manner.) Ibn `Abbas and several others said that the Ayah refers to a beating that is not violent. Al-Hasan Al-Basri said that it means, a beating that is not severe.

Chapter 4: An-Nisaa (The Women), Verses 024-147

When the Wife Obeys Her Husband, Means of Annoyance Against Her are Prohibited

Allah said,

(but if they return to obedience, seek not against them means (of annoyance),) meaning, when the wife obeys her husband in all that Allah has allowed, then no means of annoyance from the husband are allowed against his wife. Therefore, in this case, the husband does not have the right to beat her or shun her bed. Allah's statement,

(Surely, Allah is Ever Most High, Most Great.) reminds men that if they transgress against their wives without justification, then Allah, the Ever Most High, Most Great, is their Protector, and He will exert revenge on those who transgress against their wives and deal with them unjustly.

Surah: 4 Ayah: 35

﴿ وَإِنْ خِفْتُمْ شِقَاقَ بَيْنِهِمَا فَٱبْعَثُوا۟ حَكَمًا مِّنْ أَهْلِهِۦ وَحَكَمًا مِّنْ أَهْلِهَآ إِن يُرِيدَآ إِصْلَـٰحًا يُوَفِّقِ ٱللَّهُ بَيْنَهُمَآ ۗ إِنَّ ٱللَّهَ كَانَ عَلِيمًا خَبِيرًا ﴾

35. If you fear a breach between them twain (the man and his wife), appoint (two) arbitrators, one from his family and the other from her's; if they both wish for peace, Allâh will cause their reconciliation. Indeed Allâh is Ever All-Knower, Well-Acquainted with all things.

Transliteration

35. Wa-in khiftum shiqaqa baynihima faibAAathoo hakaman min ahlihi wahakaman min ahliha in yureeda islahan yuwaffiqi Allahu baynahuma inna Allaha kana AAaleeman khabeeran

Tafsir Ibn Kathir

Appointing Two Arbitrators When the Possibility of Estrangement Between Husband and Wife Occurs

Allah first mentioned the case of rebellion on the part of the wife. He then mentioned the case of estrangement and alienation between the two spouses. Allah said,

(If you fear a breach between the two, appoint (two) arbitrators, one from his family). The Fuqaha' (scholars of Fiqh) say that when estrangement occurs between the husband and wife, the judge refers them to a trusted person who examines their case in order to stop any wrongs commited between them. If the matter continues or worsens, the judge sends a trustworthy person from the woman's family and a trustworthy person from the man's family to meet with them and examine their case to determine whether it is best for them to part or to remain together. Allah gives preference to staying together, and this is why Allah said, (if they both wish for peace, Allah will cause their reconciliation.) `Ali bin Abi Talhah reported that Ibn `Abbas said, "Allah commands that a righteous man from the husband's side of the family and the wife's side of the family are appointed, so that they find out who among the spouses is in the wrong. If the man is in the wrong, they prevent him from his wife, and he pays some restitution. If the wife is in the wrong, she remains with her husband, and he does not pay any restitution. If the arbitrators decide that the marriage should remain intact or be dissolved, then their decision is upheld. If they decide that the marriage remains intact, but one of the spouses disagrees while the other agrees, and one of them dies, then the one who agreed inherits from the other, while the spouse who did not agree does not inherit from the spouse who agreed." This was collected by Ibn Abi Hatim and Ibn Jarir. Shaykh Abu `Umar bin `Abdul-Barr said, "The scholars agree that when the two arbitrators disagree, then the opinion that dissolves the marriage will not be adopted. They also agree that the decision of the arbitrators is binding, even if the two spouses did not appoint them as agents. This is the case if it is decided that they should stay together, but they disagree whether it is binding or not when they decide for separation." Then he mentioned that the majority holds the view that the decision is still binding, even if they did not appoint them to make any decision.

Surah: 4 Ayah: 36

﴿ ۞ وَٱعْبُدُواْ ٱللَّهَ وَلَا تُشْرِكُواْ بِهِۦ شَيْـًٔا ۖ وَبِٱلْوَٰلِدَيْنِ إِحْسَٰنًا وَبِذِى ٱلْقُرْبَىٰ وَٱلْيَتَٰمَىٰ وَٱلْمَسَٰكِينِ وَٱلْجَارِ ذِى ٱلْقُرْبَىٰ وَٱلْجَارِ ٱلْجُنُبِ وَٱلصَّاحِبِ بِٱلْجَنۢبِ وَٱبْنِ ٱلسَّبِيلِ وَمَا مَلَكَتْ أَيْمَٰنُكُمْ ۗ إِنَّ ٱللَّهَ لَا يُحِبُّ مَن كَانَ مُخْتَالًا فَخُورًا ﴾

36. Worship Allâh and join none with Him in worship; and do good to parents, kinsfolk, orphans, Al-Masâkîn (the poor), the neighbor who is near of kin, the neighbor who is a stranger, the companion by your side, the wayfarer (you meet), and those (slaves) whom your right hands possess. Verily, Allâh does not like such as are proud and boastful.

Transliteration

36. WaoAAbudoo Allaha wala tushrikoo bihi shay-an wabialwalidayni ihsanan wabithee alqurba waalyatama waalmasakeeni waaljari thee alqurba waaljari aljunubi waalssahibi bialjanbi waibni alssabeeli wama malakat aymanukum inna Allaha la yuhibbu man kana mukhtalan fakhooran

Tafsir Ibn Kathir

The Order to Worship Allah Alone and to Be Dutiful to Parents

Allah orders that He be worshipped Alone without partners, because He Alone is the Creator and Sustainer Who sends His favors and bounties on His creation in all situations and instances. Therefore He deserves to be singled out, without associating anything or anyone from His creation with Him in worship. Indeed, the Prophet said to Mu`adh,

$$\text{«أَتَدْرِي مَا حَقُّ اللهِ عَلَى الْعِبَادِ؟»}$$

(Do you know what Allah's right on His servants is) Mu`adh replied, "Allah and His Messenger know better." He said,

$$\text{«أَنْ يَعْبُدُوهُ وَلَا يُشْرِكُوا بِهِ شَيْئًا»}$$

(That they should worship Him and should not worship any others with Him.) The Prophet then said,

$$\text{«أَتَدْرِي مَا حَقُّ الْعِبَادِ عَلَى اللهِ إِذَا فَعَلُوا ذَلِكَ؟ أَنْ لَا يُعَذِّبَهُم»}$$

(Do you know what the right of the servants on Allah is if they do this He should not punish them.) Allah then commands the servants to be dutiful to their parents, for Allah made parents the reason for the servants to come to existence, after they did not exist. Allah joins the order to worship Him with being dutiful to parents in many places. For example, He said,

(give thanks to Me and to your parents), and,

(And your Lord has decreed that you worship none but Him. And that you be dutiful to your parents). After Allah ordained being dutiful to parents, He ordained kind treatment of relatives, males and females. A Hadith states,

$$\text{«الصَّدَقَةُ عَلَى الْمِسْكِينِ صَدَقَةٌ، وَعَلَى ذِي الرَّحِمِ صَدَقَةٌ وَصِلَةٌ»}$$

(Charity given to the poor is Sadaqah, while charity given to relatives is both Sadaqah and Silah (keeping the relations).) Allah then said,

(orphans), because they lost their caretakers who would spend on them. So Allah commands that the orphans be treated with kindness and compassion. Allah then said,

(Al-Masakin (the poor)) who have various needs and cannot find what sustains these needs. Therefore, Allah commands they should be helped in acquiring their needs in a sufficient manner that will end their inadequacy. We will further elaborate on the matter of the destitute and the poor in Surah Bara'h (9:60).

The Right of the Neighbor

Allah said,

(the neighbor who is near of kin, the neighbor who is a stranger) `Ali bin Abi Talhah said that Ibn `Abbas said that, (the neighbor who is near of kin) means, "The neighbor who is also a relative", while,

(The neighbor who is a stranger) means, "Who is not a relative." It was also reported that `Ikrimah, Mujahid, Maymun bin Mihran, Ad-Dahhak, Zayd bin Aslam, Muqatil bin Hayyan and Qatadah said similarly. Mujahid was also reported to have said that Allah's statement,

(the neighbor who is a stranger) means, "The companion during travel." There are many Hadiths that command kind treatment to the neighbors, and we will mention some of them here with Allah's help. The First Hadith Imam Ahmad recorded that `Abdullah bin `Umar said that the Messenger of Allah said,

«مَازَالَ جِبْرِيلُ يُوصِينِي بِالْجَارِ حَتَّى ظَنَنْتُ أَنَّهُ سَيُوَرِّثُهُ»

(Jibril kept reminding of the neighbor's right, until I thought that he was going to give him a share of the inheritance.) The Two Sahihs recorded this Hadith. The Second Hadith Imam Ahmad recorded that `Abdullah bin `Amr said that the Messenger of Allah said,

«مَازَالَ جِبْرِيلُ يُوصِينِي بِالْجَارِ حَتَّى ظَنَنْتُ أَنَّهُ سَيُوَرِّثُهُ»

(Jibril kept reminding me of the neighbor's right, until I thought he was going to appoint a share of the inheritance for him.) Abu Dawud and At-Tirmidhi recorded this Hadith, which At-Tirmidhi said was "Hasan Gharib through this route." The Third Hadith Imam Ahmad recorded that `Abdullah bin `Amr bin Al-`As said that the Prophet said,

«خَيْرُ الْأَصْحَابِ عِنْدَ اللهِ خَيْرُهُمْ لِصَاحِبِهِ، وَخَيْرُ الْجِيرَانِ عِنْدَ اللهِ خَيْرُهُمْ لِجَارِهِ»

(The best companions according to Allah are those who are the best with their friends, and the best neighbors according to Allah are the best with their neighbors.) At-Tirmidhi recorded this Hadith and said, "Hasan Gharib". The Fourth Hadith Imam Ahmad recorded that Al-Miqdad bin Al-Aswad said that the Messenger of Allah asked his Companions,

«مَا تَقُولُونَ فِي الزِّنَا؟»

(What do you say about adultery) They said, "It is prohibited, for Allah and His Messenger have prohibited it. So it is forbidden until the Day of Resurrection." The Messenger of Allah said,

Chapter 4: An-Nisaa (The Women), Verses 024-147

«لَأَنْ يَزْنِيَ الرَّجُلُ بِعَشْرِ نِسْوَةٍ، أَيْسَرُ عَلَيْهِ مِنْ أَنْ يَزْنِيَ بِامْرَأَةِ جَارِهِ»

(For a man to commit adultery with his neighbor's wife is worse than if he commits adultery with ten women.) He then said,

«مَا تَقُولُونَ فِي السَّرِقَةِ؟»

(What do you say about theft) They said, "It is prohibited, for Allah and His Messenger prohibited it." He said,

«لَأَنْ يَسْرِقَ الرَّجُلُ مِنْ عَشْرَةِ أَبْيَاتٍ، أَيْسَرُ عَلَيْهِ مِنْ أَنْ يَسْرِقَ مِنْ جَارِهِ»

(If a man steals from his neighbor, it is worse for him than stealing from ten homes.) Only Ahmad recorded this Hadith. A similar Hadith is recorded in the Two Sahihs, Ibn Mas`ud said, "I asked, `O Allah's Messenger! What is the greatest sin' He said,

«أَنْ تَجْعَلَ لِلَّهِ نِدًّا وَهُوَ خَلَقَكَ»

(To make a rival for Allah while He Alone created you.) I said, `Then' He said,

«أَنْ تَقْتُلَ وَلَدَكَ خَشْيَةَ أَنْ يَطْعَمَ مَعَكَ»

(To kill your offspring for fear that he might share your food with you.) I said, `Then' He said,

«أَنْ تُزَانِيَ حَلِيلَةَ جَارِكَ»

(To commit adultery with your neighbor's wife.)" The Fifth Hadith Imam Ahmad recorded that `A'ishah asked the Messenger of Allah, "I have two neighbors, so whom among them should I give my gift" He said,

«إِلَى أَقْرَبِهِمَا مِنْكِ بَابًا»

(The neighbor whose door is the closest to you.) Al-Bukhari narrated this Hadith We will elaborate on this subject in the Tafsir of Surah Bara'h, Allah willing and upon Him we depend.

Being Kind to Slaves and Servants

Allah said,

(and those (slaves) whom your right hands possess,) this is an order to be kind to them because they are weak, being held as captives by others. An authentic Hadith records that during the illness that preceded his death, the Messenger of Allah continued advising his Ummah:

»الصَّلَاةَ الصَّلَاةَ، وَمَا مَلَكَتْ أَيْمَانُكُم«

((Protect) the prayer, (protect) the prayer, and (those slaves) whom your hands possess.) He was repeating it until his tongue was still. Imam Ahmad recorded that Al-Miqdam bin Ma`dykarib said that the Messenger of Allah said,

»مَا أَطْعَمْتَ نَفْسَكَ فَهُوَ لَكَ صَدَقَةٌ، وَمَا أَطْعَمْتَ وَلَدَكَ فَهُوَ لَكَ صَدَقَةٌ، وَمَا أَطْعَمْتَ زَوْجَتَكَ فَهُوَ لَكَ صَدَقَةٌ، وَمَا أَطْعَمْتَ خَادِمَكَ فَهُوَ لَكَ صَدَقَة«

(What you feed yourself is a Sadaqah (charity) for you, what you feed your children is Sadaqah for you, what you feed your wife is Sadaqah for you and what you feed your servant is Sadaqah for you.) An-Nasa'i recorded this Hadith which has an authentic chain of narration, all the thanks are due to Allah. `Abdullah bin `Amr said to a caretaker of his, "Did you give the slaves their food yet" He said, "No." Ibn `Amr said, "Go and give it to them, for the Messenger of Allah said,

»كَفَى بِالْمَرْءِ إِثْمًا أَنْ يَحْبِسَ عَمَّنْ يَمْلِكُ قُوتَهُم«

(It is enough sin for someone to prevent whomever he is responsible for from getting their food.)" Muslim recorded this Hadith. Abu Hurayrah narrated that the Prophet said,

»لِلْمَمْلُوكِ طَعَامُهُ وَكِسْوَتُهُ، وَلَا يُكَلَّفُ مِنَ الْعَمَلِ إِلَّا مَا يُطِيق«

(The slave has the right to have food, clothing and to only be required to perform what he can bear of work.) Muslim also recorded this Hadith. Abu Hurayrah narrated that the Prophet said,

»إِذَا أَتَى أَحَدَكُمْ خَادِمُهُ بِطَعَامِهِ، فَإِنْ لَمْ يُجْلِسْهُ مَعَهُ فَلْيُنَاوِلْهُ لُقْمَةً أَوْ لُقْمَتَيْنِ أَوْ أُكْلَةً أَوْ أُكْلَتَيْنِ فَإِنَّهُ وَلِيَ حَرَّهُ وَعِلَاجَه«

Chapter 4: An-Nisaa (The Women), Verses 024-147

(When your servant brings meals to one of you, if he does not let him sit and share the meal, then he should at least give him a mouthful or two mouthfuls of that meal or a meal or two, for he has prepared it.) This is the wording collected by Al-Bukhari.

Allah Does Not Like the Arrogant

Allah said,

(Verily, Allah does not like such as are proud and boastful.) meaning, one who is proud and arrogant, insolent and boasts to others. He thinks that he is better than other people, thus thinking high of himself, even though he is insignificant to Allah and hated by people. Mujahid said that Allah's statement,

(Verily, Allah does not like such as are proud) means arrogant, while,

(boastful) means boasting about what he has, while he does not thank Allah. This Ayah indicates that such a person boasts with people about the bounty that Allah has given him, but he is actually ungrateful to Allah for this bounty. Ibn Jarir recorded that `Abdullah bin Waqid Abu Raja' Al-Harawi said, "You will find that those who are mean are also proud and boasting. He then recited,

(and those (slaves) whom your right hands possess,) You will find that he who is undutiful (to parents) is also arrogant, and deprived. He then recited,

(And dutiful to my mother, and made me not arrogant, deprived.) Once a man asked the Prophet, "O Messenger of Allah, advise me.' The Prophet said,

«إِيَّاكَ وَإِسْبَالَ الْإِزَارِ، فَإِنَّ إِسْبَالَ الْإِزَارِ مِنَ الْمَخِيلَةِ، وَإِنَّ اللهَ لَا يُحِبُّ الْمَخِيلَة»

(Avoid lengthening the dress (below the ankles), for this practice is from arrogance. Verily, Allah does not like arrogance.)"

Surah: 4 Ayah: 37, Ayah: 38 & Ayah: 39

﴿ ٱلَّذِينَ يَبْخَلُونَ وَيَأْمُرُونَ ٱلنَّاسَ بِٱلْبُخْلِ وَيَكْتُمُونَ مَآ ءَاتَىٰهُمُ ٱللَّهُ مِن فَضْلِهِۦ ۗ وَأَعْتَدْنَا لِلْكَٰفِرِينَ عَذَابًا مُّهِينًا ﴾

37. Those who are miserly and enjoin miserliness on other men and hide what Allâh has bestowed upon them of His Bounties. And We have prepared for the disbelievers a disgraceful torment.

﴿ وَٱلَّذِينَ يُنفِقُونَ أَمْوَٰلَهُمْ رِئَآءَ ٱلنَّاسِ وَلَا يُؤْمِنُونَ بِٱللَّهِ وَلَا بِٱلْيَوْمِ ٱلْءَاخِرِ ۗ وَمَن يَكُنِ ٱلشَّيْطَٰنُ لَهُۥ قَرِينًا فَسَآءَ قَرِينًا ﴾

38. And (also) those who spend of their substance to be seen of men, and believe not in Allâh and the Last Day (they are the friends of Shaitân (Satan)) and whoever takes Shaitân (Satan) as an intimate; then what a dreadful intimate he has!

﴿ وَمَاذَا عَلَيْهِمْ لَوْ ءَامَنُوا بِٱللَّهِ وَٱلْيَوْمِ ٱلْأَخِرِ وَأَنفَقُوا مِمَّا رَزَقَهُمُ ٱللَّهُ وَكَانَ ٱللَّهُ بِهِمْ عَلِيمًا ﴾

39. And what loss have they if they had believed in Allâh and in the Last Day, and they spend out of what Allâh has given them for sustenance? And Allâh is Ever All-Knower of them.

Transliteration

37. Allatheena yabkhaloona waya/muroona alnnasa bialbukhli wayaktumoona ma atahumu Allahu min fadlihi waaAAtadna lilkafireena AAathaban muheenan 38. Waallatheena yunfiqoona amwalahum ri-aa alnnasi wala yu/minoona biAllahi wala bialyawmi alakhiri waman yakuni alshshaytanu lahu qareenan fasaa qareenan 39. Wamatha AAalayhim law amanoo biAllahi waalyawmi al-akhiri waanfaqoo mimma razaqahumu Allahu wakana Allahu bihim AAaleeman

Tafsir Ibn Kathir

The Censure of Stingy Behavior

Allah chastises the stingy behavior of those who refuse to spend their money for what Allah ordered them, such as being kind to parents and compassionate to relatives, orphans, the poor, the relative who is also a neighbor, the companion during travel, the needy wayfarer, the slaves and servants. Such people do not give Allah's right from their wealth, and they assist in the spread of stingy behavior. The Messenger of Allah said,

«وَأَيُّ دَاءٍ أَدْوَأُ مِنَ الْبُخْلِ»

(What disease is more serious than being stingy) He also said,

«إِيَّاكُمْ وَالشُّحَّ، فَإِنَّهُ أَهْلَكَ مَنْ كَانَ قَبْلَكُمْ، أَمَرَهُمْ بِالْقَطِيعَةِ فَقَطَعُوا، وَأَمَرَهُمْ بِالْفُجُورِ فَفَجَرُوا»

(Beware of being stingy, for it destroyed those who were before you, as it encouraged them to cut their relations and they did, and it encouraged them to commit sin and they did.) Allah said,

Chapter 4: An-Nisaa (The Women), Verses 024-147

(and hide what Allah has bestowed upon them of His bounties,) Therefore, the miser is ungrateful for Allah's favor, for its effect does not appear on him, whether in his food, clothes or what he gives. Similarly, Allah said,

(Verily, man is ungrateful to his Lord. And to that he bears witness.) by his manners and conduct,

(And verily, he is violent in the love of wealth.) Allah said,

(and hide what Allah has bestowed upon them of His bounties) and this is why He threatened them,

(And We have prepared for the disbelievers a disgraceful torment.) Kufr means to cover something. Therefore, the Bakhil (miser) covers the favors that Allah has blessed him with, meaning he does not spread those favors. So he is described by the term Kafir (ungrateful) regarding the favors that Allah granted him. A Hadith states that,

«إِنَّ اللهَ إِذَا أَنْعَمَ نِعْمَةً عَلَى عَبْدٍ، أَحَبَّ أَنْ يَظْهَرَ أَثَرُهَا عَلَيْهِ»

(When Allah grants a servant a favor, He likes that its effect appears on him.) Some of the Salaf stated that this Ayah (4:37) is describing the Jews who hid the knowledge they had about the description of Muhammad, and there is no doubt that the general meaning of the Ayah includes this. The apparent wording for this Ayah indicates that it is talking about being stingy with money, even though miserly conduct with knowledge is also included. The Ayah talks about spending on relatives and the weak, just as the Ayah after it,

(And (also) those who spend of their wealth to be seen of men,) Allah first mentions the punished misers who do not spend, then He mentions those who spend to show off to gain the reputation that they are generous, not for the Face of Allah. A Hadith states that the first three persons on whom the fire will feed are a scholar, a fighter and a spender who shows off with their actions. For instance,

«يَقُولُ صَاحِبُ الْمَالِ: مَا تَرَكْتُ مِنْ شَيْءٍ تُحِبُّ أَنْ يُنْفَقَ فِيهِ، إِلَّا أَنْفَقْتُ فِي سَبِيلِكَ، فَيَقُولُ اللهُ: كَذَبْتَ، إِنَّمَا أَرَدْتَ أَنْ يُقَالَ: جَوَادٌ، فَقَدْ دِقيل»

(The wealthy will say, "I did not leave any area that You like to be spent on, but I spent on it in Your cause." Allah will say, "You lie, you only did that so that it is said, `He is generous.' And it was said...") meaning you acquired your reward in the life, and this is indeed what you sought with your action. This is why Allah said,

(and believe not in Allah and the Last Day,) meaning, it is Shaytan who lured them to commit this evil action, instead of performing the good deed as it should be performed. Shaytan encouraged, excited and lured them by making the evil appear good,

(And whoever takes Shaytan as an intimate; then what a dreadful intimate he has!) Allah then said,

(And what loss have they if they had believed in Allah and in the Last Day, and they spend out of what Allah has given them for sustenance) This Ayah means, what harm would it cause them if they believe in Allah, go on the righteous path, replace showing off with sincerity, have faith in Allah, and await His promise in the Hereafter, for those who do good and spend what He has given them on what He likes and is pleased with. Allah's statement:

(And Allah is Ever All-Knower of them.) means, He has perfect knowledge of their intentions, whether good or evil. Indeed, Allah knows those who deserve success, and He grants them success and guidance, directing them to perform righteous actions that will earn them His pleasure. He also knows those who deserve failure and expulsion from His great mercy, which amounts to utter failure in this life and the Hereafter for them, we seek refuge in Allah from this evil end.

Surah: 4 Ayah: 40, Ayah: 41 & Ayah: 42

﴿ إِنَّ ٱللَّهَ لَا يَظْلِمُ مِثْقَالَ ذَرَّةٍ ۖ وَإِن تَكُ حَسَنَةً يُضَٰعِفْهَا وَيُؤْتِ مِن لَّدُنْهُ أَجْرًا عَظِيمًا ﴾

40. Surely! Allâh wrongs not even of the weight of an atom (or a small ant), but if there is any good (done), He doubles it, and gives from Him a great reward.

﴿ فَكَيْفَ إِذَا جِئْنَا مِن كُلِّ أُمَّةٍ بِشَهِيدٍ وَجِئْنَا بِكَ عَلَىٰ هَٰٓؤُلَآءِ شَهِيدًا ﴾

41. How (will it be) then, when We bring from each nation a witness and We bring you (O Muhammad (peace be upon him)) as a witness against these people?

﴿ يَوْمَئِذٍ يَوَدُّ ٱلَّذِينَ كَفَرُوا۟ وَعَصَوُا۟ ٱلرَّسُولَ لَوْ تُسَوَّىٰ بِهِمُ ٱلْأَرْضُ وَلَا يَكْتُمُونَ ٱللَّهَ حَدِيثًا ﴾

42. On that day those who disbelieved and disobeyed the Messenger (Muhammad (peace be upon him)) will wish that they were buried in the earth, but they will never be able to hide a single fact from Allâh.

Transliteration

40. Inna Allaha la yathlimu mithqala tharratin wa-in taku hasanatan yudaAAifha wayu/ti min ladunhu ajran AAatheeman   41. Fakayfa itha ji/na min kulli ommatin bishaheedin waji/na bika AAala haola-i shaheedan   42. Yawma-ithin yawaddu allatheena kafaroo waAAasawoo alrrasoola law tusawwa bihimu al-ardu wala yaktumoona Allaha hadeethan

Chapter 4: An-Nisaa (The Women), Verses 024-147

Tafsir Ibn Kathir

Allah Wrongs Not Even the Weight of a Speck of Dust

Allah states that He does not treat any of His servants with injustice on the Day of Resurrection, be it the weight of a mustard seed or a speck of dust. Rather, Allah shall reward them for this action and multiply it, if it were a good deed. For instance, Allah said,

(And We shall set up balances of justice) Allah said that Luqman said,

(O my son! If it be (anything) equal to the weight of a mustard seed, and though it be in a rock, or in the heavens or in the earth, Allah will bring it forth). Allah said,

(That Day mankind will proceed in scattered groups that they may be shown their deeds. So whosoever does good equal to the weight of a speck of dust shall see it. And whosoever does evil equal to the weight of a speck of dust shall see it.) The Two Sahihs recorded the long Hadith about the intercession that Abu Sa`id Al-Khudri narrated, and in which the Messenger of Allah said,

«فَيَقُولُ اللهُ عَزَّ وَجَلَّ: ارْجِعُوا، فَمَنْ وَجَدْتُمْ فِي قَلْبِهِ مِثْقَالَ حَبَّةِ خَرْدَلٍ مِنْ إِيمَانٍ، فَأَخْرِجُوهُ مِنَ النَّارِ»

(Allah then says, "Go back, and take out of the Fire everyone in whose heart you find the weight of a mustard seed of faith") In another narration, Allah says,

«أَدْنَى أَدْنَى أَدْنَى مِثْقَالِ ذَرَّةٍ مِنْ إِيمَانٍ، فَأَخْرِجُوهُ مِنَ النَّارِ، فَيُخْرِجُونَ خَلْقًا كَثِيرًا»

("Whosoever had the least, least, least speck of faith, take him out of the Fire," and they will take out many people.) Abu Sa`id then said, "Read, if you will,

(Surely! Allah wrongs not even of the weight of a speck of dust)."

Will Punishment be Diminished for the Disbelievers

Sa`id bin Jubayr commented about Allah's statement,

(but if there is any good (done), He doubles it,) "As for the disbeliever, his punishment will be lessened for him on the Day of Resurrection, but he will never depart the Fire." He used as evidence the authentic Hadith in which Al-`Abbas said, "O Messenger of Allah! Your uncle Abu Talib used to protect and support you, did you benefit him at all" The Messenger said,

«نَعَمْ هُوَ فِي ضَحْضَاحٍ مِنْ نَارٍ، وَلَوْلَا أَنَا، لَكَانَ فِي الدَّرْكِ الْأَسْفَلِ مِنَ النَّارِ»

(Yes. He is in a shallow area in Hell-fire, and were it not for me, he would have been in the deepest depths of the Fire.) However, this Hadith only applies to Abu Talib, not the rest of the disbelievers. To support this, we mention what Abu Dawud At-Tayalisi recorded in his Musnad that Anas said that the Messenger of Allah said,

«إِنَّ اللهَ لَا يَظْلِمُ الْمُؤْمِنَ حَسَنَةً، يُثَابُ عَلَيْهَا الرِّزْقَ فِي الدُّنْيَا، وَيُجْزَى بِهَا فِي الْآخِرَةِ، وَأَمَّا الْكَافِرُ فَيُطْعَمُ بِهَا فِي الدُّنْيَا، فَإِذَا كَانَ يَوْمُ الْقِيَامَةِ لَمْ يَكُنْ لَهُ حَسَنَةٌ»

(Allah does not wrong the faithful even concerning one good action, for he will be rewarded for it by provision in this life and awarded for it in the Hereafter. As for the disbeliever, he will be provided provision in this life for his good action, and on the Day of Resurrection, he will not have any good deed.)

What Does `Great Reward' Mean

Abu Hurayrah, `Ikrimah, Sa`id bin Jubayr, Al-Hasan, Qatadah and Ad-Dahhak said that Allah's statement,

(and gives from Him a great reward.) refers to Paradise. We ask Allah for His pleasure and Paradise. Ibn Abi Hatim recorded that Abu `Uthman An-Nahdi said, "No other person accompanied Abu Hurayrah more than I. One year, he went to Hajj before me, and I found the people of Al-Basrah saying that he narrated that he heard the Messenger of Allah saying,

«إِنَّ اللهَ يُضَاعِفُ الْحَسَنَةَ أَلْفَ أَلْفِ حَسَنَةٍ»

(Allah rewards the good deed with a million deeds.) So I said, `Woe to you! No person accompanied Abu Hurayrah more than I, and I never heard him narrate this Hadith!' When I wanted to meet him, I found that he had left for Hajj so I followed him to Hajj to ask him about this Hadith." Ibn Abi Hatim also recorded this Hadith using another chain of narration leading to Abu `Uthman. In this narration, Abu `Uthman said, "I said, `O Abu Hurayrah! I heard my brethren in Al-Basrah claim that you narrated that you heard the Messenger of Allah saying,

«إِنَّ اللهَ يَجْزِي بِالْحَسَنَةِ أَلْفَ أَلْفِ حَسَنَةٍ»

(Allah rewards the good deed with a million deeds.) Abu Hurayrah said, `By Allah! I heard the Messenger of Allah saying,

Chapter 4: An-Nisaa (The Women), Verses 024-147

«إِنَّ اللهَ يَجْزِي بِالْحَسَنَةِ أَلْفَيْ أَلْفِ حَسَنَةٍ»

(Allah rewards the good deed with two million deeds.) He then recited this Ayah,

(But little is the enjoyment of the life of this world as compared to the Hereafter)."

Our Prophet will be a Witness Against, or For his Ummah on the Day of Resurrection, When the Disbelievers Will Wish for Death

Allah said,

(How (will it be) then, when We bring from each nation a witness and We bring you (O Muhammad) as a witness against these people) Allah describes the horrors, hardships and difficulties of the Day of Resurrection, saying, how would it be on that Day when there will be a witness from every nation, meaning the Prophets, just as Allah said;

(And the earth will shine with the light of its Lord, and the Book will be placed (open); and the Prophets and the witnesses will be brought forward), and,

(And (remember) the Day when We shall raise up from every nation a witness against them from amongst themselves). Al-Bukhari recorded that `Abdullah bin Mas`ud said, "The Messenger of Allah said to me, `Recite to me.' I said, `O Messenger of Allah! Should I recite (the Qur'an) to you, while it was revealed to you' He said, `Yes, for I like to hear it from other people.' I recited Surat An-Nisa' until I reached this Ayah,

(How (will it be) then, when We bring from each nation a witness and We bring you (O Muhammad) as a witness against these people) He then said, `Stop now.' I found that his eyes were tearful." Allah's statement,

(On that day those who disbelieved and disobeyed the Messenger will wish that they were buried in the earth, but they will never be able to hide a single fact from Allah.) means, they will wish that the earth would open up and swallow them because of the horror of the gathering place and the disgrace, dishonor and humiliation they will suffer on that Day. This is similar to Allah's statement,

(The Day when man will see that (the deeds) which his hands have sent forth) Allah then said,

(but they will never be able to hide a single fact from Allah.) indicating that they will admit to everything they did and will not hide any of it. `Abdur-Razzaq recorded that Sa`id bin Jubayr said, "A man came to Ibn `Abbas and said to him, `There are things that confuse me in the Qur'an.' Ibn `Abbas said, `What things do you have doubts about in the Qur'an' He said, `Not doubts, but rather confusing things.' Ibn `Abbas said, `Tell me what caused you confusion.' He said, `I hear Allah's statement,

(There will then be no test for them but to say: "By Allah, our Lord, we were not those who joined others in worship with Allah.") but He also says, (but they will never be able to hide a single fact from Allah.) They have indeed hid something.' Ibn `Abbas said, `As for Allah's statement,

(There will then be no test for them but to say: "By Allah, our Lord, we were not those who joined others in worship with Allah."), when they see that on the Day of Resurrection that Allah does not forgive, except for the people of Islam, and that He forgives the sins, no matter how big they are, except Shirk, then the Mushriks will lie. They will say,

("By Allah, our Lord, we were not those who joined others in worship with Allah."), hoping that Allah will forgive them. However, Allah will then seal their mouths, and their hands and feet will disclose what they used to do. Then,

(those who disbelieved and disobeyed the Messenger will wish that they were buried in the earth, but they will never be able to hide a single fact from Allah.)'"

Surah: 4 Ayah: 43

﴿ يَٰٓأَيُّهَا ٱلَّذِينَ ءَامَنُوا۟ لَا تَقْرَبُوا۟ ٱلصَّلَوٰةَ وَأَنتُمْ سُكَٰرَىٰ حَتَّىٰ تَعْلَمُوا۟ مَا تَقُولُونَ وَلَا جُنُبًا إِلَّا عَابِرِى سَبِيلٍ حَتَّىٰ تَغْتَسِلُوا۟ ۚ وَإِن كُنتُم مَّرْضَىٰٓ أَوْ عَلَىٰ سَفَرٍ أَوْ جَآءَ أَحَدٌ مِّنكُم مِّنَ ٱلْغَآئِطِ أَوْ لَٰمَسْتُمُ ٱلنِّسَآءَ فَلَمْ تَجِدُوا۟ مَآءً فَتَيَمَّمُوا۟ صَعِيدًا طَيِّبًا فَٱمْسَحُوا۟ بِوُجُوهِكُمْ وَأَيْدِيكُمْ ۗ إِنَّ ٱللَّهَ كَانَ عَفُوًّا غَفُورًا ﴾

43. O you who believe! Approach not As-Salât (the prayer) when you are in a drunken state until you know (the meaning) of what you utter, nor when you are in a state of Janâba, (i.e. in a state of sexual impurity and have not yet taken a bath) except when travelling on the road (without enough water, or just passing through a mosque), till you wash your whole body. And if you are ill, or on a journey, or one of you comes after answering the call of nature, or you have been in contact with women (by sexual relations) and you find no water, perform Tayammum with clean earth and rub therewith your faces and hands (Tayammum). Truly, Allâh is Ever Oft-Pardoning, Oft-Forgiving.

Transliteration

43. Ya ayyuha allatheena amanoo la taqraboo alssalata waantum sukara hatta taAAlamoo ma taqooloona wala junuban illa AAabiree sabeelin hatta taghtasiloo wa-in kuntum marda aw AAala safarin aw jaa ahadun minkum mina algha-iti aw lamastumu alnnisaa falam tajidoo maan fatayammamoo saAAeedan tayyiban faimsahoo biwujoohikum waaydeekum inna Allaha kana AAafuwwan ghafooran

Tafsir Ibn Kathir

The Prohibition of Approaching Prayer When Drunk or Junub

Allah forbade His believing servants from praying while drunk, for one does not know the meaning of what he is saying in that state, and He forbade them from attending

Chapter 4: An-Nisaa (The Women), Verses 024-147

the Masjids while sexually impure, except when one is just passing through the Masjid from one door to another. This Ayah was revealed before alcohol consumption was completely prohibited, as evident by the Hadith that we mentioned in Surat Al-Baqarah when we explained Allah's statement,

(They ask you about alcoholic drink and gambling). In that Hadith, the Messenger of Allah recited this Ayah to `Umar, who said, "O Allah! Explain the ruling about Khamr (intoxicants) for us in a plain manner." When this Ayah (4:43) was revealed, the Prophet recited it to `Umar, who still said, "O Allah! Explain the ruling about Khamr (intoxicants) for us in a plain manner." After that, they would not drink alcohol close to the time of prayer. When Allah's statement,

(O you who believe! alcoholic drinks, gambling, Al-Ansab, and Al-Azlam are an abomination of Shayatan's handiwork. So avoid that in order that you may be successful.) (5:90), until,

(So, will you not then abstain) (5:91) was revealed, `Umar said, "We abstain, we abstain." In another narration, when the Ayah in Surat An-Nisa' was revealed,

(O you who believe! Do not approach Salah while you are in a druken state until you know what you are saying,) at the time of prayer, the Messenger of Allah would have someone proclaim; "Let not any drunk approach the prayer." This is the wording collected by Abu Dawud.

Causes of Its Revelation

Ibn Abi Hatim has recorded some reports about the incident of its revelation: Sa`d said, "Four Ayat were revealed concerning me. A man from the Ansar once made some food and invited some Muhajirin and Ansar men to it, and we ate and drank until we became intoxicated. We then boasted about our status." Then a man held a camel's bone and injured Sa`d's nose, which was scarred ever since. This occurred before Al-Khamr was prohibited, and Allah later revealed,

(O you who believe! Approach not AsSalat (the prayer) when you are in a drunken state). Muslim recorded this Hadith, and the collectors of the Sunan recorded it, with the exception of Ibn Majah. Another Reason Ibn Abi Hatim narrated that `Ali bin Abi Talib said, "Abdur-Rahman bin `Awf made some food to which he invited us and served some alcohol to drink. When we became intoxicated, and the time for prayer came, they asked someone to lead us in prayer. He recited `Say, `O disbelievers! I do not worship that which you worship, but we worship that which you worship (refer to the correct wording of the Surah: 109).'" Allah then revealed,

(O you who believe! Do not approach Salah when you are in a drunken state until you know what you are saying). " This is the narration collected by Ibn Abi Hatim and At-Tirmidhi, who said "Hasan (Gharib) Sahih." Allah's statement,

(until you know what you are saying) is the best description for when one is intoxicated, that is, when he does not know the meaning of what he is saying. When a person is drunk, he makes obvious mistakes in the recitation and will not be able to be humble during the prayer. Imam Ahmad recorded that Anas said that the Messenger of Allah said,

«إِذَا نَعَسَ أَحَدُكُمْ وَهُوَ يُصَلِّي، فَلْيَنْصَرِفْ فَلْيَنَمْ، حَتَّى يَعْلَمَ مَا يَقُول»

(If one feels sleepy while he is praying, let him sleep for a while so that he knows the meaning of what he is saying.) This was also recorded by Al-Bukhari and An-Nasa'i. In some of the narrations of this Hadith, the Messenger said,

«فَلَعَلَّهُ يَذْهَبُ يَسْتَغْفِرُ فَيَسُبَّ نَفْسَه»

(...For he might want to ask for forgiveness, but instead curses himself!) Allah said,

(nor while Junub (sexually impure), except while passing through, until you bathe (your entire body),) Ibn Abi Hatim recorded that Ibn `Abbas said that Allah's statement,

(nor while Junub (sexually impure), except while passing through, until you bathe (your entire body,) means, "Do not enter the Masjid when you are Junub, unless you are just passing by, in which case, you pass through without sitting down." Ibn Abi Hatim said that similar is reported from `Abdullah bin Mas`ud, Anas, Abu `Ubaydah, Sa`id bin Al-Musayyib, Abu Ad-Duha, `Ata', Mujahid, Masruq, Ibrahim An-Nakha`i, Zayd bin Aslam, Abu Malik, `Amr bin Dinar, Al-Hakam bin `Utaybah, `Ikrimah, Al-Hasan Al-Basri, Yahya bin Sa`id Al-Ansari, Ibn Shihab and Qatadah. Ibn Jarir recorded that Yazid bin Abi Habib commented on Allah's statement,

(nor while Junub (sexually impure), except while passing through,) when some men from the Ansar, whose doors literally opened into the Masjid, were sexually impure, and they did not have water, their only way to get water was to pass through the Masjid. So, Allah sent down,

(nor while Junub (sexually impure), except while passing through,)." What supports this statement by Yazid bin Abi Habib, may Allah have mercy upon him, is Al-Bukhari's report in his Sahih, that the Messenger of Allah said,

«سُدُّوا كُلَّ خَوْخَةٍ فِي الْمَسْجِدِ إِلَّا خَوْخَةَ أَبِي بَكْر»

(Close all the small doors in this Masjid, except that of Abu Bakr.) This is what the Prophet commanded at the end of his life, knowing that Abu Bakr will be the Khalifah after him, and that he would need to enter the Masjid on numerous occasions to manage the important affairs of the Muslims. Yet, the Messenger of Allah commanded that all the small doors that open into the Masjid be closed, except Abu Bakr's door. Some of the Sunan compilers recorded the Prophet saying that only `Ali's door should remain open, but this is an error, what is in the Sahih is what is correct. In his Sahih, Muslim recorded that `A'ishah said, "The Messenger of Allah said to me,

Chapter 4: An-Nisaa (The Women), Verses 024-147

«نَاوِلِينِي الْخُمْرَةَ مِنَ الْمَسْجِدِ»

(Bring me the garment from the Masjid.) I said, `I am having my period.' He said,

«إِنَّ حَيْضَتَكِ لَيْسَتْ فِي يَدِكِ»

(Your period is not in your hand.) Muslim also collected a similar narration from Abu Hurayrah. This Hadith indicates that the woman is allowed to pass through the Masjid during menses or post-natal bleeding, and Allah knows best.

Description of Tayammum

Allah said,

(and if you are ill, or on a journey, or one of you comes from the Gha'it (toilet), or from Lamastum (touching) women, but you do not find water, then perform Tayammum with clean earth, rubbing your face and hands. Truly, Allah is Ever Oft-Pardoning, Oft-Forgiving.) As for the type of illness which would allow Tayammum, it is an illness that one fears would be aggravated by using water, which could be detrimental to a part of the body, or when doing so would prolong an illness. Some scholars said that any type of illness warrants Tayammum, because of the general indications of the Ayah. As for travelling on a journey, it is known, regardless of its length. Allah then said,

(or comes from the Gha'it). The Gha'it is, literally, the flat land, and this part of the Ayah refers to the minor impurity. Allah then said,

(or you Lamastum women), which was recited Lamastum and Lamastum, referring to sexual intercourse. For instance, Allah said in another Ayah,

(And if you divorce them before you have touched them, and you have appointed unto them the dowry, then pay half of that) (2:237), and,

(O you who believe! When you marry believing women, and then divorce them before you have touched them, no `Iddah (period of waiting) have you to count in respect of them) (33:49). Ibn Abi Hatim recorded that Ibn `Abbas said that Allah's statement,

(or Lamastum women) refers to sexual intercourse. It was reported that `Ali, Ubayy bin Ka`b, Mujahid, Tawus, Al-Hasan, `Ubayd bin `Umayr, Sa`id bin Jubayr, Ash-Sha`bi, Qatadah and Muqatil bin Hayyan said similarly. Allah said,

(but you do not find water,them perform Tayammum with clean earth,) In the Two Sahihs, it is recorded that `Imran bin Husayn said,

(Allah's Messenger saw a person sitting away from the people and not praying with them. He asked him,

«يَا فُلَانُ مَا مَنَعَكَ أَنْ تُصَلِّيَ مَعَ الْقَوْمِ، أَلَسْتَ بِرَجُلٍ مُسْلِمٍ؟»

`O so-and-so! What prevented you from offering the prayer with the people, are not you Muslim' He replied, `Yes, O Allah's Messenger! I am Junub and there is no water.' The Prophet said,

«عَلَيْكَ بِالصَّعِيدِ، فَإِنَّهُ يَكْفِيكَ»

`Perform Tayammum with clean earth and that will be sufficient for you.') The linguistic meaning of Tayammum is to intend, as Arabs say, "May Allah Tayammamaka (direct at you) His care." `Clean earth' means dust. In his Sahih, Muslim recorded that Hudhayfah bin Al-Yaman said that the Messenger of Allah said,

«فُضِّلْنَا عَلَى النَّاسِ بِثَلَاثٍ: جُعِلَتْ صُفُوفُنَا كَصُفُوفِ الْمَلَائِكَةِ، وَجُعِلَتْ لَنَا الْأَرْضُ كُلُّهَا مَسْجِدًا، وَجُعِلَتْ تُرْبَتُهَا لَنَا طَهُورًا، إِذَا لَمْ نَجِدِ الْمَاءَ»

(We were given preference over people in three things. Our lines (in prayer) were arranged in rows to resemble the rows of the angels, all of the earth was made a Masjid for us, and its dust was made clean for us when there is no water.) The Messenger mentioned the favor of making dust a purifier for us, and if there were any other substance to replace it for Tayammum, he would have mentioned it. Imam Ahmad and the collectors of Sunan, with the exception of Ibn Majah, recorded that Abu Dharr said that the Messenger of Allah said,

«الصَّعِيدُ الطَّيِّبُ طَهُورُ الْمُسْلِمِ، وَإِنْ لَمْ يَجِدِ الْمَاءَ عَشْرَ حِجَجٍ، فَإِذَا وَجَدَهُ فَلْيُمِسَّهُ بَشَرَتَهُ، فَإِنَّ ذَلِكَ خَيْرٌ»

(Clean earth is pure for the Muslim, even if he does not find water for ten years. When he finds water, let him use it for his skin, for this is better.) At-Tirmidhi said, "Hasan Sahih". Allah's statement,

(rubbing your faces and hands (Tayammum)) indicates that Tayammum is a substitute for normal ablution, not that it involves cleaning the parts that normal ablution does. Therefore, it is sufficient in Tayammum to just wipe the face and hands, as the consensus concurs. The face and hands are wiped with one strike on the sand in this case, as Imam Ahmad recorded that `Abdur-Rahman bin Abza said that a man came to `Umar and asked him, "I am Junub, but there is no water." `Umar said, "Then, do not pray." `Ammar said, "Do you not remember, O Leader of the Faithful! You and I were on a military expedition when we became Junub and did not find water. You did not pray, but I rolled myself in the sand and then prayed.

Chapter 4: An-Nisaa (The Women), Verses 024-147

When we went back to the Prophet, we mentioned to him what had happened. He said to me,

»إِنَّمَا كَانَ يَكْفِيكَ«

(This would have been sufficient for you), and the Prophet stroked his hand on the earth once, blew into it and wiped his face and hands." The Muslim Ummah, rather than all other nations, was favored with the allowance of Tayammum. In the Two Sahihs, it is recorded that Jabir bin `Abdullah said that the Messenger of Allah said,

»أُعْطِيتُ خَمْسًا لَمْ يُعْطَهُنَّ أَحَدٌ قَبْلِي: نُصِرْتُ بِالرُّعْبِ مَسِيرَةَ شَهْرٍ، وَجُعِلَتْ لِيَ الْأَرْضُ مَسْجِدًا وَطَهُورًا، فَأَيُّمَا رَجُلٍ مِنْ أُمَّتِي أَدْرَكَتْهُ الصَّلَاةُ فَلْيُصَلِّ«

(I have been given five things which were not given to any (Prophet) before me: Allah made me victorious with fright that covers a month's distance. The earth has been made for me (and for my followers) a place for praying and an object to perform purification with. Therefore let my followers pray wherever the time of a prayer is due) - and in another narration –

»فَعِنْدَهُ طَهُورُهُ وَمَسْجِدُهُ، وَأُحِلَّتْ لِيَ الْغَنَائِمُ، وَلَمْ تَحِلَّ لِأَحَدٍ قَبْلِي، وَأُعْطِيتُ الشَّفَاعَةَ، وَكَانَ النَّبِيُّ يُبْعَثُ إِلَى قَوْمِهِ، وَبُعِثْتُ إِلَى النَّاسِ عَامَّةً«

(he will have his means of purity and his Masjid. The spoils of war have been made lawful for me and it was not made so for anyone else before me. I have been given the right of intercession (on the Day of Resurrection.) Every Prophet used to be sent to his nation exclusively, but I have been sent to all mankind.) We also mentioned the Hadith of Hudhayfah that Muslim recorded;

»فُضِّلْنَا عَلَى النَّاسِ بِثَلَاثٍ، جُعِلَتْ صُفُوفُنَا كَصُفُوفِ الْمَلَائِكَةِ، وَجُعِلَتْ لَنَا الْأَرْضُ مَسْجِدًا، وَتُرْبَتُهَا طَهُورًا، إِذَا لَمْ نَجِدِ الْمَاءَ«

(We were preferred with three things over people. Our lines (in prayer) were arranged in rows to resemble the rows of the angels, all of the earth was made a Masjid for us, and its dust was made clean for us when there is no water.) Allah said in this Ayah,

(rubbing your faces and hands. Truly, Allah is Ever Oft-Pardoning, Oft-Forgiving.) meaning, a part of His pardoning and forgiving is that He allows you to use Tayammum and to pray after using it when there is no water, to make things easy for you. This Ayah sanctifies the position of the prayer, it being too sacred than to be performed in a defecient manner, like in a state of drunkenness, until one becomes aware of what he is saying, or sexually impure, until he bathes (Ghusl), or after answering the call of nature, until he performs ablution. There are exceptions when one is ill or when there is no water. In this case, Allah allows us to use Tayammum, out of His mercy and kindness for His servants, and to facilitate them, all praise is due to Allah.

The Reason behind allowing Tayammum

Al-Bukhari recorded that `A'ishah said, "We set out with Allah's Messenger on one of his journeys until we reached Al-Bayda' or Dhat-ul-Jaysh, where a necklace of mine was broken (and lost). Allah's Messenger stayed there to search for it, and so did the people along with him. There was no water source or any water with them at that place, so the people went to Abu Bakr As-Siddiq and said, `Don't you see what `A'ishah has done! She has made Allah's Messenger and the people stay where there is no source of water and they have no water with them.' Abu Bakr came while Allah's Messenger was sleeping with his head on my thigh. He said to me, `You have detained Allah's Messenger and the people where there is no source of water and they have no water with them.' So he admonished me and said what Allah wished him to say and hit me on my flank with his hand. Nothing prevented me from moving (because of pain) but the position of Allah's Messenger on my thigh. Allah's Messenger got up when dawn broke and there was no water. So Allah revealed the verses of Tayammum, and they all performed Tayammum. Usayd bin Hudayr said, `O the family of Abu Bakr! This is not the first blessing of yours.' Then the camel on which I was riding was moved from its place and the necklace was found beneath it." Al-Bukhari and Muslim recorded this Hadith.

Surah: 4 Ayah: 44, Ayah: 45 & Ayah: 46

﴿ أَلَمْ تَرَ إِلَى ٱلَّذِينَ أُوتُوا۟ نَصِيبًا مِّنَ ٱلْكِتَٰبِ يَشْتَرُونَ ٱلضَّلَٰلَةَ وَيُرِيدُونَ أَن تَضِلُّوا۟ ٱلسَّبِيلَ ﴾

44. Have you not seen those who were given a portion of the book (the Jews), purchasing the wrong path, and wish that you should go astray from the Right Path.

﴿ وَٱللَّهُ أَعْلَمُ بِأَعْدَآئِكُمْ وَكَفَىٰ بِٱللَّهِ وَلِيًّا وَكَفَىٰ بِٱللَّهِ نَصِيرًا ﴾

45. Allâh has full knowledge of your enemies, and Allâh is Sufficient as a Walî (Protector), and Allâh is Sufficient as a Helper.

﴿ مِّنَ ٱلَّذِينَ هَادُوا۟ يُحَرِّفُونَ ٱلْكَلِمَ عَن مَّوَاضِعِهِۦ وَيَقُولُونَ سَمِعْنَا وَعَصَيْنَا وَٱسْمَعْ غَيْرَ مُسْمَعٍ وَرَٰعِنَا لَيًّۢا بِأَلْسِنَتِهِمْ وَطَعْنًا فِى ٱلدِّينِ ۚ وَلَوْ أَنَّهُمْ قَالُوا۟ سَمِعْنَا وَأَطَعْنَا

Chapter 4: An-Nisaa (The Women), Verses 024-147

وَٱسْمَعْ وَٱنظُرْنَا لَكَانَ خَيْرًا لَّهُمْ وَأَقْوَمَ وَلَٰكِن لَّعَنَهُمُ ٱللَّهُ بِكُفْرِهِمْ فَلَا يُؤْمِنُونَ إِلَّا قَلِيلًا ﴿٤٦﴾

46. Among those who are Jews, there are some who displace words from (their) right places and say: "We hear your word (O Muhammad (peace be upon him)) and disobey," and "Hear and let you (O Muhammad (peace be upon him)) hear nothing." And Râ'ina with a twist of their tongues and as a mockery of the religion (Islâm). And if only they had said: "We hear and obey", and "Do make us understand," it would have been better for them, and more proper; but Allâh has cursed them for their disbelief, so they believe not except a few.

Transliteration

44. Alam tara ila allatheena ootoo naseeban mina alkitabi yashtaroona alddalalata wayureedoona an tadilloo alssabeela 45. WaAllahu aAAlamu bi-aAAda-ikum wakafa biAllahi waliyyan wakafa biAllahi naseeran 46. Mina allatheena hadoo yuharrifoona alkalima AAan mawadiAAihi wayaqooloona samiAAna waAAsayna waismaAA ghayra musmaAAin waraAAina layyan bi-alsinatihim wataAAnan fee alddeeni walaw annahum qaloo samiAAna waataAAna waismaAA waonthurna lakana khayran lahum waaqwama walakin laAAanahumu Allahu bikufrihim fala yu/minoona illa qaleelan

Tafsir Ibn Kathir

Chastising the Jews for Choosing Misguidance, Altering Allah's Words, and Mocking Islam

Allah states that the Jews, may Allah's continued curse fall on them until the Day of Resurrection, have purchased the wrong path instead of guidance, and ignored what Allah sent down to His Messenger Muhammad . They also ignored the knowledge that they inherited from previous Prophets, about the description of Muhammad , so that they may have a small amount of the delights of this life.

(and wishing that you should go astray from the right path.) for they would like that you disbelieve in what was sent down to you, O believers, and that you abandon the guidance and beneficial knowledge that you have.

(Allah has full knowledge of your enemies) meaning, Allah has better knowledge of your enemies, and He warns you against them.

(and Allah is sufficient as a Wali (Protector), and Allah is Sufficient as a Helper) He is a Sufficient Protector for those who seek refuge with Him and a Sufficient Supporter for those who seek His help. Allah then said,

(there are some who displace words from (their) right places) meaning, they intentionally and falsely alter the meanings of the Words of Allah and explain them in a different manner than what Allah meant,

(And say: "We hear your word and disobey) saying, "We hear what you say, O Muhammad, but we do not obey you in it," as Mujahid and Ibn Zayd explained. This is the implied meaning of the Ayah, and it demonstrates the Jews' disbelief, stubbornness and disregard for Allah's Book after they understood it, all the while aware of the sin and punishment that this behavior will earn for them. Allah's statement,

(And "Hear and let you hear nothing.") means, hear our words, may you never hear anything, as Ad-Dahhak reported from Ibn `Abbas. This is the Jews' way of mocking and jesting, may Allah's curse descend on them.

(And Ra`ina, with a twist of their tongues and as a mockery of the religion.) meaning, they pretend to say, `Hear us,' when they say, Ra`ina (an insult in Hebrew, but in Arabic it means `Listen to us.').' Yet, their true aim is to curse the Prophet . We mentioned this subject when we explained Allah's statement,

(O you who believe! Say not Ra`ina but say Unzurna (make us understand)). Therefore, Allah said about them, while they pretend to say other than what they truly mean,

(With a twist of their tongues and as a mockery of the religion) because of their cursing the Prophet . Allah then said,

(And if only they had said: "We hear and obey", and "Do make us understand," it would have been better for them, and more proper; but Allah has cursed them for their disbelief, so they believe not except a few.) meaning, their hearts are cast away from the path of righteousness and therefore, no beneficial part of faith enters it. Earlier, when we explained,

(so little is that which they believe) which means they do not have beneficial faith.

Surah: 4 Ayah: 47 & Ayah: 48

﴿ يَٰٓأَيُّهَا ٱلَّذِينَ أُوتُواْ ٱلْكِتَٰبَ ءَامِنُواْ بِمَا نَزَّلْنَا مُصَدِّقًا لِّمَا مَعَكُم مِّن قَبْلِ أَن نَّطْمِسَ وُجُوهًا فَنَرُدَّهَا عَلَىٰٓ أَدْبَارِهَآ أَوْ نَلْعَنَهُمْ كَمَا لَعَنَّآ أَصْحَٰبَ ٱلسَّبْتِ وَكَانَ أَمْرُ ٱللَّهِ مَفْعُولًا ﴿٤٧﴾ ﴾

47. O you who have been given the Scripture (Jews and Christians)! Believe in what We have revealed (to Muhammad (peace be upon him)) confirming what is (already) with you, before We efface faces (by making them like the back of necks; without nose, mouth) and turn them hindwards, or curse them as We cursed the Sabbath-breakers. And the Commandment of Allâh is always executed.

﴿ إِنَّ ٱللَّهَ لَا يَغْفِرُ أَن يُشْرَكَ بِهِۦ وَيَغْفِرُ مَا دُونَ ذَٰلِكَ لِمَن يَشَآءُ وَمَن يُشْرِكْ بِٱللَّهِ فَقَدِ ٱفْتَرَىٰٓ إِثْمًا عَظِيمًا ﴿٤٨﴾ ﴾

Chapter 4: An-Nisaa (The Women), Verses 024-147

48. Verily, Allâh forgives not that partners should be set up with Him (in worship), but He forgives except that (anything else) to whom He wills; and whoever sets up partners with Allâh in worship, he has indeed invented a tremendous sin.

Transliteration

47. Ya ayyuha allatheena ootoo alkitaba aminoo bima nazzalna musaddiqan lima maAAakum min qabli an natmisa wujoohan fanaruddaha AAala adbariha aw nalAAanahum kama laAAanna as-haba alssabti wakana amru Allahi mafAAoolan 48. Inna Allaha la yaghfiru an yushraka bihi wayaghfiru ma doona thalika liman yashao waman yushrik biAllahi faqadi iftara ithman AAatheeman

Tafsir Ibn Kathir

Calling the People of the Book to Embrace the Faith, Warning them Against Doing Otherwise

Allah commands the People of the Scriptures to believe in what He has sent down to His servant and Messenger, Muhammad , the Glorious Book that conforms to the good news that they already have about Muhammad . He also warns them,

(before We efface faces and turn them backwards) Al-`Awfi said that Ibn `Abbas said that `effacing' here refers to blindness,

(and turn them backwards) meaning, We put their faces on their backs, and make them walk backwards, since their eyes will be in their backs. Similar was said by Qatadah and `Atiyah Al-`Awfi. This makes the punishment even more severe, and it is a parable that Allah set for ignoring the truth, preferring the wrong way and turning away from the plain path for the paths of misguidance. Therefore, such people walk backwards. Similarly, some said that Allah's statement,

(Verily, We have put on their necks iron collars reaching to the chins, so that their heads are raised up. And We have put a barrier before them) that is a parable that Allah gave for their deviation and hindrance from guidance.

Ka`b Al-Ahbar Embraces Islam Upon Hearing this Ayah [4:47]

It was reported that Ka`b Al-Ahbar became Muslim when he heard this Ayah (4:47). Ibn Jarir recorded that `Isa bin Al-Mughirah said: We were with Ibrahim when we talked about the time when Ka`b became Muslim. He said, `Ka`b became Muslim during the reign of `Umar, for he passed by Al-Madinah intending to visit Jerusalem, and `Umar said to him, "Embrace Islam, O Ka`b.' Ka`b said, `Do you not read in your Book,

(The likeness of those who were entrusted with the Tawrah...) (62:5) until,

(Books) I am among those who were entrusted with the Tawrah.' `Umar left him alone and Ka`b went on to Hims (in Syria) and heard one of its inhabitants recite this Ayah while feeling sad,

(O you who have been given the Scripture (Jews and Christians)! Believe in what We have revealed confirming what is with you, before We efface faces and turn them backwards). Ka`b said, `I believe, O Lord! I embraced Islam, O Lord!' for He feared that this might be struck by this threat. He then went back to his family in Yemen and returned with them all as Muslims." Allah's statement,

(or curse them as We cursed the people of the Sabbath.) refers to those who breached the sanctity of the Sabbath, using deceit, for the purpose of doing more work. Allah changed these people into apes and swine, as we will come to know in the explanation of Surat Al-A`raf (7). Allah's statement,

(And the commandment of Allah is always executed.) means, when He commands something, then no one can dispute or resist His command.

Allah Does not Forgive Shirk, Except After Repenting From it

Allah said that He,

(forgives not that partners should be set up with Him (in worship),) meaning, He does not forgive a servant if he meets Him while he is associating partners with Him,

(but He forgives except that) of sins,

(to whom He wills) of His servants. Imam Ahmad recorded that Abu Dharr said that the Messenger of Allah said,

«إِنَّ اللهَ يَقُولُ: يَا عَبْدِي مَا عَبَدْتَنِي وَرَجَوْتَنِي، فَإِنِّي غَافِرٌ لَكَ عَلَى مَا كَانَ فِيكَ، يَا عَبْدِي إِنَّكَ إِنْ لَقِيتَنِي بِقُرَابِ الْأَرْضِ خَطِيئَةً مَا لَمْ تُشْرِكْ بِي، لَقِيتُكَ بِقُرَابِهَا مَغْفِرَةً»

(Allah said, "O My servant! As long as you worship and beg Me, I will forgive you, no matter your shortcomings. O My servant! If you meet Me with the earth's fill of sin, yet you do not associate any partners with Me, I will meet you with its fill of forgiveness.") Only Ahmad recorded this Hadith with this chain of narration. Imam Ahmad recorded that Abu Dharr said, "I came to the Messenger of Allah and he said,

«مَا مِنْ عَبْدٍ قَالَ: لَا إِلَهَ إِلَّا اللهُ ثُمَّ مَاتَ عَلَى ذَلِكَ، إِلَّا دَخَلَ الْجَنَّةَ»

("No servant proclaims, `There is no deity worthy of worship except Allah,' and dies on that belief, but will enter Paradise." I said, "Even if he committed adultery and theft" He said,

«وَإِنْ زَنَى وَإِنْ سَرَقَ»

Chapter 4: An-Nisaa (The Women), Verses 024-147

"Even if he committed adultery and theft." I asked again, "Even if he committed adultery and theft" He said,

《وَإِنْ زَنَى وَإِنْ سَرَقَ》

"Even if he committed adultery and theft." The fourth time, he said,

《عَلَى رَغْمِ أَنْفِ أَبِي ذَر》

"Even if Abu Dharr's nose was put in the dust.") Abu Dharr departed while pulling his Izar and saying, "Even if Abu Dharr's nose was put in the dust." Ever since that happened, Abu Dharr used to narrate the Hadith and then comment, "Even if Abu Dharr's nose was put in dust." The Two Sahihs recorded this Hadith Al-Bazzar recorded that Ibn `Umar said, "We used to refrain from begging (Allah) for forgiveness for those who commit major sins until we heard our Prophet reciting,

(Verily, Allah forgives not that partners should be set up with Him (in worship), but He forgives except that (anything else) to whom He wills;), and his saying,

《أَخَّرْتُ شَفَاعَتِي لِأَهْلِ الْكَبَائِرِ مِنْ أُمَّتِي يَوْمَ الْقِيَامَة》

(I have reserved my intercession on the Day of Resurrection for those among my Ummah who commit major sins.)" Allah's statement,

(and whoever sets up partners with Allah in worship, he has indeed invented a tremendous sin.) is similar to His statement,

(Verily, joining others in worship with Allah is a great Zulm (wrong) indeed.) In the Two Sahihs, it is recorded that Ibn Mas`ud said, "I said, `O Messenger of Allah! Which is the greatest sin' He said,

《أَنْ تَجْعَلَ لِلَّهِ نِدًّا وَهُوَ خَلَقَكَ》

(To make a rival with Allah, while He Alone created you.)"

Surah: 4 Ayah: 49, Ayah: 50, Ayah: 51 & Ayah: 52

﴿ أَلَمْ تَرَ إِلَى ٱلَّذِينَ يُزَكُّونَ أَنفُسَهُم بَلِ ٱللَّهُ يُزَكِّى مَن يَشَآءُ وَلَا يُظْلَمُونَ فَتِيلًا ﴾

49. Have you not seen those (Jews and Christians) who claim sanctity for themselves. Nay, but Allâh sanctifies whom He wills, and they will not be dealt

with injustice even equal to the extent of a scalish thread in the long slit of a date-stone.

﴿ ٱنظُرْ كَيْفَ يَفْتَرُونَ عَلَى ٱللَّهِ ٱلْكَذِبَ وَكَفَىٰ بِهِ إِثْمًا مُّبِينًا ﴾

50. Look, how they invent a lie against Allâh, and enough is that as a manifest sin.

﴿ أَلَمْ تَرَ إِلَى ٱلَّذِينَ أُوتُواْ نَصِيبًا مِّنَ ٱلْكِتَـٰبِ يُؤْمِنُونَ بِٱلْجِبْتِ وَٱلطَّـٰغُوتِ وَيَقُولُونَ لِلَّذِينَ كَفَرُواْ هَـٰٓؤُلَآءِ أَهْدَىٰ مِنَ ٱلَّذِينَ ءَامَنُواْ سَبِيلًا ﴾

51. Have you not seen those who were given a portion of the Scripture? They believe in Jibt and Tâghût and say to the disbelievers that they are better guided as regards the way than the believers (Muslims).

﴿ أُوْلَـٰٓئِكَ ٱلَّذِينَ لَعَنَهُمُ ٱللَّهُ وَمَن يَلْعَنِ ٱللَّهُ فَلَن تَجِدَ لَهُۥ نَصِيرًا ﴾

52. They are those whom Allâh curses, and he whom Allâh curses, you will not find for him (any) helper,

Transliteration

49. Alam tara ila allatheena yuzakkoona anfusahum bali Allahu yuzakkee man yashao wala yuthlamoona fateelan 50. Onthur kayfa yaftaroona AAala Allahi alkathiba wakafa bihi ithman mubeenan 51. Alam tara ila allatheena ootoo naseeban mina alkitabi yu/minoona bialjibti waalttaghooti wayaqooloona lillatheena kafaroo haola-i ahda mina allatheena amanoo sabeelan 52. Ola-ika allatheena laAAanahumu Allahu waman yalAAani Allahu falan tajida lahu naseeran

Tafsir Ibn Kathir

Chastising and Cursing the Jews for Claiming Purity for Themselves and Believing in Jibt and Taghut

Al-Hasan and Qatadah said, "This Ayah,

(Have you not seen those who claim sanctity for themselves) was revealed about the Jews and Christians when they said, `We are Allah's children and His loved ones.'" Ibn Zayd also said, "This Ayah was revealed concerning their statement,

(We are the children of Allah and His loved ones) and their statement,

(None shall enter Paradise unless he be a Jew or a Christian)." This is why Allah said,

(Nay, but Allah sanctifies whom He wills,) meaning, the decision in this matter is with Allah Alone, because He has perfect knowledge of the true reality and secrets of all things. Allah then said,

(And they will not be dealt with injustice even equal to the extent of a Fatil,) meaning, He does no injustice with anyone's compensation in any part of his reward,

Chapter 4: An-Nisaa (The Women), Verses 024-147

even if it was the weight of a Fatil. Ibn `Abbas, Mujahid, `Ikrimah, `Ata', Al-Hasan, Qatadah and others among the Salaf said that Fatil means, "The scalish thread in the long slit of the date-stone." Allah said,

(Look, how they invent a lie against Allah,) claiming purity for themselves, their claim that they are Allah's children and His loved ones, their statement;

(None shall enter Paradise unless he be a Jew or a Christian) their statement;

(The Fire shall not touch us but for a number of days) and their reliance on the righteous deeds of their forefathers. Allah has decreed that the good actions of the fathers do not help the children, when He said,

(That was a nation who has passed away. They shall receive the reward of what they earned and you of what you earn). Allah then said,

(and enough is that as a manifest sin.) meaning, these lies and fabrications of theirs are sufficent. Allah's statement,

(Have you not seen those who were given a portion of the Scripture They believe in Jibt and Taghut). Muhammad bin Ishaq said from Hassan bin Fa'id that `Umar bin Al-Khattab said, "Jibt is sorcery and Taghut is the Shaytan." Abu Nasr Isma`il bin Hammad Al-Jawhari, the renowned scholar, said in his book As-Sihah, "Al-Jibt means idol, soothsayer and sorcerer." Ibn Abi Hatim recorded that Jabir bin `Abdullah was asked about Taghut, and he said, "They are soothsayers upon whom the devils descend." Mujahid said "Taghut is a devil in the shape of man, and they refer to him for judgment." Imam Malik said, "Taghut is every object that is worshipped instead of Allah, the Exalted and Most Honored."

Disbelievers Are not Better Guided Than Believers

Allah said,

(and say to those who disbelieve, "These people are better guided on the way," than the believers.) preferring the disbelievers over Muslims, because of their ignorance, un-religious nature and disbelief in Allah's Book which is before them. Ibn Abi Hatim recorded that `Ikrimah said, "Huyay bin Akhtab and Ka`b bin Al-Ashraf (two Jewish leaders) came to the people of Makkah, who said to them, `You (Jews) are people of the Book and knowledge, so judge us and Muhammad.' They said, `Describe yourselves and describe Muhammad.' They said, `We keep relation with kith and kin, slaughter camels (for the poor), release the indebted and provide water for the pilgrims. As for Muhammad he is without male children, he severed our relations, and the thieves who rob pilgrims (the tribe of) Ghifar follow him. So who is better, we or him' They said, `You are more righteous and better guided.' Thereafter, Allah sent down,

(Have you not seen those who were given a portion)." This story was also reported from Ibn `Abbas and several others among the Salaf. Allah's Curse on the Jews This Ayah (4:52) contains a curse for the Jews and informs them that they have no supporter in this life or the Hereafter, because they sought the help of the idolators.

They uttered this statement (in Ayah 4:51) to lure the disbelievers into supporting them, and they ultimately gathered their forces for the battle of Al-Ahzab, forcing the Prophet and his Companions to dig a defensive tunnel around Al-Madinah. But, Allah saved the Muslims from their evil,

(And Allah drove back those who disbelieved in their rage, they gained no advantage (booty). Allah sufficed for the believers in the fighting. And Allah is Ever All-Strong, All-Mighty).

Surah: 4 Ayah: 53, Ayah: 54 & Ayah: 55

﴿ أَمْ لَهُمْ نَصِيبٌ مِّنَ ٱلْمُلْكِ فَإِذًا لَّا يُؤْتُونَ ٱلنَّاسَ نَقِيرًا ۝ ﴾

53. Or have they a share in the dominion? Then in that case they would not give mankind even a speck on the back of a date-stone.

﴿ أَمْ يَحْسُدُونَ ٱلنَّاسَ عَلَىٰ مَآ ءَاتَىٰهُمُ ٱللَّهُ مِن فَضْلِهِۦ ۖ فَقَدْ ءَاتَيْنَآ ءَالَ إِبْرَٰهِيمَ ٱلْكِتَٰبَ وَٱلْحِكْمَةَ وَءَاتَيْنَٰهُم مُّلْكًا عَظِيمًا ۝ ﴾

54. Or do they envy men (Muhammad (peace be upon him) and his followers) for what Allâh has given them of His Bounty? Then We had already given the family of Ibrâhîm (Abraham) the Book and Al-Hikmah (As-Sunnah - Divine Revelation to those Prophets not written in the form of a book), and conferred upon them a great kingdom.

﴿ فَمِنْهُم مَّنْ ءَامَنَ بِهِۦ وَمِنْهُم مَّن صَدَّ عَنْهُ ۚ وَكَفَىٰ بِجَهَنَّمَ سَعِيرًا ۝ ﴾

55. Of them were (some) who believed in him (Muhammad (peace be upon him)) and of them were (some) who averted their faces from him (Muhammad (peace be upon him)) and enough is Hell for burning (them).

Transliteration

53. Am lahum naseebun mina almulki fa-ithan la yu/toona alnnasa naqeeran 54. Am yahsudoona alnnasa AAala ma atahumu Allahu min fadlihi faqad atayna ala ibraheema alkitaba waalhikmata waataynahum mulkan AAatheeman 55. Faminhum man amana bihi waminhum man sadda AAanhu wakafa bijahannama saAAeeran

Tafsir Ibn Kathir

The Envy and Miserly Conduct of the Jews

Allah asked the Jews if they have a share in the dominion. That is merely a statement of rebuke, since they do not have any share in the dominion. Allah then described them as misers,

(Then in that case they would not give mankind even a Naqir.) Meaning, if they had a share in the sovereignty and dominion, they would not give anyone anything, especially Muhammad, even if it was the speck on the back of a date-stone, which is

Chapter 4: An-Nisaa (The Women), Verses 024-147

the meaning of Naqir according to Ibn `Abbas and the majority of the scholars. This Ayah is similar to another of Allah's statements,

(Say: "If you possessed the treasure of the mercy of my Lord, then you would surely withold it out of fear of spending it.) meaning, for fear that what you have might end, although there is no such possibility here. This only demonstrates their greedy and stingy nature. This is why Allah said,

(And man is ever Qatur) meaning Bakhil (stingy). Allah then said,

(Or do they envy men for what Allah has given them of His Bounty) referring to their envy of the Prophet for the great prophethood that Allah entrusted him with. Their envy made them reject him, because he was an Arab and not from the Children of Israel. At-Tabarani recorded that Ibn `Abbas said that,

(Or do they envy men) means, "We are the worthy people, rather than the rest of the people." Allah said,

(Then, We have already given the family of Ibrahim the Book and Al-Hikmah, and conferred upon them a great kingdom.) meaning, We gave the prophethood to the tribes of the Children of Israel, who are among the offspring of Ibrahim and sent down the Books to them. These Prophets ruled the Jews with the prophetic tradition, and We made kings among them. Yet,

(Of them were (some) who believed in it;) referring to Allah's favor and bounty (Prophets, Books, kingship),

(and of them were (some) who rejected it) by disbelieving in it, ignoring it, and hindering the people from its path, although this bounty was from and for them, the Children of Israel. They disputed with their own Prophets; so what about you, O Muhammad , especially since you are not from the Children of Israel Mujahid said,

(Of them were (some) who believed in (him),) "Muhammad ,

(and of them were (some) who rejected (him).)" Therefore, O Muhammad, the rejection of you because of their disbelief is even more severe and they are even further from the truth that you brought them. This is why Allah threatened them,

(and enough is Hell for burning (them).), meaning, the Fire is a just punishment for them because of their disbelief, rebellion and defiance of Allah's Books and Messengers.

Surah: 4 Ayah: 56 & Ayah: 57

﴿ إِنَّ ٱلَّذِينَ كَفَرُوا۟ بِـَٔايَٰتِنَا سَوْفَ نُصْلِيهِمْ نَارًا كُلَّمَا نَضِجَتْ جُلُودُهُم بَدَّلْنَٰهُمْ جُلُودًا غَيْرَهَا لِيَذُوقُوا۟ ٱلْعَذَابَ ۗ إِنَّ ٱللَّهَ كَانَ عَزِيزًا حَكِيمًا ﴾

56. Surely! Those who disbelieved in Our Ayât (proofs, evidences, verses, lessons, signs, revelations, etc.), We shall burn them in Fire. As often as their skins are

roasted through, We shall change them for other skins that they may taste the punishment. Truly, Allâh is Ever Most Powerful, All-Wise.

﴿ وَٱلَّذِينَ ءَامَنُواْ وَعَمِلُواْ ٱلصَّٰلِحَٰتِ سَنُدْخِلُهُمْ جَنَّٰتٍ تَجْرِى مِن تَحْتِهَا ٱلْأَنْهَٰرُ خَٰلِدِينَ فِيهَآ أَبَدًا لَّهُمْ فِيهَآ أَزْوَٰجٌ مُّطَهَّرَةٌ وَنُدْخِلُهُمْ ظِلًّا ظَلِيلًا ﴾

57. But those who believe (in the Oneness of Allâh - Islâmic Monotheism) and do deeds of righteousness, We shall admit them to Gardens under which rivers flow (Paradise), abiding therein forever. Therein they shall have Azwâjun Mutahharatun (purified mates or wives, and We shall admit them to shades wide and ever deepening (Paradise).

Transliteration

56. Inna allatheena kafaroo bi-ayatina sawfa nusleehim naran kullama nadijat julooduhum baddalnahum juloodan ghayraha liyathooqoo alAAathaba inna Allaha kana AAazeezan hakeeman 57. Waallatheena amanoo waAAamiloo alssalihati sanudkhiluhum jannatin tajree min tahtiha alanharu khalideena feeha abadan lahum feeha azwajun mutahharatun wanudkhiluhum thillan thaleelan

Tafsir Ibn Kathir

The Punishment of Those Who Disbelieve in Allah's Books and Messengers

Allah describes the torment in the Fire of Jahannam for those who disbelieve in His Ayat and hinder from the path of His Messengers. Allah said,

(Surely, those who disbelieved in Our Ayat ,) meaning, We will place them in the Fire which will encompass every part of their bodies. Allah then states that their punishment and torment are everlasting,

(We shall burn them in Fire. As often as their skins are roasted through, We shall change them for other skins that they may taste the punishment). Al-A`mash said that Ibn `Umar said, "When their skin are burned, they will be given another skin in replacement, and this skin will be as white as paper." This was collected by Ibn Abi Hatim, who also recorded that Al-Hasan said,

(As often as their skins are roasted through,) "Their skin will be roasted through, seventy thousand times every day." Husayn said; Fudayl added that Hisham said that Al-Hasan also said that,

(As often as their skins are roasted through,) means, "Whenever the Fire has roasted them through and consumed their flesh, they will be told, `Go back as you were before,' and they will."

The Wealth of the Righteous; Paradise and its Joy

Allah said,

(But those who believe and do deeds of righteousness, We shall admit them to Gardens under which rivers flow (Paradise), abiding therein forever.) describing the destination of the happy ones in the gardens of Eden, beneath which rivers flow in all of its areas, spaces and corners, wherever they desire and wish. They will reside in it for eternity, and they will not be transferred or removed from it, nor would they want to move from it. Allah said,

(Therein they shall have Azwajun Mutahharatun (purified mates),) free of menstruation, postnatal bleeding, filth, bad manners and shortcomings. Ibn `Abbas said that the Ayah means, "They are purified of filth and foul things." Similar was said by `Ata', Al-Hasan, Ad-Dahhak, An-Nakha`i, Abu Salih, `Atiyah, and As-Suddi. Mujahid said that they are, free of urine, menstruation, spit, mucous and pregnancies." Allah's statement,

(And We shall admit them to shades, wide and ever deepening (Paradise).) means, wide, extensive, pure and elegant shade. Ibn Jarir recorded that Abu Hurayrah said that the Prophet said,

«إِنَّ فِي الْجَنَّةِ لَشَجَرَةً يَسِيرُ الرَّاكِبُ فِي ظِلِّهَا مِائَةَ عَامٍ لَا يَقْطَعُهَا: شَجَرَةُ الْخُلْدِ»

(There is a tree in Paradise, that if a rider travels under its shade for a hundred years, he will not cross it. It is the Tree of Everlasting Life.)

Surah: 4 Ayah: 58

﴿إِنَّ ٱللَّهَ يَأْمُرُكُمْ أَن تُؤَدُّواْ ٱلْأَمَٰنَٰتِ إِلَىٰٓ أَهْلِهَا وَإِذَا حَكَمْتُم بَيْنَ ٱلنَّاسِ أَن تَحْكُمُواْ بِٱلْعَدْلِ إِنَّ ٱللَّهَ نِعِمَّا يَعِظُكُم بِهِۦٓ إِنَّ ٱللَّهَ كَانَ سَمِيعَۢا بَصِيرًا﴾

58. Verily! Allâh commands that you should render back the trusts to those to whom they are due; and that when you judge between men, you judge with justice. Verily, how excellent is the teaching which He (Allâh) gives you! Truly, Allâh is Ever All-Hearer, All-Seer.

Transliteration

58. Inna Allaha ya/murukum an tu-addoo al-amanati ila ahliha wa-itha hakamtum bayna alnnasi an tahkumoo bialAAadli inna Allaha niAAimma yaAAithukum bihi inna Allaha kana sameeAAan baseeran

Tafsir Ibn Kathir

The Command to Return the Trusts to Whomever They Are Due

Allah commands that the trusts be returned to their rightful owners. Al-Hasan narrated that Samurah said that the Messenger of Allah said,

«أَدِّ الْأَمَانَةَ إِلَى مَنِ ائْتَمَنَكَ، وَلَا تَخُنْ مَنْ خَانَكَ»

(Return the trust to those who entrusted you, and do not betray those who betrayed you.) Imam Ahmad and the collectors of Sunan recorded this Hadith. This command refers to all things that one is expected to look after, such as Allah's rights on His servants: praying, Zakah, fasting, penalties for sins, vows and so forth. The command also includes the rights of the servants on each other, such as what they entrust each other with, including the cases that are not recorded or documented. Allah commands that all types of trusts be fulfillled. Those who do not implement this command in this life, it will be extracted from them on the Day of Resurrection. It is recorded in the Sahih that the Messenger of Allah said,

«لَتُؤَدَّنَّ الْحُقُوقُ إِلَى أَهْلِهَا حَتَّى يُقْتَصَّ لِلشَّاةِ الْجَمَّاءِ مِنَ الْقَرْنَاءِ»

(The rights will be rendered back to those to whom they are due, and even the sheep that does not have horns will take revenge from the horned sheep.) Ibn Jarir recorded that Ibn Jurayj said about this Ayah, "It was revealed concerning `Uthman bin Talhah from whom the Messenger of Allah took the key of the Ka`bah and entered it on the Day of the victory of Makkah. When the Prophet went out, he was reciting this Ayah,

(Verily, Allah commands that you should render back the trusts to those, to whom they are due). He then called `Uthman and gave the key back to him." Ibn Jarir also narrated that `Umar bin Al-Khattab said, "When the Messenger of Allah went out of the Ka`bah, he was reciting this Ayah,

(Verily, Allah commands that you should render back the trusts to those, to whom they are due). May I sacrifice my father and mother for him, I never heard him recite this Ayah before that." It is popular that this is the reason behind revealing the Ayah (4:58). Yet, the application of the Ayah is general, and this is why Ibn `Abbas and Muhammad bin Al-Hanafiyyah said, "This Ayah is for the righteous and wicked," meaning it is a command that encompasses everyone.

The Order to Be Just

Allah said,

(and that when you judge between men, you judge with justice.) commanding justice when judging between people. Muhammad bin Ka`b, Zayd bin Aslam and Shahr bin Hawshab said; "This Ayah was revealed about those in authority", meaning those who judge between people. A Hadith states,

«إِنَّ اللهَ مَعَ الْحَاكِمِ مَا لَمْ يَجُرْ، فَإِذَا جَارَ وَكَلَهُ اللهُ إِلَى نَفْسِهِ»

Chapter 4: An-Nisaa (The Women), Verses 024-147

(Allah is with the judge as long as he does not commit injustice, for when he does, Allah will make him reliant on himself.) A statement goes, "One day of justice equals forty years of worship." Allah said,

(Verily, how excellent is the teaching which He (Allah) gives you!) meaning, His commands to return the trusts to their owners, to judge between people with justice, and all of His complete, perfect and great commandments and laws. Allah's statement,

(Truly, Allah is Ever All-Hearer, All-Seer.) means, He hears your statements and knows your actions.

Surah: 4 Ayah: 59

﴿ يَـٰٓأَيُّهَا ٱلَّذِينَ ءَامَنُوٓاْ أَطِيعُواْ ٱللَّهَ وَأَطِيعُواْ ٱلرَّسُولَ وَأُوْلِى ٱلْأَمْرِ مِنكُمْ ۖ فَإِن تَنَـٰزَعْتُمْ فِى شَىْءٍ فَرُدُّوهُ إِلَى ٱللَّهِ وَٱلرَّسُولِ إِن كُنتُمْ تُؤْمِنُونَ بِٱللَّهِ وَٱلْيَوْمِ ٱلْأَخِرِ ذَٰلِكَ خَيْرٌ وَأَحْسَنُ تَأْوِيلًا ﴾

59. O you who believe! Obey Allâh and obey the Messenger (Muhammad (peace be upon him)) and those of you (Muslims) who are in authority. (And) if you differ in anything amongst yourselves, refer it to Allâh and His Messenger (peace be upon him), if you believe in Allâh and in the Last Day. That is better and more suitable for final determination.

Transliteration

59. Ya ayyuha allatheena amanoo ateeAAoo Allaha waateeAAoo alrrasoola waolee al-amri minkum fain tanazaAAtum fee shay-in faruddoohu ila Allahi waalrrasooli in kuntum tu/minoona biAllahi waalyawmi al-akhiri thalika khayrun waahsanu ta/weelan

Tafsir Ibn Kathir

The Necessity of Obeying the Rulers in Obedience to Allah

Al-Bukhari recorded that Ibn `Abbas said that the Ayah,

(Obey Allah and obey the Messenger, and those of you who are in authority.) "Was revealed about `Abdullah bin Hudhafah bin Qays bin `Adi, who the Messenger of Allah sent on a military expedition." This statement was collected by the Group, with the exception of Ibn Majah At-Tirmidhi said, "Hasan, Gharib". Imam Ahmad recorded that `Ali said, "The Messenger of Allah sent a troop under the command of a man from Al-Ansar. When they left, he became angry with them for some reason and said to them, `Has not the Messenger of Allah commanded you to obey me' They said, `Yes.' He said, `Collect some wood,' and then he started a fire with the wood, saying, `I command you to enter the fire.' The people almost entered the fire, but a young man among them said, `You only ran away from the Fire to Allah's Messenger. Therefore, do not rush until you go back to Allah's Messenger, and if he commands you to enter it, then enter it.' When they went back to Allah's Messenger, they told him what had happened, and the Messenger said,

»لَوْ دَخَلْتُمُوهَا مَا خَرَجْتُمْ مِنْهَا أَبَدًا، إِنَّمَا الطَّاعَةُ فِي الْمَعْرُوفِ«

(Had you entered it, you would never have departed from it. Obedience is only in righteousness.)" This Hadith is recorded in the Two Sahihs. Abu Dawud recorded that `Abdullah bin `Umar said that the Messenger of Allah said,

»السَّمْعُ وَالطَّاعَةُ عَلَى الْمَرْءِ الْمُسْلِمِ فِيمَا أَحَبَّ وَكَرِهَ، مَا لَمْ يُؤْمَرْ بِمَعْصِيَةٍ، فَإِذَا أُمِرَ بِمَعْصِيَةٍ فَلَا سَمْعَ وَلَا طَاعَةَ«

(The Muslim is required to hear and obey in that which he likes and dislikes, unless he was commanded to sin. When he is commanded with sin, then there is no hearing or obeying.) This Hadith is recorded in the Two Sahihs. `Ubadah bin As-Samit said, "We gave our pledge to Allah's Messenger to hear and obey (our leaders), while active and otherwise, in times of ease and times of difficulty, even if we were deprived of our due shares, and to not dispute this matter (leadership) with its rightful people. The Prophet said,

»إِلَّا أَنْ تَرَوْا كُفْرًا بَوَاحًا، عِنْدَكُمْ فِيهِ مِنَ اللهِ بُرْهَانٌ«

(Except when you witness clear Kufr about which you have clear proof from Allah.)" This Hadith is recorded in the Two Sahihs. Another Hadith narrated by Anas states that the Messenger of Allah said,

»اسْمَعُوا وَأَطِيعُوا، وَإِنْ أُمِّرَ عَلَيْكُمْ عَبْدٌ حَبَشِيٌّ كَأَنَّ رَأْسَهُ زَبِيبَةٌ«

(Hear and obey (your leaders), even if an Ethiopian slave whose head is like a raisin, is made your chief.) Al-Bukhari recorded this Hadith. Umm Al-Husayn said that she heard the Messenger of Allah giving a speech during the Farewell Hajj, in which he said;

»وَلَوِ اسْتُعْمِلَ عَلَيْكُمْ عَبْدٌ يَقُودُكُمْ بِكِتَابِ اللهِ، اسْمَعُوا لَهُ وَأَطِيعُوا«

(Even if a slave was appointed over you, and he rules you with Allah's Book, then listen to him and obey him.) Muslim recorded this Hadith. In another narration with Muslim, the Prophet said,

$$«عَبْدًا حَبَشِيًّا مَجْدُوعًا»$$

(Even if an Ethiopian slave, whose nose was mutilated...) In the Two Sahihs, it is recorded that Abu Hurayrah said that the Messenger of Allah said,

$$«مَنْ أَطَاعَنِي فَقَدْ أَطَاعَ اللهَ، وَمَنْ عَصَانِي فَقَدْ عَصَى اللهَ، وَمَنْ أَطَاعَ أَمِيرِي فَقَدْ أَطَاعَنِي، وَمَنْ عَصَى أَمِيرِي فَقَدْ عَصَانِي»$$

(Whoever obeys me, obeys Allah, and whoever disobeys me, disobeys Allah. Whoever obeys my commander, obeys me, and whoever disobeys my commander, disobeys me.) This is why Allah said,

(Obey Allah), adhere to His Book,

(and obey the Messenger), adhere to his Sunnah,

(And those of you who are in authority) in the obedience to Allah which they command you, not what constitutes disobedience of Allah, for there is no obedience to anyone in disobedience to Allah, as we mentioned in the authentic Hadith,

$$«إِنَّمَا الطَّاعَةُ فِي الْمَعْرُوفِ»$$

(Obedience is only in righteousness.)

The Necessity of Referring to the Qur'an and Sunnah for Judgment

Allah said,

((And) if you differ in anything amongst yourselves, refer it to Allah and His Messenger). Mujahid and several others among the Salaf said that the Ayah means, "(Refer) to the Book of Allah and the Sunnah of His Messenger." This is a command from Allah that whatever areas the people dispute about, whether major or minor areas of the religion, they are required to refer to the Qur'an and Sunnah for judgment concerning these disputes. In another Ayah, Allah said,

(And in whatsoever you differ, the decision thereof is with Allah). Therefore, whatever the Book and Sunnah decide and testify to the truth of, then it, is the plain truth. What is beyond truth, save falsehood This is why Allah said,

(if you believe in Allah and in the Last Day.) meaning, refer the disputes and conflicts that arise between you to the Book of Allah and the Sunnah of His Messenger for judgment. Allah's statement, (if you believe in Allah and in the Last Day.) indicates that those who do not refer to the Book and Sunnah for judgment in their disputes, are not believers in Allah or the Last Day. Allah said,

(That is better) meaning, referring to the Book of Allah and the Sunnah of His Messenger for judgment in various disputes is better,

(and more suitable for final determination.) meaning, "Has a better end and destination," as As-Suddi and several others have stated while Mujahid said, "Carries a better reward."

Surah: 4 Ayah: 60, Ayah: 61, Ayah: 62 & Ayah: 63

﴿ أَلَمْ تَرَ إِلَى ٱلَّذِينَ يَزْعُمُونَ أَنَّهُمْ ءَامَنُوا۟ بِمَآ أُنزِلَ إِلَيْكَ وَمَآ أُنزِلَ مِن قَبْلِكَ يُرِيدُونَ أَن يَتَحَاكَمُوٓا۟ إِلَى ٱلطَّٰغُوتِ وَقَدْ أُمِرُوٓا۟ أَن يَكْفُرُوا۟ بِهِۦ وَيُرِيدُ ٱلشَّيْطَٰنُ أَن يُضِلَّهُمْ ضَلَٰلًۢا بَعِيدًا ۝ ﴾

60. Have you seen those (hypocrites) who claim that they believe in that which has been sent down to you, and that which was sent down before you, and they wish to go for judgement (in their disputes) to the Tâghût (false judges) while they have been ordered to reject them. But Shaitân (Satan) wishes to lead them far astray.

﴿ وَإِذَا قِيلَ لَهُمْ تَعَالَوْا۟ إِلَىٰ مَآ أَنزَلَ ٱللَّهُ وَإِلَى ٱلرَّسُولِ رَأَيْتَ ٱلْمُنَٰفِقِينَ يَصُدُّونَ عَنكَ صُدُودًا ۝ ﴾

61. And when it is said to them: "Come to what Allâh has sent down and to the Messenger (Muhammad (peace be upon him))" you (Muhammad (peace be upon him)) see the hypocrites turn away from you (Muhammad (peace be upon him)) with aversion.

﴿ فَكَيْفَ إِذَآ أَصَٰبَتْهُم مُّصِيبَةٌۢ بِمَا قَدَّمَتْ أَيْدِيهِمْ ثُمَّ جَآءُوكَ يَحْلِفُونَ بِٱللَّهِ إِنْ أَرَدْنَآ إِلَّآ إِحْسَٰنًا وَتَوْفِيقًا ۝ ﴾

62. How then, when a catastrophe befalls them because of what their hands have sent forth, they come to you swearing by Allâh, "We meant no more than goodwill and conciliation!"

﴿ أُو۟لَٰٓئِكَ ٱلَّذِينَ يَعْلَمُ ٱللَّهُ مَا فِى قُلُوبِهِمْ فَأَعْرِضْ عَنْهُمْ وَعِظْهُمْ وَقُل لَّهُمْ فِىٓ أَنفُسِهِمْ قَوْلًۢا بَلِيغًا ۝ ﴾

Chapter 4: An-Nisaa (The Women), Verses 024-147

63. They (hypocrites) are those of whom Allâh knows what is in their hearts; so turn aside from them (do not punish them) but admonish them, and speak to them an effective word (i.e. to believe in Allâh, worship Him, obey Him, and be afraid of Him) to reach their innerselves.

Transliteration

60. Alam tara ila allatheena yazAAumoona annahum amanoo bima onzila ilayka wama onzila min qablika yureedoona an yatahakamoo ila alttaghooti waqad omiroo an yakfuroo bihi wayureedu alshshaytanu an yudillahum dalalan baAAeedan 61. Wa-itha qeela lahum taAAalaw ila ma anzala Allahu wa-ila alrrasooli raayta almunafiqeena yasuddoona AAanka sudoodan 62. Fakayfa itha asabat-hum museebatun bima qaddamat aydeehim thumma jaooka yahlifoona biAllahi in aradna illa ihsanan watawfeeqan 63. Ola-ika allatheena yaAAlamu Allahu ma fee quloobihim faaAArid AAanhum waAAithhum waqul lahum fee anfusihim qawlan baleeghan

Kathir's Tafsir

Referring to Other than the Qur'an and Sunnah for Judgment is Characteristic of Non-Muslims

Allah chastises those who claim to believe in what Allah has sent down to His Messenger and to the earlier Prophets, yet they refer to other than the Book of Allah and the Sunnah of His Messenger for judgment in various disputes. It was reported that the reason behind revealing this Ayah was that a man from the Ansar and a Jew had a dispute, and the Jew said, "Let us refer to Muhammad to judge between us." However, the Muslim man said, "Let us refer to Ka`b bin Al-Ashraf (a Jew) to judge between us." It was also reported that the Ayah was revealed about some hypocrites who pretended to be Muslims, yet they sought to refer to the judgment of Jahiliyyah. Other reasons were also reported behind the revelation of the Ayah. However, the Ayah has a general meaning, as it chastises all those who refrain from referring to the Qur'an and Sunnah for judgment and prefer the judgment of whatever they chose of falsehood, which befits the description of Taghut here. This is why Allah said,

(and they wish to go for judgment to the Taghut) until the end of the Ayah. Allah's statement,

(turn away from you with aversion) means, they turn away from you in arrogance, just as Allah described the polytheists,

(When it is said to them: "Follow what Allah has sent down." They say: "Nay! We shall follow what we found our fathers following.") This is different from the conduct of the faithful believers, whom Allah describes as,

(The only saying of the faithful believers, when they are called to Allah and His Messenger, to judge between them, is that they say: "We hear and we obey.")

Chastising the Hypocrites

Chastising the hypocrites, Allah said,

(How then, when a catastrophe befalls them because of what their hands have sent forth,) meaning, how about it if they feel compelled to join you because of disasters that they suffer due to their sins, then they will be in need of you.

(They come to you swearing by Allah, "We meant no more than goodwill and conciliation!") apologizing and swearing that they only sought goodwill and reconciliation when they referred to other than the Prophet for judgment, not that they believe in such alternative judgment, as they claim. Allah describes these people to us further in His statement,

(And you see those in whose hearts there is a disease (of hypocrisy), they hurry to their friendship, saying: "We fear"), until,

(Then they will become regretful for what they have been keeping as a secret in themselves). At-Tabarani recorded that Ibn `Abbas said, "Abu Barzah Al-Aslami used to be a soothsayer who judged between the Jews in their disputes. When some Muslims came to him to judge between them, Allah sent down,

(Have you not seen those (hyprocrites) who claim that they believe in that which has been sent down to you, and that which was sent down before you), until,

("We meant no more than goodwill and conciliation!") Allah then said,

(They (hypocrites) are those of whom Allah knows what is in their hearts;) These people are hypocrites, and Allah knows what is in their hearts and will punish them accordingly, for nothing escapes Allah's watch. Consequently, O Muhammad! Let Allah be sufficient for you in this regard, because He has perfect knowledge of their apparent and hidden affairs. This is why Allah said,

(so turn aside from them (do not punish them)) meaning, do not punish them because of what is in their hearts.

(but admonish them) means, advise them against the hypocrisy and evil that reside in their hearts,

(and speak to them an effective word to reach their inner selves) advise them, between you and them, using effective words that might benefit them.

Surah: 4 Ayah: 64 & Ayah: 65

﴿ وَمَا أَرْسَلْنَا مِن رَّسُولٍ إِلَّا لِيُطَاعَ بِإِذْنِ ٱللَّهِ ۚ وَلَوْ أَنَّهُمْ إِذ ظَّلَمُوٓا۟ أَنفُسَهُمْ جَآءُوكَ فَٱسْتَغْفَرُوا۟ ٱللَّهَ وَٱسْتَغْفَرَ لَهُمُ ٱلرَّسُولُ لَوَجَدُوا۟ ٱللَّهَ تَوَّابًا رَّحِيمًا ﴾

64. We sent no Messenger, but to be obeyed by Allâh's Leave. If they (hypocrites), when they had been unjust to themselves, had come to you (Muhammad (peace be upon him)) and begged Allâh's Forgiveness, and the Messenger had begged forgiveness for them: indeed, they would have found Allâh All-Forgiving (One Who accepts repentance), Most Merciful.

Chapter 4: An-Nisaa (The Women), Verses 024-147

$$\text{﴿ فَلَا وَرَبِّكَ لَا يُؤْمِنُونَ حَتَّىٰ يُحَكِّمُوكَ فِيمَا شَجَرَ بَيْنَهُمْ ثُمَّ لَا يَجِدُوا فِي أَنفُسِهِمْ حَرَجًا مِّمَّا قَضَيْتَ وَيُسَلِّمُوا تَسْلِيمًا ﴾}$$

65. But no, by your Lord, they can have no Faith, until they make you (O Muhammad (peace be upon him)) judge in all disputes between them, and find in themselves no resistance against your decisions, and accept (them) with full submission.

Transliteration

64. Wama arsalna min rasoolin illa liyutaAAa bi-ithni Allahi walaw annahum ith thalamoo anfusahum jaooka faistaghfaroo Allaha waistaghfara lahumu alrrasoolu lawajadoo Allaha tawwaban raheeman 65. Fala warabbika la yu/minoona hatta yuhakkimooka feema shajara baynahum thumma la yajidoo fee anfusihim harajan mimma qadayta wayusallimoo tasleeman

Tafsir Ibn Kathir

The Necessity of Obeying the Messenger

Allah said,

(We sent no Messenger, but to be obeyed) meaning, obeying the Prophet was ordained for those to whom Allah sends the Prophet. Allah's statement,

(by Allah's leave) means, "None shall obey, except by My leave," according to Mujahid. This Ayah indicates that the Prophets are only obeyed by whomever Allah directs to obedience. In another Ayah, Allah said,

(And Allah did indeed fulfill His promise to you when you were killing them (your enemy) with His permission) meaning, by His command, decree, will and because He granted you superiority over them. Allah's statement,

(If they (hypocrites), when they had been unjust to themselves,) directs the sinners and evildoers, when they commit errors and mistakes, to come to the Messenger , so that they ask Allah for forgiveness in his presence and ask him to supplicate to Allah to forgive them. If they do this, Allah will forgive them and award them His mercy and pardon. This is why Allah said,

(they would have found Allah All-Forgiving (One Who forgives and accepts repentance), Most Merciful).

One Does not Become a Believer Unless He Refers to the Messenger for Judgment and Submits to his Decisions

Allah said,

(But no, by your Lord, they can have no faith, until they make you judge in all disputes between them,) Allah swears by His Glorious, Most Honorable Self, that no one shall attain faith until he refers to the Messenger for judgment in all matters.

Thereafter, whatever the Messenger commands, is the plain truth that must be submitted to inwardly and outwardly. Allah said,

(and find in themselves no resistance against your decisions, and accept (them) with full submission.) meaning: they adhere to your judgment, and thus do not feel any hesitation over your decision, and they submit to it inwardly and outwardly. They submit to the Prophet's decision with total submission without any rejection, denial or dispute. Al-Bukhari recorded that `Urwah said, "Az-Zubayr quarreled with a man about a stream which both of them used for irrigation. Allah's Messenger said to Az-Zubayr,

«اسْقِ يَا زُبَيْرُ ثُمَّ أَرْسِلِ الْمَاءَ إِلَى جَارِكَ»

(O Zubayr! Irrigate (your garden) first, and then let the water flow to your neighbor.) The Ansari became angry and said, `O Allah's Messenger! Is it because he is your cousin' On that, the face of Allah's Messenger changed color (because of anger) and said,

«اسْقِ يَا زُبَيْرُ ثُمَّ احْبِسِ الْمَاءَ حَتَّى يَرْجِعَ إِلَى الْجَدْرِ، ثُمَّ أَرْسِلِ الْمَاءَ إِلَى جَارِكَ»

(Irrigate (your garden), O Zubayr, and then withhold the water until it reaches the walls (surrounding the palms). Then, release the water to your neighbor.) So, Allah's Messenger gave Az-Zubayr his full right when the Ansari made him angry. Before that, Allah's Messenger had given a generous judgment, beneficial for Az-Zubayr and the Ansari. Az-Zubayr said, `I think the following verse was revealed concerning that case,

(But no, by your Lord, they can have no faith, until they make you (O Muhammad) judge in all disputes between them.)"' Another Reason In his Tafsir, Al-Hafiz Abu Ishaq Ibrahim bin `Abdur-Rahman bin Ibrahim bin Duhaym recorded that Damrah narrated that two men took their dispute to the Prophet , and he gave a judgment to the benefit of whoever among them had the right. The person who lost the dispute said, "I do not agree." The other person asked him, "What do you want then" He said, "Let us go to Abu Bakr As-Siddiq." They went to Abu Bakr and the person who won the dispute said, "We went to the Prophet with our dispute and he issued a decision in my favor." Abu Bakr said, "Then the decision is that which the Messenger of Allah issued." The person who lost the dispute still rejected the decision and said, "Let us go to `Umar bin Al-Khattab." When they went to `Umar, the person who won the dispute said, "We took our dispute to the Prophet and he decided in my favor, but this man refused to submit to the decision." `Umar bin Al-Khattab asked the second man and he concurred. `Umar went to his house and emerged from it holding aloft his sword. He struck the head of the man who rejected the Prophet's decision with the sword and killed him. Consequently, Allah revealed,

(But no, by your Lord, they can have no faith).

Surah: 4 Ayah: 66, Ayah: 67, Ayah: 68, Ayah: 69 & Ayah: 70

﴿ وَلَوْ أَنَّا كَتَبْنَا عَلَيْهِمْ أَنِ اقْتُلُوا أَنفُسَكُمْ أَوِ اخْرُجُوا مِن دِيَارِكُم مَّا فَعَلُوهُ إِلَّا قَلِيلٌ مِّنْهُمْ وَلَوْ أَنَّهُمْ فَعَلُوا مَا يُوعَظُونَ بِهِ لَكَانَ خَيْرًا لَّهُمْ وَأَشَدَّ تَثْبِيتًا ۝ ﴾

66. And if We had ordered them (saying), "Kill yourselves (i.e. the innocent ones kill the guilty ones) or leave your homes," very few of them would have done it; but if they had done what they were told, it would have been better for them, and would have strengthened their (Faith);

﴿ وَإِذًا لَّآتَيْنَاهُم مِّن لَّدُنَّا أَجْرًا عَظِيمًا ۝ ﴾

67. And indeed We should then have bestowed upon them a great reward from Ourselves.

﴿ وَلَهَدَيْنَاهُمْ صِرَاطًا مُّسْتَقِيمًا ۝ ﴾

68. And indeed We should have guided them to a Straight Way.

﴿ وَمَن يُطِعِ اللَّهَ وَالرَّسُولَ فَأُولَٰئِكَ مَعَ الَّذِينَ أَنْعَمَ اللَّهُ عَلَيْهِم مِّنَ النَّبِيِّينَ وَالصِّدِّيقِينَ وَالشُّهَدَاءِ وَالصَّالِحِينَ وَحَسُنَ أُولَٰئِكَ رَفِيقًا ۝ ﴾

69. And whoso obey Allâh and the Messenger (Muhammad (peace be upon him)) then they will be in the company of those on whom Allâh has bestowed His Grace, of the Prophets, the Siddiqûn (those followers of the Prophets who were first and foremost to believe in them, like Abu Bakr As-Siddiq (may Allah be pleased with him), the martyrs, and the righteous. And how excellent these companions are!

﴿ ذَٰلِكَ الْفَضْلُ مِنَ اللَّهِ وَكَفَىٰ بِاللَّهِ عَلِيمًا ۝ ﴾

70. Such is the Bounty from Allâh, and Allâh is Sufficient as All-Knower.

Transliteration

66. Walaw anna katabna AAalayhim ani oqtuloo anfusakum awi okhrujoo min diyarikum ma faAAaloohu illa qaleelun minhum walaw annahum faAAaloo ma yooAAathoona bihi lakana khayran lahum waashadda tathbeetan   67. Wa-ithan laataynahum min ladunna ajran AAatheeman   68. Walahadaynahum siratan mustaqeeman   69. Waman yutiAAi Allaha waalrrasoola faola-ika maAAa allatheena anAAama Allahu AAalayhim mina alnnabiyyeena waalssiddeeqeena waalshshuhada-i waalssaliheena wahasuna ola-ika rafeeqan   70. Thalika alfadlu mina Allahi wakafa biAllahi AAaleeman

Tafsir Ibn Kathir

Most People Disobey What They Are Ordered

Allah states that even if the people were commanded to commit what they were prohibited from doing, most of them would not submit to this command, for their wicked nature is such that they dispute orders. Allah has complete knowledge of what has not occured, and how it would be if and when it did occur. This is why Allah said,

(And if We had ordered them (saying), "Kill yourselves (i.e. the innnocent ones kill the guilty ones)) until the end of the Ayah. This is why Allah said,

(but if they had done what they were told,) meaning, if they do what they were commanded and refrain from what they were prohibited,

(it would have been better for them,) than disobeying the command and committing the prohibition,

(and would have strengthened their conviction), stronger Tasdiq (conviction of faith), according to As-Suddi.

(And indeed We should then have bestowed upon them from Ladunna) from Us,

(A great reward), Paradise,

(And indeed We should have guided them to the straight way.) in this life and the Hereafter.

Whoever Obeys Allah and His Messenger Will Be Honored by Allah

Allah then said,

(And whoever obeys Allah and the Messenger, then they will be in the company of those on whom Allah has bestowed His grace, of the Prophets, the Siddiqin, the martyrs, and the righteous. And how excellent these companions are!) Consequently, whosoever implements what Allah and His Messenger have commanded him and avoids what Allah and His Messenger have prohibited, then Allah will grant him a dwelling in the Residence of Honor. There, Allah will place him in the company of the Prophets, and those who are lesser in grade, the true believers, then the martyrs and then the righteous, who are righteous inwardly and outwardly. Allah then praised this company,

(And how excellent these companions are!) Al-Bukhari recorded that `A'ishah said, "I heard the Messenger of Allah saying,

«مَا مِنْ نَبِيٍ يَمْرَضُ إِلَّا خُيِّرَ بَيْنَ الدُّنْيَا وَالْآخِرَةِ»

(Every Prophet who falls ill is given the choice between this life and the Hereafter.) During the illness that preceded his death, his voice became weak and I heard him saying,

Chapter 4: An-Nisaa (The Women), Verses 024-147

[مَعَ الَّذِينَ أَنْعَمَ اللَّهُ عَلَيْهِم مِّنَ النَّبِيِّينَ وَالصِّدِّيقِينَ وَالشُّهَدَآءِ وَالصَّالِحِينَ]

(in the company of those on whom Allah has bestowed His grace, the Prophets, the true believers (Siddiqin), the martyrs and the righteous) I knew then that he was being given the choice." Muslim recorded this Hadith. This Hadith explains the meaning of another Hadith; the Prophet said before his death;

«اللَّهُمَّ (فِي) الرَّفِيقِ الْأَعْلَى»

(O Allah! In the Most High Company) three times, and he then died, may Allah's best blessings be upon him.

The Reason Behind Revealing this Honorable Ayah

Ibn Jarir recorded that Sa`id bin Jubayr said, "An Ansari man came to the Messenger of Allah while feeling sad. The Prophet said to him, `Why do I see you sad' He said, `O Allah's Prophet! I was contemplating about something.' The Prophet said, `What is it' The Ansari said, `We come to you day and night, looking at your face and sitting by you. Tomorrow, you will be raised with the Prophets, and we will not be able to see you.' The Prophet did not say anything, but later Jibril came down to him with this Ayah,

(And whoever obeys Allah and the Messenger then they will be in the company of those on whom Allah has bestowed His grace, of the Prophets), and the Prophet sent the good news to the Ansari man." This Hadith was narrated in Mursal form from Masruq, `Ikrimah, `Amir Ash-Sha`bi, Qatadah and Ar-Rabi` bin Anas. This is the version with the best chain of narrators. Abu Bakr bin Marduwyah recorded it with a different chain from `A'ishah, who said; "A man came to the Prophet and said to him, `O Messenger of Allah! You are more beloved to me than myself, my family and children. Sometimes, when I am at home, I remember you, and I cannot wait until I come and look at you. When I contemplate about my death and your death, I know that you will be with the Prophets when you enter Paradise. I fear that I might not see you when I enter Paradise.' The Prophet did not answer him until the Ayah,

(And whoever obeys Allah and the Messenger, then they will be in the company of those on whom Allah has bestowed His grace, of the Prophets, the true believers, the martyrs, and the righteous. And how excellent these companions are!) was revealed to him." This was collected by Al-Hafiz Abu `Abdullah Al-Maqdisi in his book, Sifat Al-Jannah, he then commented, "I do not see problems with this chain." And Allah knows best. Muslim recorded that Rabi`ah bin Ka`b Al-Aslami said, "I used to sleep at the Prophet's house and bring him his water for ablution and his needs. He once said to me, `Ask me.' I said, `O Messenger of Allah! I ask that I be your companion in Paradise.' He said, `Anything except that' I said, `Only that.' He said,

«فَأَعِنِّي عَلَى نَفْسِكَ بِكَثْرَةِ السُّجُودِ»

(Then help me (fulfill this wish) for you by performing many prostrations.)" Imam Ahmad recorded that `Amr bin Murrah Al-Juhani said, "A man came to the Prophet and said, `O Allah's Messenger! I bear witness that there is no deity worthy of worship except Allah and that you are the Messenger of Allah, pray the five (daily prayers), give the Zakah due on my wealth and fast the month of Ramadan.' The Messenger of Allah said,

«مَنْ مَاتَ عَلَى هَذَا كَانَ مَعَ النَّبِيِّينَ وَالصِّدِّيقِينَ وَالشُّهَدَاءِ يَوْمَ الْقِيَامَةِ، هَكَذَا وَنَصَبَ أُصْبُعَيْهِ مَا لَمْ يَعُقَّ وَالِدَيْهِ»

(Whoever dies in this state will be with the Prophets, the truthful and martyrs on the Day of Resurrection, as long as - and he raised his finger - he is not disobedient to his parents.)" Only Ahmad recorded this Hadith. Greater news than this is in the authentic Hadith collected in the Sahih and Musnad compilations, in Mutawatir form, narrated by several Companions that the Messenger of Allah was asked about the person who loves a people, but his status is not close to theirs. The Messenger said,

«الْمَرْءُ مَعَ مَنْ أَحَبَّ»

(One is with those whom he loves.) Anas commented, "Muslims were never happier than with this Hadith." In another narration, Anas said, "I love the Messenger of Allah, Abu Bakr and `Umar, and I hope that Allah will resurrect me with them, even though I did not perform actions similar to theirs." Allah said,

(Such is the bounty from Allah) meaning, from Allah by His mercy, for it is He who made them suitable for this, not their good deeds.

(and Allah is sufficient as All-Knower), He knows those who deserve guidance and success.

Surah: 4 Ayah: 71, Ayah: 72, Ayah: 73 & Ayah: 74

﴿يَٰٓأَيُّهَا ٱلَّذِينَ ءَامَنُواْ خُذُواْ حِذْرَكُمْ فَٱنفِرُواْ ثُبَاتٍ أَوِ ٱنفِرُواْ جَمِيعًا ۝﴾

71. O you who believe! Take your precautions, and either go forth (on an expedition) in parties, or go forth all together.

﴿وَإِنَّ مِنكُمْ لَمَن لَّيُبَطِّئَنَّ فَإِنْ أَصَٰبَتْكُم مُّصِيبَةٌ قَالَ قَدْ أَنْعَمَ ٱللَّهُ عَلَىَّ إِذْ لَمْ أَكُن مَّعَهُمْ شَهِيدًا ۝﴾

72. There is certainly among you he who would linger behind (from fighting in Allâh's Cause). If a misfortune befalls you, he says, "Indeed Allâh has favored me in that I was not present among them."

﴿ وَلَئِنْ أَصَابَكُمْ فَضْلٌ مِّنَ ٱللَّهِ لَيَقُولَنَّ كَأَن لَّمْ تَكُن بَيْنَكُمْ وَبَيْنَهُۥ مَوَدَّةٌ يَٰلَيْتَنِى كُنتُ مَعَهُمْ فَأَفُوزَ فَوْزًا عَظِيمًا ﴾

73. But if a bounty (victory and booty) comes to you from Allâh, he would surely say - as if there had never been ties of affection between you and him - "Oh! I wish I had been with them; then I would have achieved a great success (a good share of booty)."

﴿ ۞ فَلْيُقَٰتِلْ فِى سَبِيلِ ٱللَّهِ ٱلَّذِينَ يَشْرُونَ ٱلْحَيَوٰةَ ٱلدُّنْيَا بِٱلْأَخِرَةِ وَمَن يُقَٰتِلْ فِى سَبِيلِ ٱللَّهِ فَيُقْتَلْ أَوْ يَغْلِبْ فَسَوْفَ نُؤْتِيهِ أَجْرًا عَظِيمًا ﴾

74. Let those (believers) who sell the life of this world for the Hereafter fight in the Cause of Allâh, and whoso fights in the Cause of Allâh, and is killed or gets victory, We shall bestow on him a great reward.

Transliteration

71. Ya ayyuha allatheena amanoo khuthoo hithrakum fainfiroo thubatin awi infiroo jameeAAan 72. Wa-inna minkum laman layubatti-anna fa-in asabatkum museebatun qala qad anAAama Allahu AAalayya ith lam akun maAAahum shaheedan 73. Wala-in asabakum fadlun mina Allahi layaqoolanna kaan lam takun baynakum wabaynahu mawaddatun ya laytanee kuntu maAAahum faafooza fawzan AAatheeman 74. Falyuqatil fee sabeeli Allahi allatheena yashroona alhayata alddunya bial-akhirati waman yuqatil fee sabeeli Allahi fayuqtal aw yaghlib fasawfa nu/teehi ajran AAatheeman

Tafsir Ibn Kathir

The Necessity of Taking Necessary Precautions Against the Enemy

Allah commands His faithful servants to take precautions against their enemies, by being prepared with the necessary weapons and supplies, and increasing the number of troops fighting in His cause.

(in parties) means, group after group, party after party, and expedition after expedition. `Ali bin Talhah reported that Ibn `Abbas said that,

(and either go forth in parties) means, "In groups, expedition after expedition,

(or go forth all together), means, all of you." Similar was reported from Mujahid, `Ikrimah, As-Suddi, Qatadah, Ad-Dahhak, `Ata' Al-Khurrasani, Muqatil bin Hayyan and Khusayf Al-Jazari.

Refraining from Joining Jihad is a Sign of Hypocrites

Allah said,

(There is certainly among you he who would linger behind.) Mujahid and others said that this Ayah was revealed about the hypocrites. Muqatil bin Hayyan said that,

(linger behind) means, stays behind and does not join Jihad. It is also possible that this person himself lingers behind, while luring others away from joining Jihad. For instance, `Abdullah bin Ubayy bin Salul, may Allah curse him, used to linger behind and lure other people to do the same and refrain from joining Jihad, as Ibn Jurayj and Ibn Jarir stated. This is why Allah said about the hypocrite, that when he lingers behind from Jihad, then:

(If a misfortune befalls you) death, martyrdom, or - by Allah's wisdom - being defeated by the enemy,

(he says, "Indeed Allah has favored me that I was not present among them.") meaning, since I did not join them in battle. Because he considers this one of Allah's favors on him, unaware of the reward that he might have gained from enduring war or martyrdom, if he was killed.

(But if a bounty comes to you from Allah) such as victory, triumph and booty,

(he would surely say - as if there had never been ties of affection between you and him,) meaning, as if he was not a follower of your religion,

("Oh! I wish I had been with them; then I would have achieved a great success.") by being assigned a share of the booty and taking possession of that share. This is his ultimate aim and objective.

The Encouragement to Participation in Jihad

Allah then said,

(So fight) the believer with an aversion (to fighting),

(those who trade the life of this world with the Hereafter) referring to those sell their religion for the meager goods of the world, and they only do this because of their disbelief and lack of faith. Allah then said;

(And whoever fights in the cause of Allah, and is killed or gets victory, We shall bestow on him a great reward.) meaning, whoever fights in the cause of Allah, whether he was killed or triumphant, he will earn an immense compensation and a great reward with Allah. The Two Sahihs recorded,

«وَتَكَفَّلَ اللهُ لِلْمُجَاهِدِ فِي سَبِيلِهِ، إِنْ تَوَفَّاهُ أَنْ يُدْخِلَهُ الْجَنَّةَ، أَوْ يَرْجِعَهُ إِلَى مَسْكَنِهِ الَّذِي خَرَجَ مِنْهُ، بِمَا نَالَ مِنْ أَجْرٍ أَوْ غَنِيمَة»

Chapter 4: An-Nisaa (The Women), Verses 024-147

(Allah has guaranteed the Mujahid in His cause that He will either bring death to him, admitting into Paradise; or, He will help him return safely to his home with whatever reward and booty he gained.)

Surah: 4 Ayah: 75 & Ayah: 76

﴿ وَمَا لَكُمْ لَا تُقَـٰتِلُونَ فِى سَبِيلِ ٱللَّهِ وَٱلْمُسْتَضْعَفِينَ مِنَ ٱلرِّجَالِ وَٱلنِّسَآءِ وَٱلْوِلْدَٰنِ ٱلَّذِينَ يَقُولُونَ رَبَّنَآ أَخْرِجْنَا مِنْ هَـٰذِهِ ٱلْقَرْيَةِ ٱلظَّالِمِ أَهْلُهَا وَٱجْعَل لَّنَا مِن لَّدُنكَ وَلِيًّا وَٱجْعَل لَّنَا مِن لَّدُنكَ نَصِيرًا ﴾ ۝

75. And what is wrong with you that you fight not in the Cause of Allâh, and for those weak, ill-treated and oppressed among men, women, and children, whose cry is: "Our Lord! Rescue us from this town whose people are oppressors; and raise for us from You one who will protect, and raise for us from You one who will help."

﴿ ٱلَّذِينَ ءَامَنُواْ يُقَـٰتِلُونَ فِى سَبِيلِ ٱللَّهِ وَٱلَّذِينَ كَفَرُواْ يُقَـٰتِلُونَ فِى سَبِيلِ ٱلطَّـٰغُوتِ فَقَـٰتِلُوٓاْ أَوْلِيَآءَ ٱلشَّيْطَـٰنِ إِنَّ كَيْدَ ٱلشَّيْطَـٰنِ كَانَ ضَعِيفًا ﴾ ۝

76. Those who believe, fight in the Cause of Allâh, and those who disbelieve, fight in the cause of Tâghût (Satan). So fight you against the friends of Shaitân (Satan). Ever feeble indeed is the plot of Shaitân (Satan).

Transliteration

75. Wama lakum la tuqatiloona fee sabeeli Allahi waalmustadAAafeena mina alrrijali waalnnisa-i waalwildani allatheena yaqooloona rabbana akhrijna min hathihi alqaryati alththalimi ahluha waijAAal lana min ladunka waliyyan waijAAal lana min ladunka naseeran 76. Allatheena amanoo yuqatiloona fee sabeeli Allahi waallatheena kafaroo yuqatiloona fee sabeeli alttaghooti faqatiloo awliyaa alshshaytani inna kayda alshshaytani kana daAAeefan

Tafsir Ibn Kathir

Encouraging Jihad to Defend the Oppressed

Allah encouraged His believing servants to perform Jihad in His cause and to strive hard to save the oppressed Muslims in Makkah, men, women and children who were restless because of having to remain there. This is why Allah said,

(whose cry is: "Our Lord! Rescue us from this town), referring to Makkah. In a similar Ayah, Allah said,

(And many a town, stronger than your town which has driven you out) Allah then describes this town, (whose people are oppressors; and raise for us from You one who will protect, and raise for us from You one who will help) meaning, send protectors and helpers for us. Al-Bukhari recorded that Ibn `Abbas said, "I and my mother were from the oppressed (in Makkah)." Allah then said,

(Those who believe, fight in the cause of Allah, and those who disbelieve, fight in the cause of the Taghut.) Therefore, the believers fight in obedience to Allah and to gain His pleasure, while the disbelievers fight in obedience to Shaytan. Allah then encourages the believers to fight His enemies,

(So fight against the friends of Shaytan; ever feeble indeed is the plot of Shaytan).

Surah: 4 Ayah: 77, Ayah: 78 & Ayah: 79

﴿ أَلَمْ تَرَ إِلَى ٱلَّذِينَ قِيلَ لَهُمْ كُفُّوٓاْ أَيْدِيَكُمْ وَأَقِيمُواْ ٱلصَّلَوٰةَ وَءَاتُواْ ٱلزَّكَوٰةَ فَلَمَّا كُتِبَ عَلَيْهِمُ ٱلْقِتَالُ إِذَا فَرِيقٌ مِّنْهُمْ يَخْشَوْنَ ٱلنَّاسَ كَخَشْيَةِ ٱللَّهِ أَوْ أَشَدَّ خَشْيَةً وَقَالُواْ رَبَّنَا لِمَ كَتَبْتَ عَلَيْنَا ٱلْقِتَالَ لَوْلَآ أَخَّرْتَنَآ إِلَىٰٓ أَجَلٍ قَرِيبٍ قُلْ مَتَٰعُ ٱلدُّنْيَا قَلِيلٌ وَٱلْأَخِرَةُ خَيْرٌ لِّمَنِ ٱتَّقَىٰ وَلَا تُظْلَمُونَ فَتِيلًا ﴾

77. Have you not seen those who were told to hold back their hands (from fighting) and perform As-Salât (Iqâmat-as-Salât), and give Zakât, but when the fighting was ordained for them, behold! a section of them fear men as they fear Allâh or even more. They say: "Our Lord! Why have You ordained for us fighting? Would that You had granted us respite for a short period?" Say: "Short is the enjoyment of this world. The Hereafter is (far) better for him who fears Allâh, and you shall not be dealt with unjustly even equal to a scalish thread in the long slit of a date-stone.

﴿ أَيْنَمَا تَكُونُواْ يُدْرِككُّمُ ٱلْمَوْتُ وَلَوْ كُنتُمْ فِى بُرُوجٍ مُّشَيَّدَةٍ وَإِن تُصِبْهُمْ حَسَنَةٌ يَقُولُواْ هَٰذِهِۦ مِنْ عِندِ ٱللَّهِ وَإِن تُصِبْهُمْ سَيِّئَةٌ يَقُولُواْ هَٰذِهِۦ مِنْ عِندِكَ قُلْ كُلٌّ مِّنْ عِندِ ٱللَّهِ فَمَالِ هَٰٓؤُلَآءِ ٱلْقَوْمِ لَا يَكَادُونَ يَفْقَهُونَ حَدِيثًا ﴾

78. "Wheresoever you may be, death will overtake you even if you are in fortresses built up strong and high!" And if some good reaches them, they say, "This is from Allâh," but if some evil befalls them, they say, "This is from you (O Muhammad (peace be upon him))" Say: "All things are from Allâh," so what is wrong with these people that they fail to understand any word?

﴿ مَّآ أَصَابَكَ مِنْ حَسَنَةٍ فَمِنَ ٱللَّهِ وَمَآ أَصَابَكَ مِن سَيِّئَةٍ فَمِن نَّفْسِكَ وَأَرْسَلْنَٰكَ لِلنَّاسِ رَسُولًا وَكَفَىٰ بِٱللَّهِ شَهِيدًا ﴾

79. Whatever of good reaches you, is from Allâh, but whatever of evil befalls you, is from yourself. And We have sent you (O Muhammad (peace be upon him)) as a Messenger to mankind, and Allâh is Sufficient as a Witness.

Transliteration

77. Alam tara ila allatheena qeela lahum kuffoo aydiyakum waaqeemoo alssalata waatoo alzzakata falamma kutiba AAalayhimu alqitalu itha fareequn minhum yakhshawna alnnasa kakhashyati Allahi aw ashadda khashyatan waqaloo rabbana lima katabta AAalayna alqitala lawla akhkhartana ila ajalin qareebin qul mataAAu alddunya qaleelun waal-akhiratu khayrun limani ittaqa wala tuthlamoona fateelan   78. Aynama takoonoo yudrikkumu almawtu walaw kuntum fee buroojin mushayyadatin wa-in tusibhum hasanatun yaqooloo hathihi min AAindi Allahi wa-in tusibhum sayyi-atun yaqooloo hathihi min AAindika qul kullun min AAindi Allahi famali haola-i alqawmi la yakadoona yafqahoona hadeethan   79. Ma asabaka min hasanatin famina Allahi wama asabaka min sayyi-atin famin nafsika waarsalnaka lilnnasi rasoolan wakafa biAllahi shaheedan

Tafsir Ibn Kathir

The Wish that the Order for Jihad be Delayed

In the beginning of Islam, Muslims in Makkah were commanded to perform the prayer and pay some charity, so as to comfort the poor among them. They were also commanded to be forgiving and forbearing with the idolators and to observe patience with them at the time. However, they were eager and anticipating the time when they would be allowed to fight, so that they could punish their enemies. The situation at that time did not permit armed conflict for many reasons. For instance, Muslims were few at the time, compared to their numerous enemies. The Muslims' city was a sacred one and the most honored area on the earth, and this is why the command to fight was not revealed in Makkah. Later on when the Muslims controlled a town of their own, Al-Madinah, and had strength, power and support, Jihad was then legislated. Yet, when the command to fight was revealed, just as Muslims wished, some of them became weary and were very fearful of facing the idolators in battle.

(They say: "Our Lord! Why have You ordained for us fighting Would that You had granted us respite for a short period") meaning, we wish that Jihad was delayed until a later time, because it means bloodshed, orphans and widows. In a similar Ayah, Allah said,

(Those who believe say: "Why is not a Surah sent down (for us) But when a decisive is sent down, and fighting is mentioned). Ibn Abi Hatim recorded that Ibn `Abbas said that `Abdur-Rahman bin `Awf and several of his companions came to the Prophet while in Makkah and said, "O Allah's Prophet! We were mighty when we were pagans, but when we embraced the faith, we became weak." The Prophet said,

«إِنِّي أُمِرْتُ بِالْعَفْوِ فَلَا تُقَاتِلُوا الْقَوْمَ»

(I was commanded to pardon the people, so do not fight them.) When Allah transferred the Prophet to Al-Madinah, He commanded him to fight (the idolators), but they (some Muslims) held back. So, Allah revealed the Ayah;

(Have you not seen those who were told to hold back their hands) This Hadith was collected by An-Nasa'i and Al-Hakim. Allah's statement,

(Say: "Short is the enjoyment of this world. The Hereafter is (far) better for him who fears Allah,) means, the destination of the one who with Taqwa is better for him than this life.

(and you shall not be dealt with unjustly even equal to the Fatil.) for your good deeds. Rather, you will earn your full rewards for them. This promise directs the focus of believers away from this life and makes them eager for the Hereafter, all the while encouraging them to fight in Jihad.

There is No Escaping Death

Allah said,

(Wheresoever you may be, death will overtake you even if you are in fortresses built up strong and high!) meaning, you shall certainly die and none of you shall ever escape death. Allah said,

(Whatsooever is on it (the earth) will perish),

(Everyone shall taste death), and,

(And We granted not to any human being immortality before you). Therefore, every soul shall taste death and nothing can save any person from it, whether he performed Jihad or not. Everyone has an appointed time, and a limited term of life. In the illness that preceded his death, Khalid bin Al-Walid said, while in his bed, "I participated in so and so number of battles, and every part of my body sustained an injury due to a stab or a shot. Yet here I am, I die in my bed! Let not the eyes of the cowards ever taste sleep." Allah's statement,

(even if you are in fortresses built up strong and high!) means, entrenched, fortified, high and towering. No caution or fortification can ever avert death.

The Hypocrites Sense a Bad Omen Because of the Prophet!

Allah said,

(And if some good reaches them) meaning, fertile years and provision of fruits, produce, children, etc., as said by Ibn `Abbas, Abu Al-`Aliyah and As-Suddi.

(they say, "This is from Allah," but if some evil befalls them) drought, famine, shortages of fruits and produce, death that strikes their children or animals, and so forth, as Abu Al-`Aliyah and As-Suddi stated.

Chapter 4: An-Nisaa (The Women), Verses 024-147

(they say, "This is from you,") meaning, because of you and because we followed you and embraced your religion. Allah said about the people of Fir`awn,

(But whenever good came to them, they said: "Ours is this." And if evil afflicted them, they ascribed it to evil omens connected with Musa and those with him.) Allah said,

(And among mankind is he who worships Allah as it were upon the edge (i. e. in doubt)). The same is the statement uttered by the hypocrites, who embraced Islam outwardly, but disliked it inwardly. This is why when a calamity befell them, they attributed it to following the Prophet . Consequently, Allah revealed,

Say: All things are from AllaOh, Allah's statement that all things are from Him means, everything occurs by the decision and decree of Allah, and His decision shall come to pass for both the righteous and the wicked, the faithful and the disbelievers. Allah then said while addressing His Messenger , but refering to mankind in general,

(Whatever of good reaches you, is from Allah,) meaning, of Allah's bounty, favor, kindness and mercy.

(But whatever of evil befalls you, is from yourself.), meaning because of you and due to your actions. Similarly, Allah said,

(And whatever of misfortune befalls you, it is because of what your hands have earned. And He pardons much.) As-Suddi, Al-Hasan Al-Basri, Ibn Jurayj and Ibn Zayd said that,

(from yourself) means, because of your errors. Qatadah said that,

(From yourself) means, as punishment for you, O son of Adam, because of your sins. Allah said,

(And We have sent you as a Messenger to mankind,) so that you convey to them Allah's commandments, what He likes and is pleased with, and what He dislikes and refuses.

(and Allah is sufficient as a Witness.) that He has sent you. He is also Witness over you and them, having full knowledge in what you convey to them and the disbelief and rebellion with which they respond to the truth.

Surah: 4 Ayah: 80 & Ayah: 81

﴿ مَّن يُطِعِ ٱلرَّسُولَ فَقَدْ أَطَاعَ ٱللَّهَ وَمَن تَوَلَّىٰ فَمَآ أَرْسَلْنَٰكَ عَلَيْهِمْ حَفِيظًا ﴾

80. He who obeys the Messenger (Muhammad (peace be upon him)) has indeed obeyed Allâh, but he who turns away, then we have not sent you (O Muhammad (peace be upon him)) as a watcher over them.

﴿ وَيَقُولُونَ طَاعَةٌ فَإِذَا بَرَزُواْ مِنْ عِندِكَ بَيَّتَ طَآئِفَةٌ مِّنْهُمْ غَيْرَ ٱلَّذِى تَقُولُ وَٱللَّهُ يَكْتُبُ مَا يُبَيِّتُونَ فَأَعْرِضْ عَنْهُمْ وَتَوَكَّلْ عَلَى ٱللَّهِ وَكَفَىٰ بِٱللَّهِ وَكِيلاً ﴿٨١﴾ ﴾

81. They say: "We are obedient," but when they leave you (Muhammad (peace be upon him)) a section of them spend all night in planning other than what you say. But Allâh records their nightly (plots). So turn aside from them (do not punish them), and put your trust in Allâh. And Allâh is Ever All-Sufficient as a Disposer of affairs.

Transliteration

80. Man yutiAAi alrrasoola faqad ataAAa Allaha waman tawalla fama arsalnaka AAalayhim hafeethan   81. Wayaqooloona taAAatun fa-itha barazoo min AAindika bayyata ta-ifatun minhum ghayra allathee taqoolu waAllahu yaktubu ma yubayyitoona faaAArid AAanhum watawakkal AAala Allahi wakafa biAllahi wakeelan

Tafsir Ibn Kathir

Obeying the Messenger is Obeying Allah

Allah states that whoever obeys His servant and Messenger, Muhammad , obeys Allah; and whoever disobeys him, disobeys Allah. Verily, whatever the Messenger utters is not of his own desire, but a revelation inspired to him. Ibn Abi Hatim recorded that Abu Hurayrah said that the Messenger of Allah said,

«مَنْ أَطَاعَنِي فَقَدْ أَطَاعَ اللهَ، وَمَنْ عَصَانِي فَقَدْ عَصَى اللهَ، وَمَنْ أَطَاعَ الْأَمِيرَ فَقَدْ أَطَاعَنِي، وَمَنْ عَصَى الْأَمِيرَ فَقَدْ عَصَانِي»

(Whoever obeys me, obeys Allah; and whoever disobeys me, disobeys Allah. Whoever obeys the Amir (leader, ruler), obeys me; and whoever disobeys the Amir, disobeys me.) This Hadith was recorded in the Two Sahihs. Allah's statement,

(But he who turns away, then We have not sent you as a watcher over them.) means, do not worry about him. Your job is only to convey, and whoever obeys you, he will acquire happiness and success and you will gain a similar reward to that he earns. As for the one who turns away from you, he will gain failure and loss and you will not carry a burden because of what he does. A Hadith states,

«مَنْ يُطِعِ اللهَ وَرَسُولَهُ فَقَدْ رَشَدَ، وَمَنْ يَعْصِ اللهَ وَرَسُولَهُ فَإِنَّهُ لَا يَضُرُّ إِلَّا نَفْسَهُ»

(Whoever obeys Allah and His Messenger, will acquire guidance; and whoever disobeys Allah and His Messenger, will only harm himself.)

The Foolishness of the Hypocrites

Allah said,

(They say: "We are obedient,"). Allah states that the hypocrites pretend to be loyal and obedient.

(but when they leave you), meaning, when they depart and are no longer with you,

(a section of them spends all night in planning other than what you say). They plot at night among themselves for other than what they pretend when they are with you. Allah said,

(But Allah records their nightly (plots).) meaning, He has full knowledge of their plots and records it through His command to His scribes, the angels who are responsible for recording the actions of the servants. This is a threat from Allah, stating that He knows what the hypocrites try to hide, their plotting in the night to defy the Messenger and oppose him, even though they pretend to be loyal and obedient to him. Allah will certainly punish them for this conduct. In a similar Ayah, Allah said,

(They (hypocrites) say: "We have believed in Allah and in the Messenger, and we obey,") until the end of the Ayah. Allah's statement,

(So turn aside from them) means, pardon them, be forbearing with them, do not punish them, do not expose them to the people and do not fear them.

(and put your trust in Allah. And Allah is Ever All-Sufficient as a Disposer of affairs.) meaning, He is sufficient as Protector, Supporter and Helper for those who rely on Him and return to Him.

Surah: 4 Ayah: 82 & Ayah: 83

﴿ أَفَلَا يَتَدَبَّرُونَ ٱلْقُرْءَانَ ۚ وَلَوْ كَانَ مِنْ عِندِ غَيْرِ ٱللَّهِ لَوَجَدُوا۟ فِيهِ ٱخْتِلَٰفًا كَثِيرًا ﴾

82. Do they not then consider the Qur'ân carefully? Had it been from other than Allâh, they would surely have found therein many a contradiction.

﴿ وَإِذَا جَآءَهُمْ أَمْرٌ مِّنَ ٱلْأَمْنِ أَوِ ٱلْخَوْفِ أَذَاعُوا۟ بِهِۦ ۖ وَلَوْ رَدُّوهُ إِلَى ٱلرَّسُولِ وَإِلَىٰٓ أُو۟لِى ٱلْأَمْرِ مِنْهُمْ لَعَلِمَهُ ٱلَّذِينَ يَسْتَنۢبِطُونَهُۥ مِنْهُمْ ۗ وَلَوْلَا فَضْلُ ٱللَّهِ عَلَيْكُمْ وَرَحْمَتُهُۥ لَٱتَّبَعْتُمُ ٱلشَّيْطَٰنَ إِلَّا قَلِيلًا ﴾

83. When there comes to them some matter touching (public) safety or fear, they make it known (among the people); if only they had referred it to the Messenger or to those charged with authority among them, the proper investigators would

have understood it from them (directly). Had it not been for the Grace and Mercy of Allâh upon you, you would have followed Shaitân (Satan), save a few of you.

Transliteration

82. Afala yatadabbaroona alqur-ana walaw kana min AAindi ghayri Allahi lawajadoo feehi ikhtilafan katheeran 83. Wa-itha jaahum amrun mina al-amni awi alkhawfi athaAAoo bihi walaw raddoohu ila alrrasooli waila olee al-amri minhum laAAalimahu allatheena yastanbitoonahu minhum walawla fadlu Allahi AAalaykum warahmatuhu laittabaAAtumu alshshaytana illa qaleelan

Tafsir Ibn Kathir

The Qur'an is True

Allah commands them to contemplate about the Qur'an and forbids them from ignoring it, or ignoring its wise meanings and eloquent words. Allah states that there are no inconsistencies, contradictions, conflicting statements or discrepancies in the Qur'an, because it is a revelation from the Most-Wise, Worthy of all praise. Therefore, the Qur'an is the truth coming from the Truth, Allah. This is why Allah said in another Ayah,

(Do they not then think deeply in the Qur'an, or are their hearts locked up (from understanding it)) Allah then said,

(Had it been from other than Allah,) meaning, had it been fraudulent and made up, as the ignorant idolators and hypocrites assert in their hearts,

(they would surely, have found therein contradictions), discrepancies and inconsistencies,

(in abundance). However, this Qur'an is free of shortcomings, and therefore, it is from Allah. Similarly, Allah describes those who are firmly grounded in knowledge,

(We believe in it, all of it is from our Lord.)(3:7) meaning, the Muhkam sections (entirely clear) and the Mutashabih sections (not entirely clear) of the Qur'an are all true. So they understand the not entirely clear from the clear, and thus gain guidance. As for those in whose heart is the disease of hypocrisy, they understand the Muhkam from the Mutashabih; thus only gaining misguidance. Allah praised those who have knowledge and criticized the wicked. Imam Ahmad recorded that `Amr bin Shu`ayb said that his father said that his grandfather said, "I and my brother were present in a gathering, which is more precious to me than red camels. My brother and I came and found that some of the leaders of the Companions of the Messenger of Allah were sitting close to a door of his. We did not like the idea of being separate from them, so we sat near the room. They then mentioned an Ayah and began disputing until they raised their voices. The Messenger of Allah was so angry that when he went out his face was red. He threw sand on them and said to them,

Chapter 4: An-Nisaa (The Women), Verses 024-147

«مَهْلًا يَا قَوْمِ، بِهَذَا أَهْلَكَتِ الْأُمَمُ مِنْ قَبْلِكُمْ، بِاخْتِلَافِهِمْ عَلَى أَنْبِيَائِهِمْ، وَضَرْبِهِمِ الْكُتُبَ بَعْضَهَا بِبَعْضٍ، إِنَّ الْقُرْآنَ لَمْ يَنْزِلْ يُكَذِّبُ بَعْضُهُ بَعْضًا، إِنَّمَا يُصَدِّقُ بَعْضُهُ بَعْضًا، فَمَا عَرَفْتُمْ مِنْهُ فَاعْمَلُوا بِهِ، وَمَا جَهِلْتُمْ مِنْهُ فَرُدُّوهُ إِلَى عَالِمِهِ»

(Behold, O people! This is how the nations before you were destroyed, because of their disputing with their Prophets and their contradicting parts of the Books with other parts. The Qur'an does not contradict itself. Rather, it testifies to the truth of itself. Therefore, whatever of it you have knowledge in, then implement it, and whatever you do not know of it, then refer it to those who have knowledge in it.)" Ahmad recorded that `Abdullah bin `Amr said, "I went to the Messenger of Allah one day. When we were sitting, two men disputed about an Ayah, and their voices became loud. The Prophet said,

«إِنَّمَا هَلَكَتِ الْأُمَمُ قَبْلَكُمْ بِاخْتِلَافِهِمْ فِي الْكِتَابِ»

(Verily, the nations before you were destroyed because of their disagreements over the Book.) Muslim and An-Nasa'i recorded this Hadith.

The Prohibition of Disclosing Unreliable and Uninvestigated News

Allah said,

(When there comes to them some matter touching (public) safety or fear, they make it known (among the people);) chastising those who indulge in things before being sure of their truth, disclosing them, making them known and spreading their news, even though such news might not be true at all. In the introduction to his Sahih, Imam Muslim recorded that Abu Hurayrah said that the Prophet said,

«كَفَى بِالْمَرْءِ كَذِبًا أَنْ يُحَدِّثَ بِكُلِّ مَا سَمِعَ»

(Narrating everything one hears is sufficient to make a person a liar.) This is the same narration collected by Abu Dawud in the section of Adab (manners) in his Sunan. In the Two Sahihs, it is recorded that Al-Mughirah bin Shu`bah said that the Messenger of Allah prohibited, "It was said," and, "So-and-so said." This Hadith refers to those who often convey the speech that people utter without investigating the reliability and truth of what he is disclosing. The Sahih also records,

«مَنْ حَدَّثَ بِحَدِيثٍ وَهُوَ يَرَى أَنَّهُ كَذِبٌ، فَهُوَ أَحَدُ الْكَاذِبَيْنِ»

(Whoever narrates a Hadith while knowing it is false, then he is one of the two liars (who invents and who spreads the lie).) We should mention here the Hadith of `Umar bin Al-Khattab collected in the Two Sahihs. When `Umar was informed that the Messenger of Allah divorced his wives, he came from his house, entered the Masjid and found the people talking about this news. He could not wait and went to the Prophet to ask him about what had truly happened, asking him, "Have you divorced your wives" The Prophet said, "No." `Umar said, "I said, Allahu Akbar..." and mentioned the rest of the Hadith. In the narration that Muslim collected, `Umar said, "I asked, `Have you divorced them' He said, `No.' So, I stood by the door of the Masjid and shouted with the loudest voice, `The Messenger of Allah did not divorce his wives.' Then, this Ayah was revealed,

(When there comes to them some matter touching (public) safety or fear, they make it known (among the people), if only they had referred it to the Messenger or to those charged with authority among them, the proper investigators would have understood it from them (directly).) So I properly investigated that matter." This Ayah refers to proper investigation, or extraction of matters from their proper resources. Allah's statement,

(you would have followed Shaytan except a few of you.) refers to the believers, as `Ali bin Abi Talhah reported from Ibn `Abbas.

Surah: 4 Ayah: 84, Ayah: 85, Ayah: 86 & Ayah: 87

﴿ فَقَٰتِلْ فِى سَبِيلِ ٱللَّهِ لَا تُكَلَّفُ إِلَّا نَفْسَكَ وَحَرِّضِ ٱلْمُؤْمِنِينَ عَسَى ٱللَّهُ أَن يَكُفَّ بَأْسَ ٱلَّذِينَ كَفَرُوا۟ وَٱللَّهُ أَشَدُّ بَأْسًا وَأَشَدُّ تَنكِيلًا ﴾

84. Then fight (O Muhammad (peace be upon him)) in the Cause of Allâh, you are not tasked (held responsible) except for yourself, and incite the believers (to fight along with you), it may be that Allâh will restrain the evil might of the disbelievers. And Allâh is Stronger in Might and Stronger in punishing.

﴿ مَّن يَشْفَعْ شَفَٰعَةً حَسَنَةً يَكُن لَّهُۥ نَصِيبٌ مِّنْهَا وَمَن يَشْفَعْ شَفَٰعَةً سَيِّئَةً يَكُن لَّهُۥ كِفْلٌ مِّنْهَا وَكَانَ ٱللَّهُ عَلَىٰ كُلِّ شَىْءٍ مُّقِيتًا ﴾

85. Whosoever intercedes for a good cause will have the reward thereof, and whosoever intercedes for an evil cause will have a share in its burden. And Allâh is Ever All-Able to do (and also an All-Witness to) everything.

﴿ وَإِذَا حُيِّيتُم بِتَحِيَّةٍ فَحَيُّوا۟ بِأَحْسَنَ مِنْهَآ أَوْ رُدُّوهَآ إِنَّ ٱللَّهَ كَانَ عَلَىٰ كُلِّ شَىْءٍ حَسِيبًا ﴾

86. When you are greeted with a greeting, greet in return with what is better than it, or (at least) return it equally. Certainly, Allâh is Ever a Careful Account Taker of all things.

Chapter 4: An-Nisaa (The Women), Verses 024-147

﴿ ٱللَّهُ لَآ إِلَٰهَ إِلَّا هُوَ لَيَجْمَعَنَّكُمْ إِلَىٰ يَوْمِ ٱلْقِيَٰمَةِ لَا رَيْبَ فِيهِ ۗ وَمَنْ أَصْدَقُ مِنَ ٱللَّهِ حَدِيثًا ﴿٨٧﴾ ﴾

87. Allâh! Lâ ilâha illa Huwa (none has the right to be worshipped but He). Surely, He will gather you together on the Day of Resurrection about which there is no doubt. And who is truer in statement than Allâh?

Transliteration

84. Faqatil fee sabeeli Allahi la tukallafu illa nafsaka waharridi almu/mineena AAasa Allahu an yakuffa ba/sa allatheena kafaroo waAllahu ashaddu ba/san waashaddu tankeelan 85. Man yashfaAA shafaAAatan hasanatan yakun lahu naseebun minha waman yashfaAA shafaAAatan sayyi-atan yakun lahu kiflun minha wakana Allahu AAala kulli shay-in muqeetan 86. Wa-itha huyyeetum bitahiyyatin fahayyoo bi-ahsana minha aw ruddooha inna Allaha kana AAala kulli shay-in haseeban 87. Allahu la ilaha illa huwa layajmaAAannakum ila yawmi alqiyamati la rayba feehi waman asdaqu mina Allahi hadeethan

Tafsir Ibn Kathir

Allah Commands His Messenger to Perform Jihad

Allah commands His servant and Messenger, Muhammad , to himself fight in Jihad and not to be concerned about those who do not join Jihad. Hence Allah's statement,

(you are not tasked (held responsible except for yourself,) Ibn Abi Hatim recorded that Abu Ishaq said, "I asked Al-Bara bin `Azib about a man who meets a hundred enemies and still fights them, would he be one of those referred to in Allah's statement,

(And do not throw yourselves into destruction (by not spending your wealth in the cause of Allah)) He said, `Allah said to His Prophet,

(Then fight in the cause of Allah, you are not tasked (held responsible) except for yourself, and incite the believers (to fight along with you))." Imam Ahmad recorded Sulayman bin Dawud saying that Abu Bakr bin `Ayyash said that Abu Ishaq said, "I asked Al-Bara', `If a man attacks the lines of the idolators, would he be throwing himself to destruction' He said, `No because Allah has sent His Messenger and commanded him,

(Then fight in the cause of Allah, you are not tasked (held responsible) except for yourself,) That Ayah is about spending (in Allah's cause)."

Inciting the Believers to Fight

Allah said,

(and incite the believers) to fight, by encouraging them and strengthening their resolve in this regard. For instance, the Prophet said to the believers at the battle of Badr, while organizing their lines,

«قُومُوا إِلَى جَنَّةٍ عَرْضُهَا السَّموَاتُ وَالْأَرْضُ»

(Stand up and march forth to a Paradise, as wide as the heavens and Earth.) There are many Hadiths that encourage Jihad. Al-Bukhari recorded that Abu Hurayrah said that the Messenger of Allah said,

«مَنْ آمَنَ بِاللهِ وَرَسُولِهِ، وَأَقَامَ الصَّلَاةَ، وَآتَى الزَّكَاةَ، وَصَامَ رَمَضَانَ، كَانَ حَقًّا عَلَى اللهِ أَنْ يُدْخِلَهُ الْجَنَّةَ، هَاجَرَ فِي سَبِيلِ اللهِ أَوْ جَلَسَ فِي أَرْضِهِ الَّتِي وُلِدَ فِيهَا»

(Whoever believes in Allah and His Messenger, offers prayer, pays the Zakah and fasts the month of Ramadan, will rightfully be granted Paradise by Allah, no matter whether he migrates in Allah's cause or remains in the land where he is born.) The people said, `O Allah's Messenger! Shall we acquaint the people with this good news' He said,

«إِنَّ فِي الْجَنَّةِ مِائَةَ دَرَجَةٍ أَعَدَّهَا اللهُ لِلْمُجَاهِدِينَ فِي سَبِيلِ اللهِ، بَيْنَ كُلِّ دَرَجَتَيْنِ كَمَا بَيْنَ السَّمَاءِ وَالْأَرْضِ، فَإِذَا سَأَلْتُمُ اللهَ فَاسْأَلُوهُ الْفِرْدَوْسَ، فَإِنَّهُ وَسَطُ الْجَنَّةِ، وَأَعْلَى الْجَنَّةِ، وَفَوْقَهُ عَرْشُ الرَّحْمنِ، وَمِنْهُ تَفَجَّرُ أَنْهَارُ الْجَنَّةِ»

(Paradise has one hundred grades which Allah has reserved for the Mujahidin who fight in His cause, the distance between each two grades is like the distance between the heaven and the Earth. So, when you ask Allah, ask for Al-Firdaws, which is the best and highest part of Paradise, above it is the Throne of the Most Beneficent (Allah) and from it originate the rivers of Paradise.) There are various narrations for this Hadith from `Ubadah, Mu`adh, and Abu Ad-Darda'. Abu Sa`id Al-Khudri narrated that the Messenger of Allah said,

«يَا أَبَا سَعِيدٍ مَنْ رَضِيَ بِاللهِ رَبًّا، وَبِالْإِسْلَامِ دِينًا، وَبِمُحَمَّدٍ صلى الله عليه وسلّم نَبِيًّا، وَجَبَتْ لَهُ الْجَنَّةُ»

(O Abu Sa`id! Whoever accepts Allah as his Lord, Islam as his religion and Muhammad as the Prophet, then he would rightfully acquire Paradise.) Abu Sa`id liked these words and said, "O Allah's Messenger! Repeat them for me." The Prophet repeated his words, then said,

«وَأُخْرَى يَرْفَعُ اللهُ الْعَبْدَ بِهَا مِائَةَ دَرَجَةٍ فِي الْجَنَّةِ، مَا بَيْنَ كُلِّ دَرَجَتَيْنِ كَمَا بَيْنَ السَّمَاءِ وَالْأَرْضِ»

(And (there is) another deed for which Allah raises the servant a hundred grades in Paradise, between each two grades is the distance between heaven and Earth.) Abu Sa`id said, "What is it, O Allah's Messenger " He said,

«الْجِهَادُ فِي سَبِيلِ الله»

(Jihad in Allah's cause.) This Hadith was collected by Muslim. Allah's statement,

(it may be that Allah will restrain the evil might of the disbelievers.) means, by your encouraging them to fight, their resolve will be strengthened to meet the enemy in battle, to defend Islam and its people and to endure and be patient against the enemy. Allah's statement,

(And Allah is Stronger in might and Stronger in punishing.) means, He is able over them in this life and the Hereafter, just as He said in another Ayah,

(But if it had been Allah's will, He Himself could certainly have punished them (without you). But (He lets you fight) in order to test some of you with others) (47:4).

Interceding for a Good or an Evil Cause

Allah said,

(Whosoever intercedes for a good cause, will have the reward thereof;) meaning, whoever intercedes in a matter that produces good results, will acquire a share in that good.

(And whosoever intercedes for an evil cause, will have a share in its burden.) meaning, he will carry a burden due to what resulted from his intercession and intention. For instance, it is recorded in the Sahih that the Prophet said,

«اشْفَعُوا تُؤْجَرُوا، وَيَقْضِي اللهُ عَلَى لِسَانِ نَبِيِّهِ مَا شَاءَ»

(Intercede and you will gain a reward of it. Yet, Allah shall decide whatever He wills by the words of His Prophet.) Mujahid bin Jabr said, "This Ayah was revealed about the intercession of people on behalf of each other." Allah then said,

(And Allah is Ever Muqit over everything.) Ibn `Abbas, `Ata', `Atiyah, Qatadah and Matar Al-Warraq said that,

(Muqit) means, "Watcher." Mujahid said that Muqit means, `Witness', and in another narration, `Able to do.'

Returning the Salam, With a Better Salam

Allah said,

(When you are greeted with a greeting, greet in return with what is better than it, or (at least) return it equally.) meaning, if the Muslim greets you with the Salam, then return the greeting with a better Salam, or at least equal to the Salam that was given. Therefore, the better Salam is recommended, while returning it equally is an obligation. Imam Ahmad recorded that Abu Raja' Al-`Utaridi said that `Imran bin Husayn said that a man came to the Messenger of Allah and said, "As-Salamu `Alaykum". The Prophet returned the greeting, and after the man sat down he said, "Ten." Another man came and said, "As-Salamu `Alaykum wa Rahmatullah, O Allah's Messenger." The Prophet returned the greeting, and after the man sat down he said, "Twenty." Then another man came and said, "As-Salamu `Alaykum wa Rahmatullah wa Barakatuh." The Prophet returned the greeting, and after the man sat down he said, "Thirty." This is the narration recorded by Abu Dawud. At-Tirmidhi, An-Nasa'i and Al-Bazzar also recorded it. At-Tirmidhi said, "Hasan Gharib". There are several other Hadiths on this subject from Abu Sa`id, `Ali, and Sahl bin Hanif. When the Muslim is greeted with the full form of Salam, he is obliged to return the greeting equally. As for Ahl Adh-Dhimmah the Salam should not be initiated nor should the greeting be added to when returning their greeting. Rather, as recorded in the Two Sahihs their greeting is returned to them equally. Ibn `Umar narrated that the Messenger of Allah said,

«إِذَا سَلَّمَ عَلَيْكُمُ الْيَهُودُ، فَإِنَّمَا يَقُولُ أَحَدُهُمْ: السَّامُ عَلَيْكَ، فَقُلْ: وَعَلَيْكَ»

(When the Jews greet you, one of them would say, `As-Samu `Alayka (death be unto you).' Therefore, say, `Wa `Alayka (and the same to you).') In his Sahih, Muslim recorded that Abu Hurayrah said that the Messenger of Allah said,

«لَا تَبْدَأُوا الْيَهُودَ وَالنَّصَارَى بِالسَّلَامِ، وَإِذَا لَقِيتُمُوهُمْ فِي طَرِيقٍ فَاضْطَرُّوهُمْ إِلَى أَضْيَقِهِ»

(Do not initiate greeting the Jews and Christians with the Salam, and when you pass by them on a road, force them to its narrowest path.) Abu Dawud recorded that Abu Hurayrah said that the Messenger of Allah said,

Chapter 4: An-Nisaa (The Women), Verses 024-147

«وَالَّذِي نَفْسِي بِيَدِهِ، لَا تَدْخُلُوا الْجَنَّةَ حَتَّى تُؤْمِنُوا، وَلَا تُؤْمِنُوا حَتَّى تَحَابُّوا، أَفَلَا أَدُلُّكُمْ عَلَى أَمْرٍ إِذَا فَعَلْتُمُوهُ تَحَابَبْتُمْ؟ أَفْشُوا السَّلَامَ بَيْنَكُمْ»

(By He in Whose Hand is my soul! You will not enter Paradise until you believe, and you will not believe until you love each other. Should I direct you to an action that would direct you to love each other Spread the Salam among yourselves.) Allah said,

(Allah! none has the right to be worshipped but He) informing that He is singled out as the sole God of all creation. Allah then said,

(Surely, He will gather you together on the Day of Resurrection about which there is no doubt.) swearing that He will gather the earlier and latter generations in one area, rewarding or punishing each person according to his or her actions. Allah said,

(And who is truer in statement than Allah) meaning, no one utters more truthful statements than Allah, in His promise, warning, stories of the past and information of what is to come; there is no deity worthy of worship nor Lord except Him.

Surah: 4 Ayah: 88, Ayah: 89, Ayah: 90 & Ayah: 91

﴿ ۞ فَمَا لَكُمْ فِى ٱلْمُنَٰفِقِينَ فِئَتَيْنِ وَٱللَّهُ أَرْكَسَهُم بِمَا كَسَبُوٓا۟ ۚ أَتُرِيدُونَ أَن تَهْدُوا۟ مَنْ أَضَلَّ ٱللَّهُ ۖ وَمَن يُضْلِلِ ٱللَّهُ فَلَن تَجِدَ لَهُۥ سَبِيلًا ﴾

88. Then what is the matter with you that you are divided into two parties about the hypocrites? Allâh has cast them back (to disbelief) because of what they have earned. Do you want to guide him whom Allâh has made to go astray? And he whom Allâh has made to go astray, you will never find for him any way (of guidance).

﴿ وَدُّوا۟ لَوْ تَكْفُرُونَ كَمَا كَفَرُوا۟ فَتَكُونُونَ سَوَآءً ۖ فَلَا تَتَّخِذُوا۟ مِنْهُمْ أَوْلِيَآءَ حَتَّىٰ يُهَاجِرُوا۟ فِى سَبِيلِ ٱللَّهِ ۚ فَإِن تَوَلَّوْا۟ فَخُذُوهُمْ وَٱقْتُلُوهُمْ حَيْثُ وَجَدتُّمُوهُمْ ۖ وَلَا تَتَّخِذُوا۟ مِنْهُمْ وَلِيًّا وَلَا نَصِيرًا ﴾

89. They wish that you reject Faith, as they have rejected (Faith), and thus that you all become equal (like one another). So take not Auliyâ' (protectors or friends) from them, till they emigrate in the Way of Allâh (to Muhammad (peace be upon him)) But if they turn back (from Islâm), take (hold) of them and kill them wherever you find them, and take neither Auliyâ' (protectors or friends) nor helpers from them.

﴿ إِلَّا ٱلَّذِينَ يَصِلُونَ إِلَىٰ قَوْمٍ بَيْنَكُمْ وَبَيْنَهُم مِّيثَـٰقٌ أَوْ جَآءُوكُمْ حَصِرَتْ صُدُورُهُمْ أَن يُقَـٰتِلُوكُمْ أَوْ يُقَـٰتِلُوا۟ قَوْمَهُمْ ۚ وَلَوْ شَآءَ ٱللَّهُ لَسَلَّطَهُمْ عَلَيْكُمْ فَلَقَـٰتَلُوكُمْ ۚ فَإِنِ ٱعْتَزَلُوكُمْ فَلَمْ يُقَـٰتِلُوكُمْ وَأَلْقَوْا۟ إِلَيْكُمُ ٱلسَّلَمَ فَمَا جَعَلَ ٱللَّهُ لَكُمْ عَلَيْهِمْ سَبِيلًا ﴿٩٠﴾

90. Except those who join a group, between you and whom there is a treaty (of peace), or those who approach you with their breasts restraining from fighting you as well as fighting their own people. Had Allâh willed, indeed He would have given them power over you, and they would have fought you. So if they withdraw from you, and fight not against you, and offer you peace, then Allâh has opened no way for you against them.

﴿ سَتَجِدُونَ ءَاخَرِينَ يُرِيدُونَ أَن يَأْمَنُوكُمْ وَيَأْمَنُوا۟ قَوْمَهُمْ كُلَّ مَا رُدُّوٓا۟ إِلَى ٱلْفِتْنَةِ أُرْكِسُوا۟ فِيهَا ۚ فَإِن لَّمْ يَعْتَزِلُوكُمْ وَيُلْقُوٓا۟ إِلَيْكُمُ ٱلسَّلَمَ وَيَكُفُّوٓا۟ أَيْدِيَهُمْ فَخُذُوهُمْ وَٱقْتُلُوهُمْ حَيْثُ ثَقِفْتُمُوهُمْ ۚ وَأُو۟لَـٰٓئِكُمْ جَعَلْنَا لَكُمْ عَلَيْهِمْ سُلْطَـٰنًا مُّبِينًا ﴿٩١﴾

91. You will find others that wish to have security from you and security from their people. Every time they are sent back to temptation, they yield thereto. If they withdraw not from you, nor offer you peace, nor restrain their hands, take (hold) of them and kill them wherever you find them. In their case, We have provided you with a clear warrant against them.

Transliteration

88. Fama lakum fee almunafiqeena fi-atayni waAllahu arkasahum bima kasaboo atureedoona an tahdoo man adalla Allahu waman yudlili Allahu falan tajida lahu sabeelan   89. Waddoo law takfuroona kama kafaroo fatakoonoona sawaan fala tattakhithoo minhum awliyaa hatta yuhajiroo fee sabeeli Allahi fa-in tawallaw fakhuthoohum waoqtuloohum haythu wajadtumoohum wala tattakhithoo minhum waliyyan wala naseeran   90. Illa allatheena yasiloona ila qawmin baynakum wabaynahum meethaqun aw jaookum hasirat sudooruhum an yuqatilookum aw yuqatiloo qawmahum walaw shaa Allahu lasallatahum AAalaykum falaqatalookum fa-ini iAAtazalookum falam yuqatilookum waalqaw ilaykumu alssalama fama jaAAala Allahu lakum AAalayhim sabeelan   91. Satajidoona akhareena yureedoona an ya/manookum waya/manoo qawmahum kulla ma ruddoo ila alfitnati orkisoo feeha fa-in lam yaAAtazilookum wayulqoo ilaykumu alssalama wayakuffoo aydiyahum fakhuthoohum waoqtuloohum haythu thaqiftumoohum waola-ikum jaAAalna lakum AAalayhim sultanan mubeenan

Chapter 4: An-Nisaa (The Women), Verses 024-147

Tafsir Ibn Kathir

Censuring the Companions for Disagreeing over the Hypocrites who Returned to Al-Madinah Before Uhud

Allah criticizes the believers for disagreeing over the hypocrites. There are conflicting opinions over the reason behind revealing this Ayah. Imam Ahmad recorded that Zayd bin Thabit said that Messenger of Allah marched towards Uhud. However, some people who accompanied him went back to Al-Madinah, and the Companions of the Messenger of Allah divided into two groups concerning them, one saying they should be killed and the other objecting. Allah sent down,

(Then what is the matter with you that you are divided into two parties about the hypocrites) The Messenger of Allah said,

«إِنَّهَا طَيْبَةٌ، وَإِنَّهَا تَنْفِي الْخَبَثَ، كَمَا يَنْفِي الْكِيرُ خَبَثَ الْحَدِيدِ»

(She (Al-Madinah) is Taybah, and she expels filth, just as the billow expels rust from iron.) The Two Sahihs also recorded this Hadith. Al-`Awfi reported that Ibn `Abbas said that the Ayah was revealed about some people in Makkah who said they embraced Islam, yet they gave their support to the idolators. One time, theses people went out of Makkah to fulfill some needs and said to each other, "If we meet the Companions of Muhammad, there will be no harm for us from their side." When the believers got news that these people went out of Makkah, some of them said, "Let us march to these cowards and kill them, because they support your enemy against you." However, another group from the believers said, "Glory be to Allah! Do you kill a people who say as you have said, just because they did not perform Hijrah or leave their land Is it allowed to shed their blood and confiscate their money in this case" So they divided to two groups, while the Messenger was with them, and did not prohibit either group from reiterating their argument. Thereafter, Allah revealed,

(Then what is the matter with you that you are divided into two parties about the hypocrites) Ibn Abi Hatim recorded this Hadith. Allah said,

(Allah has cast them back because of what they have earned.) meaning, He made them revert to, and fall into error. Ibn `Abbas said that,

(Arkasahum) means, `cast them'. Allah's statement,

(because of what they have earned) means, because of their defiance and disobedience to the Messenger and following falsehood.

(Do you want to guide him whom Allah has made to go astray And he whom Allah has made to go astray, you will never find for him a way.) meaning, there will be no path for him, or way to guidance. Allah's statement,

(They wish that you reject faith, as they have rejected, and thus that you all become equal.) means, they wish that you fall into misguidance, so that you and they are equal in that regard. This is because of their extreme enmity and hatred for you. Therefore, Allah said,

(So take not Awliya' from them, till they emigrate in the way of Allah. But if they turn back,) if they abandon Hijrah, as Al-`Awfi reported from Ibn `Abbas. As-Suddi said that this part of the Ayah means, "If they make their disbelief public."

Combatants and Noncombatants

Allah excluded some people;

(Except those who join a group, between you and whom there is a treaty (of peace),) meaning, except those who join and take refuge with a people with whom you have a pact of peace, or people of Dhimmah, then treat them as you treat the people with whom you have peace. This is the saying of As-Suddi, Ibn Zayd and Ibn Jarir. In his Sahih, Al-Bukhari recorded the story of the treaty of Al-Hudaybiyyah, where it was mentioned that whoever liked to have peace with Quraysh and conduct a pact with them, then they were allowed. Those who liked to have peace with Muhammad and his Companions and enter a pact with them were allowed. It was reported that Ibn `Abbas said that this Ayah was later abrogated by Allah's statement,

(Then when the Sacred Months have passed, kill the idolators wherever you find them) Allah said,

(or those who approach you with their breasts restraining) referring to another type of people covered by the exclusion from fighting. They are those who approach the Muslims with hesitation in their hearts because of their aversion to fighting the Muslims. They do not have the heart to fight with the Muslims against their own people. Therefore, they are neither with nor against Muslims.

(Had Allah willed, indeed He would have given them power over you, and they would have fought you.) meaning, it is from Allah's mercy that He has stopped them from fighting you.

(So, if they withdraw from you, and fight not against you, and offer you peace,) meaning, they revert to peace,

(then Allah has opened no way for you against them), you do not have the right to kill them, as long as they take this position. This was the position of Banu Hashim (the tribe of the Prophet), such as Al-`Abbas, who accompanied the idolators in the battle of Badr, for they joined the battle with great hesitation. This is why the Prophet commanded that Al-`Abbas not be killed, but only captured. Allah's statement,

(You will find others that wish to have security from you and security from their people.) refers to a type of people who on the surface appear to be like the type we just mentioned. However, the intention of each type is different, for the latter are hypocrites. They pretend to be Muslims with the Prophet and his Companions, so that they could attain safety with the Muslims for their blood, property and families. However, they support the idolators in secret and worship what they worship, so that

Chapter 4: An-Nisaa (The Women), Verses 024-147

they are at peace with them also. These people have secretly sided with the idolators, just as Allah described them,

(But when they are alone with their Shayatin, they say: "Truly, we are with you."). In this Ayah, Allah said,

(Every time they are sent back to Fitnah, they yield thereto.) meaning, they dwell in Fitnah. As-Suddi said that the Fitnah mentioned here refers to Shirk. Ibn Jarir recorded that Mujahid said that the Ayah was revealed about a group from Makkah who used to go to the Prophet (in Al-Madinah) pretending to be Muslims. However, when they went back to Quraysh, they reverted to worshipping idols. They wanted to be at peace with both sides. Allah commanded they should be fought against, unless they withdraw from combat and resort to peace. This is why Allah said,

(If they withdraw not from you, nor offer you peace) meaning, revert to peaceful and complacent behavior,

(nor restrain their hands) refrain from fighting you,

(take (hold of) them), capture them,

(and kill them wherever you Thaqiftumuhum.), wherever you find them,

(In their case, We have provided you with a clear warrant against them), meaning an unequivocal and plain warrant.

Surah: 4 Ayah: 92 & Ayah: 93

﴿ وَمَا كَانَ لِمُؤْمِنٍ أَن يَقْتُلَ مُؤْمِنًا إِلَّا خَطَأً وَمَن قَتَلَ مُؤْمِنًا خَطَأً فَتَحْرِيرُ رَقَبَةٍ مُّؤْمِنَةٍ وَدِيَةٌ مُّسَلَّمَةٌ إِلَىٰ أَهْلِهِ إِلَّا أَن يَصَّدَّقُواْ فَإِن كَانَ مِن قَوْمٍ عَدُوٍّ لَّكُمْ وَهُوَ مُؤْمِنٌ فَتَحْرِيرُ رَقَبَةٍ مُّؤْمِنَةٍ وَإِن كَانَ مِن قَوْمٍ بَيْنَكُمْ وَبَيْنَهُم مِّيثَاقٌ فَدِيَةٌ مُّسَلَّمَةٌ إِلَىٰ أَهْلِهِ وَتَحْرِيرُ رَقَبَةٍ مُّؤْمِنَةٍ فَمَن لَّمْ يَجِدْ فَصِيَامُ شَهْرَيْنِ مُتَتَابِعَيْنِ تَوْبَةً مِّنَ ٱللَّهِ وَكَانَ ٱللَّهُ عَلِيمًا حَكِيمًا ۝ ﴾

92. It is not for a believer to kill a believer except (that it be) by mistake; and whosoever kills a believer by mistake, (it is ordained that) he must set free a believing slave and a compensation (blood money, i.e. Diya) be given to the deceased's family, unless they remit it. If the deceased belonged to a people at war with you and he was a believer, the freeing of a believing slave (is prescribed); and if he belonged to a people with whom you have a treaty of mutual alliance, compensation (blood money - Diya) must be paid to his family, and a believing slave must be freed. And whoso finds this (the penance of freeing a slave) beyond his means, he must fast for two consecutive months in order to seek repentance from Allâh. And Allâh is Ever All-Knowing, All-Wise.

$$\left\{ \text{وَمَن يَقْتُلْ مُؤْمِنًا مُّتَعَمِّدًا فَجَزَآؤُهُ جَهَنَّمُ خَالِدًا فِيهَا وَغَضِبَ اللَّهُ عَلَيْهِ وَلَعَنَهُ وَأَعَدَّ لَهُ عَذَابًا عَظِيمًا} \right\}$$

93. And whoever kills a believer intentionally, his recompense is Hell to abide therein; and the Wrath and the Curse of Allâh are upon him, and a great punishment is prepared for him.

Transliteration

92. Wama kana limu/minin an yaqtula mu/minan illa khataan waman qatala mu/minan khataan fatahreeru raqabatin mu/minatin wadiyatun musallamatun ila ahlihi illa an yassaddaqoo fa-in kana min qawmin AAaduwwin lakum wahuwa mu/minun fatahreeru raqabatin mu/minatin wa-in kana min qawmin baynakum wabaynahum meethaqun fadiyatun musallamatun ila ahlihi watahreeru raqabatin mu/minatin faman lam yajid fasiyamu shahrayni mutatabiAAayni tawbatan mina Allahi wakana Allahu AAaleeman hakeeman 93. Waman yaqtul mu/minan mutaAAammidan fajazaohu jahannamu khalidan feeha waghadiba Allahu AAalayhi walaAAanahu waaAAadda lahu AAathaban AAatheeman

Tafsir Ibn Kathir

The Ruling Concerning Killing a Believer by Mistake

Allah states that the believer is not allowed to kill his believing brother under any circumstances. In the Two Sahihs, it is recorded that Ibn Mas`ud said that the Messenger of Allah said,

$$\text{«لَا يَحِلُّ دَمُ امْرِىءٍ مُسْلِمٍ يَشْهَدُ أَنْ لَا إِلَهَ إِلَّا اللهُ، وَأَنِّي رَسُولُ اللهِ، إِلَّا بِإِحْدَى ثَلَاثٍ: النَّفْسُ بِالنَّفْسِ، وَالثَّيِّبُ الزَّانِي، وَالتَّارِكُ لِدِينِهِ الْمُفَارِقُ لِلْجَمَاعَةِ»}$$

(The blood of a Muslim who testifies that there is no deity worthy of worship except Allah and that I am the Messenger of Allah, is sacred, except in three instances. (They are:) life for life, the married adulterer, and whoever reverts from the religion and abandons the Jama`ah (community of the faithful believers).) When one commits any of these three offenses, it is not up to ordinary citizens to kill him or her, because this is the responsibility of the Muslim Leader or his deputy. Allah said,

(except by mistake). There is a difference of opinion concerning the reason behind revealing this part of the Ayah. Mujahid and others said that it was revealed about `Ayyash bin Abi Rabi`ah, Abu Jahl's half brother, from his mother's side, Asma' bint Makhrabah. `Ayyash killed a man called Al-Harith bin Yazid Al-`Amiri, out of revenge for torturing him and his brother because of their Islam. That man later embraced Islam and performed Hijrah, but `Ayyash did not know this fact. On the Day of the

Chapter 4: An-Nisaa (The Women), Verses 024-147

Makkan conquest, `Ayyash saw that man and thought that he was still a disbeliever, so he attacked and killed him. Later, Allah sent down this Ayah. `Abdur-Rahman bin Zayd bin Aslam said that this Ayah was revealed about Abu Ad-Darda' because he killed a man after he embraced the faith, just as Abu Ad-Darda' held the sword above him. When this matter was conveyed to the Messenger of Allah , Abu Ad-Darda' said, "He only said that to avert death." The Prophet said to him,

«هَلَّا شَقَقْتَ عَنْ قَلْبِهِ»

(Have you opened his heart) The basis for this story is in the Sahih, but it is not about Abu Ad-Darda'. Allah said,

(and whosoever kills a believer by mistake, he must set free a believing slave and submit compensation (blood money) to the deceased's family) thus, ordaining two requirements for murder by mistake. The first requirement is the Kaffarah (fine) for the great sin that has been committed, even if it was a mistake. The Kaffarah is to free a Muslim slave, not a non-Muslim slave. Imam Ahmad recorded that a man from the Ansar said that he brought a slave and said, "O Messenger of Allah! I have to free a believing slave, so if you see that this slave is a believer, I will free her." The Messenger of Allah asked her,

«أَتَشْهَدِينَ أَنْ لَا إِلَهَ إِلَّا اللهُ؟»

(Do you testify that there is no deity worthy of worship except Allah) She said, "Yes." He asked her,

«أَتَشْهَدِينَ أَنِّي رَسُولُ اللهِ؟»

(Do you testify that I am the Messenger of Allah) She said, "Yes." He asked,

«أَتُؤْمِنِينَ بِالْبَعْثِ بَعْدَ الْمَوْتِ؟»

(Do you believe in Resurrection after death) She said, "Yes." The Prophet said,

«أَعْتِقْهَا»

(Then free her.) This is an authentic chain of narration, and not knowing the name of the Ansari Companion does not lessen its authenticity. Allah's statement,

(and submit compensation (blood money) to the deceased's family) is the second obligation which involves the killer and the family of the deceased, who will receive blood money as compensation for their loss. The compensation is only obligatory for the one who possesses one of five; as Imam Ahmad, and the Sunan compilers recorded from Ibn Mas`ud. He said; "Allah's Messenger determined that the Diyah (blood money) for unintentional murder is twenty camels which entered their fourth year, twenty camels which entered their fifth year, twenty camels which entered their second year, and twenty camels which entered their third year." This is the wording of An-Nasa'i. This Diyah is required from the elders of the killer's tribe, not from his own money. In the Two Sahihs, it is recorded that Abu Hurayrah said, "Two women from Hudhayl quarreled and one of them threw a stone at the other and killed her and her unborn fetus. They disputed before the Messenger of Allah and he decided that the Diyah of the fetus should be to free a male or a female slave. He also decided that the Diyah of the deceased is required from the elders of the killer's tribe." This Hadith indicates that in the case of what appears to be intentional murder, the Diyah is the same as that for killing by virtual mistake. The former type requires three types of Diyah, just like intentional murder, because it is somewhat similar to intentional murder. Al-Bukhari recorded in his Sahih that `Abdullah bin `Umar said, "The Messenger of Allah sent Khalid bin Al-Walid to Banu Jadhimah and he called them to Islam, but they did not know how to say, `We became Muslims.' They started saying, `Saba'na, Saba'na (we became Sabians). Khalid started killing them, and when this news was conveyed to the Messenger of Allah , he raised his hands and said,

»اللَّهُمَّ إِنِّي أَبْرَأُ إِلَيْكَ مِمَّا صَنَعَ خَالِدٌ«

(O Allah! I declare my innocence before You of what Khalid did.) The Messenger sent `Ali to pay the Diyah of those who were killed and to compensate for the property that was destroyed, to the extent of replacing the dog's bowl. This Hadith indicates that the mistake of the Leader or his deputy (Khalid in this case) is paid from the Muslim Treasury. Allah said,

(unless they remit it), meaning, the Diyah must be delivered to the family of the deceased, unless they forfeit their right, in which case the Diyah does not become necessary. Allah's statement,

(If the deceased belonged to a people at war with you and he was a believer, the freeing of a believing slave (is prescribed);) means, if the murdered person was a believer, yet his family were combatant disbelievers, then they will receive no Diyah. In this case, the murderer only has to free a believing slave. Allah's statement,

(and if he belonged to a people with whom you have a treaty of mutual alliance,) meaning, if the family of the deceased were from Ahl Adh-Dhimmah or with whom there is a peace treaty, then they deserve his Diyah; full Diyah if the deceased was a believer, in which case the killer is required to free a believing slave also.

(And whoso finds this beyond his means, he must fast for two consecutive months) without breaking the fast (in the days of) the two months. If he breaks the fast without justification, i.e. illness, menstruation, post-natal bleeding, then he has to start all over again. Allah's statement,

Chapter 4: An-Nisaa (The Women), Verses 024-147

(to seek repentance from Allah. And Allah is Ever All-Knowing, All-Wise.) means, this is how the one who kills by mistake can repent, he fasts two consecutive months if he does not find a slave to free.

(And Allah is Ever All-Knowing, All-Wise), we mentioned the explanation of this before.

Warning Against Intentional Murder

After Allah mentioned the ruling of unintentional murder, He mentioned the ruling for intentional murder. Allah said,

(And whoever kills a believer intentionally,) This Ayah carries a stern warning and promise for those who commit so grave a sin that it is mentioned along with Shirk in several Ayat of Allah's Book. For instance, in Surat Al-Furqan, Allah said,

(And those who invoke not any other god along with Allah, nor kill such person as Allah has forbidden, except for just cause). Allah said,

(Say: "Come, I will recite what your Lord has prohibited you from: Join not anything in worship with Him.) (6:151). There are many Ayat and Hadiths that prohibit murder. In the Two Sahihs, it is recorded that Ibn Mas`ud said that the Messenger of Allah said,

«أَوَّلُ مَا يُقْضَى بَيْنَ النَّاسِ يَوْمَ الْقِيَامَةِ فِي الدِّمَاءِ»

(Blood offenses are the first disputes to be judged between the people on the Day of Resurrection.) In a Hadith that Abu Dawud recorded, `Ubadah bin As-Samit states that the Messenger of Allah said,

«لَا يَزَالُ الْمُؤْمِنُ مُعْنِقًا صَالِحًا، مَا لَمْ يُصِبْ دَمًا حَرَامًا، فَإِذَا أَصَابَ دَمًا حَرَامًا بَلَّحَ»

(The believer will remain unburdened in righteousness as long as he does not shed prohibited blood. When he sheds forbidden blood, he will become burdened.) Another Hadith, states,

«لَزَوَالُ الدُّنْيَا أَهْوَنُ عِنْدَ اللهِ مِنْ قَتْلِ رَجُلٍ مُسْلِمٍ»

(The destruction of this earthly life is less significant before Allah than killing a Muslim man (or woman).)

Will the Repentance of those who Commit Intentional Murder be Accepted

Ibn `Abbas held the view that the repentance of one who intentionally murders a believer, will not be accepted. Al-Bukhari recorded that Ibn Jubayr said, "The people of knowledge of Al-Kufah differed on this subject, I traveled to Ibn `Abbas to ask him about it. He said, `This Ayah,

(And whoever kills a believer intentionally, his recompense is Hell) was the last revealed (on this subject) and nothing abrogated it.'" Muslim and An-Nasa'i also recorded it. However, the majority of scholars of the earlier and later generations said that the killer's repentance can be accepted. If he repents, and goes back to Allah humbly, submissively, and performing righteous deeds, then Allah will change his evil deeds into good deeds and compensate the deceased for his loss by rewarding him for his suffering. Allah said, R

(And those who invoke not any other god along with Allah), until,

(Except those who repent and believe, and do righteous deeds). The Ayah we just mentioned should not be considered abrogated or only applicable to the disbelievers (who become Muslim), for this contradicts the general, encompassing indications of the Ayah and requires evidence to support it. Allah knows best. Allah said,

(Say: "O My servants who have transgressed against themselves! Despair not of the mercy of Allah). This Ayah is general, covering all types of sins, including Kufr, Shirk, doubt, hypocrisy, murder, sin, and so forth. Therefore, everyone who repents sincerely from any of these errors, then Allah will forgive him. Allah said,

(Verily, Allah forgives not that partners should be set up with Him (in worship), but He forgives except that (anything else) to whom He wills). This Ayah is general and includes every sin except Shirk, and it has been mentioned in this Surah, both after this Ayah and before it, in order to encourage hope in Allah, and Allah knows best. It is confirmed in the Two Sahihs, that an Israeli killed one hundred people then he asked a scholar, "Is it possible for me to repent" So he replied, "What is there that would prevent you from repentance" So he told him to go to another land where Allah was worshipped. He began to emigrate to it but died on the way, and the angel of mercy was the one to take him. Although this Hadith is about an Israeli, it is even more suitable for the Muslim community that their repentance be accepted. Indeed, Allah relieved Muslims from the burdens and restrictions that were placed on the Jews, and He sent our Prophet with the easy Hanifiyyah way (Islamic Monotheism). As for the honorable Ayah,

(And whoever kills a believer intentionally), Abu Hurayrah and several among the Salaf said that this is his punishment, if Allah decides to punish him. And this is the case with every threat that is issued for every sin. For instance, there could be good deeds that this person has done that would prevent him from being punished for that, and Allah knows best. Even if the murderer inevitably enters the Fire -- as Ibn `Abbas stated because his repentance was not accepted, or he did not have good deeds to save him, he will not remain there for eternity, but only for a long time. There are Mutawatir Hadiths stating that the Messenger of Allah said,

«إِنَّهُ يَخْرُجُ مِنَ النَّارِ مَنْ كَانَ فِي قَلْبِهِ أَدْنَى ذَرَّةٍ مِنْ إِيمَانٍ»

(Whoever has the least speck of faith in his heart shall ultimately depart the Fire.)

Surah: 4 Ayah: 94

﴿ يَـٰٓأَيُّهَا ٱلَّذِينَ ءَامَنُوٓا۟ إِذَا ضَرَبْتُمْ فِى سَبِيلِ ٱللَّهِ فَتَبَيَّنُوا۟ وَلَا تَقُولُوا۟ لِمَنْ أَلْقَىٰٓ إِلَيْكُمُ ٱلسَّلَـٰمَ لَسْتَ مُؤْمِنًا تَبْتَغُونَ عَرَضَ ٱلْحَيَوٰةِ ٱلدُّنْيَا فَعِندَ ٱللَّهِ مَغَانِمُ كَثِيرَةٌ كَذَٰلِكَ كُنتُم مِّن قَبْلُ فَمَنَّ ٱللَّهُ عَلَيْكُمْ فَتَبَيَّنُوٓا۟ إِنَّ ٱللَّهَ كَانَ بِمَا تَعْمَلُونَ خَبِيرًا ﴾

94. O you who believe! When you go (to fight) in the Cause of Allâh, verify (the truth), and say not to anyone who greets you (by embracing Islâm): "You are not a believer"; seeking the perishable goods of the worldly life. There are much more profits and booties with Allâh. Even as he is now, so were you yourselves before till Allâh conferred on you His Favors (i.e. guided you to Islâm), therefore, be cautious in discrimination. Allâh is Ever Well-Aware of what you do.

Transliteration

94. Ya ayyuha allatheena amanoo itha darabtum fee sabeeli Allahi fatabayyanoo wala taqooloo liman alqa ilaykumu alssalama lasta mu/minan tabtaghoona AAarada alhayati alddunya faAAinda Allahi maghanimu katheeratun kathalika kuntum min qablu famanna Allahu AAalaykum fatabayyanoo inna Allaha kana bima taAAmaloona khabeeran

Tafsir Ibn Kathir

Greeting with the Salam is a Sign of Islam

Imam Ahmad recorded that `Ikrimah said that Ibn `Abbas said, "A man from Bani Sulaym, who was tending a flock of sheep, passed by some of the Companions of the Prophet and said Salam to them. They said (to each other), `He only said Salam to protect himself from us.' Then they attacked him and killed him. They brought his sheep to the Prophet , and this Ayah was revealed,

(O you who believe!), until the end of the Ayah." At-Tirmidhi recorded this in his (chapter on) Tafsir, and said, "This Hadith is Hasan, and it is also reported from Usamah bin Zayd." Al-Hakim also recorded it and said, "Its chain is Sahih, but they did not collect it." Al-Bukhari recorded that Ibn `Abbas commented;

(and say not to anyone who greets you: "You are not a believer;"), "A man was tending his sheep and the Muslims caught up with him. He said, `As-Salamu `Alaykum.' However, they killed him and took his sheep. Allah revealed the Ayah;

(And say not to anyone who greets you: "You are not a believer; seeking the perishable goods of the worldly life). " Ibn `Abbas said; "The goods of this world were those sheep." And he recited,

(Peace) Imam Ahmad recorded that Al-Qa`qa` bin Abdullah bin Abi Hadrad narrated that his father `Abdullah bin Abi Hadrad said, "The Messenger of Allah sent us to (the area of) Idam. I rode out with a group of Muslims that included Abu Qatadah, Al-Harith bin Rab`i and Muhallam bin Juthamah bin Qays. We continued on until we reached the area of Idam, where `Amr bin Al-Adbat Al-Ashja`i passed by us on his camel. When he passed by us he said Salam to us, and we did not attack him. Because of some previous problems with him, Muhallam bin Juthamah killed him and took his camel. When we went back to the Messenger of Allah and told him what had happened, a part of the Qur'an was revealed about us,

(O you who believe! When you go (to fight) in the cause of Allah), until,

(Well-Aware)." Only Ahmad recorded this Hadith. Al-Bukhari recorded that Ibn `Abbas said that the Messenger of Allah said to Al-Miqdad,

«إِذَا كَانَ رَجُلٌ مُؤْمِنٌ يُخْفِي إِيمَانَهُ مَعَ قَوْمٍ كُفَّارٍ فَأَظْهَرَ إِيمَانَهُ فَقَتَلْتَهُ، فَكَذَلِكَ كُنْتَ أَنْتَ تُخْفِي إِيمَانَكَ بِمَكَّةَ مِنْ قَبْلُ»

(You killed a believing man who hid his faith with disbelieving people, after he had announced his faith to you. Remember that you used to hide your faith in Makkah before.) Al-Bukhari recorded this shorter version without a complete chain of narrators. However a longer version with a connected chain of narrators has also been recorded. Al-Hafiz Abu Bakr Al-Bazzar recorded that Ibn `Abbas said, "The Messenger of Allah sent a military expedition under the authority of Al-Miqdad bin Al-Aswad and when they reached the designated area, they found the people had dispersed. However, a man with a lot of wealth did not leave and said, `I bear witness that there is no deity worthy of worship except Allah.' Yet, Al-Miqdad killed him, and a man said to him, `You killed a man after he proclaimed: "There is no deity worthy of worship except Allah. By Allah I will mention what you did to the Prophet .' When they went back to the Messenger of Allah, they said, `O Messenger of Allah! Al-Miqdad killed a man who testified that there is no deity worthy of worship except Allah.' He said,

«ادْعُوا لِيَ الْمِقْدَادَ، يَا مِقْدَادُ أَقَتَلْتَ رَجُلًا يَقُولُ: لَا إِلَهَ إِلَّا اللهُ، فَكَيْفَ لَكَ بِلَا إِلَهَ إِلَّا اللهُ غَدًا؟»

(Summon Al-Miqdad before me. O Miqdad! Did you kill a man who proclaimed, "There is no deity worthy of worship except Allah" What would you do when you face, "There is no deity worthy of worship except Allah tomorrow") Allah then revealed;

Chapter 4: An-Nisaa (The Women), Verses 024-147

(O you who believe! When you go (to fight) in the cause of Allah, verify (the truth), and say not to anyone who greets you: "You are not a believer;" seeking the perishable goods of the worldly life. There are much more profits and booties with Allah. Even as he is now, so were you yourselves before till Allah conferred on you His Favors, therefore, be cautious in discrimination). The Messenger of Allah said to Al-Miqdad,

«كَانَ رَجُلٌ مُؤْمِنٌ يُخْفِي إِيمَانَهُ مَعَ قَوْمٍ كُفَّارٍ فَأَظْهَرَ إِيمَانَهُ فَقَتَلْتَهُ، فَكَذَلِكَ كُنْتَ أَنْتَ تُخْفِي إِيمَانَكَ بِمَكَّةَ مِنْ قَبْلُ»

(He was a believing man who hid his faith among disbelieving people, and he announced his faith to you, but you killed him, although you used to hide your faith before, in Makkah.)" Allah's statement,

(There is much more benefit with Allah.) means, better than what you desired of worldly possessions which made you kill the one who greeted you with the Salam and pronounced his faith to you. Yet, you ignored all this and accused him of hypocrisy, to acquire the gains of this life. However, the pure wealth with Allah is far better than what you acquired. Allah's statement,

(so were you yourselves before, till Allah conferred on you His Favors.) means, beforehand, you used to be in the same situation like this person who hid his faith from his people. We mentioned the relevant Hadiths above. Allah said,

(And remember when you were few and were reckoned weak in the land). `Abdur-Razzaq recorded that Sa`id bin Jubayr commented about Allah's statement,

(so were you yourselves before), "You used to hide your faith, just as this shepherd hid his faith." Allah said,

(therefore, be cautious in discrimination), then said,

(Allah is Ever Well-Aware of what you do.) and this part of the Ayah contains a threat and a warning, as Sa`id bin Jubayr stated.

Surah: 4 Ayah: 95 & Ayah: 96

﴿لَّا يَسْتَوِي ٱلْقَٰعِدُونَ مِنَ ٱلْمُؤْمِنِينَ غَيْرُ أُوْلِي ٱلضَّرَرِ وَٱلْمُجَٰهِدُونَ فِى سَبِيلِ ٱللَّهِ بِأَمْوَٰلِهِمْ وَأَنفُسِهِمْ ۚ فَضَّلَ ٱللَّهُ ٱلْمُجَٰهِدِينَ بِأَمْوَٰلِهِمْ وَأَنفُسِهِمْ عَلَى ٱلْقَٰعِدِينَ دَرَجَةً ۚ وَكُلًّا وَعَدَ ٱللَّهُ ٱلْحُسْنَىٰ ۚ وَفَضَّلَ ٱللَّهُ ٱلْمُجَٰهِدِينَ عَلَى ٱلْقَٰعِدِينَ أَجْرًا عَظِيمًا ۝﴾

95. Not equal are those of the believers who sit (at home), except those who are disabled (by injury or are blind or lame), and those who strive hard and fight in the Cause of Allâh with their wealth and their lives. Allâh has preferred in grades those who strive hard and fight with their wealth and their lives above those who sit (at home). Unto each, Allâh has promised good (Paradise), but Allâh has preferred those who strive hard and fight, above those who sit (at home) by a huge reward.

﴿دَرَجَـٰتٍ مِّنْهُ وَمَغْفِرَةً وَرَحْمَةً وَكَانَ ٱللَّهُ غَفُورًا رَّحِيمًا ۞﴾

96. Degrees of (higher) grades from Him, and Forgiveness and Mercy. And Allâh is Ever Oft-Forgiving, Most Merciful.

Transliteration

95. La yastawee alqaAAidoona mina almu/mineena ghayru olee alddarari waalmujahidoona fee sabeeli Allahi bi-amwalihim waanfusihim faddala Allahu almujahideena bi-amwalihim waanfusihim AAala alqaAAideena darajatan wakullan waAAada Allahu alhusna wafaddala Allahu almujahideena AAala alqaAAideena ajran AAatheeman   96. Darajatin minhu wamaghfiratan warahmatan wakana Allahu ghafooran raheeman

Tafsir Ibn Kathir

The Mujahid and those Who Do not Join Jihad are Not the Same, [and Jihad is Fard Kifayah]

Al-Bukhari recorded that Al-Bara' said, "When the Ayah,

(Not equal are those of the believers who sit (at home),) was revealed, the Messenger of Allah called Zayd and commanded him to write it. Then, Ibn Umm Maktum came and mentioned that he was blind. Allah revealed,

(except those who are disabled (by injury or are blind or lame))." Al-Bukhari recorded that Sahl bin Sa`d As-Sa`di said, "I saw Marwan bin Al-Hakam sitting in the Masjid. I came and sat by his side. He told us that Zayd bin Thabit told him that Allah's Messenger dictated this Ayah to him,

(Not equal are those of the believers who sit (at home), except those who are disabled, and those who strive hard and fight in the cause of Allah) Ibn Umm Maktum came to the Prophet as he was dictating that very Ayah to me. Ibn Umm Maktum said, `O Allah's Messenger! By Allah, if I had power, I would surely take part in Jihad.' He was a blind man. So Allah sent down revelation to His Messenger while his thigh was on mine and it became so heavy for me that I feared that my thigh would be broken. That ended after Allah revealed,

(except those who are disabled)." This was recorded by Al-Bukhari. At-Tirmidhi recorded that Ibn `Abbas said,

(Not equal are those of the believers who sit (at home), except those who are disabled), refers to those who did not go to the battle of Badr and those who went to Badr. When the battle of Badr was about to occur, Abu Ahmad bin Jahsh and Ibn Umm Maktum said, `We are blind, O Messenger of Allah! Do we have an excuse' The Ayah,

(Not equal are those of the believers who sit (at home), except those who are disabled) was revealed. Allah made those who fight, above those who sit in their homes not hindered by disability.

(but Allah has preferred those who strive hard and fight, above those who sit (at home), by a huge reward. Degrees of (higher) grades from Him), above the believers who sit at home without a disability hindering them." This is the wording recorded by At-Tirmidhi, who said, "Hasan Gharib. Allah's statement,

(Not equal are those of the believers who sit (at home),) this is general. Soon after, the revelation came down with,

(except those who are disabled). So whoever has a disability, such as blindness, a limp, or an illness that prevents them from joining Jihad, they were not compared to the Mujahidin who strive in Allah's cause with their selves and wealth, as those who are not disabled and did not join the Jihad were. In his Sahih, Al-Bukhari recorded that Anas said that the Messenger of Allah said,

«إِنَّ بِالْمَدِينَةِ أَقْوَامًا مَا سِرْتُمْ مِنْ مَسِيرٍ، وَلَا قَطَعْتُمْ مِنْ وَادٍ، إِلَّا وَهُمْ مَعَكُمْ فِيهِ»

(There are people who remained in Al-Madinah, who were with you in every march you marched and every valley you crossed.) They said, "While they are still in Al-Madinah, O Messenger of Allah" He said,

«نَعَمْ حَبَسَهُمُ الْعُذْرُ»

(Yes. Only their disability hindered them (from joining you).) Allah said,

(Unto each, Allah has promised good) meaning, Paradise and tremendous rewards. This Ayah indicates that Jihad is not Fard on each and every individual, but it is Fard Kifayah (which is a collective duty). Allah then said,

(but Allah has preferred those who strive hard and fight, above those who sit (at home), by a huge reward). Allah mentions what He has given them rooms in Paradise, along with His forgiveness and the descent of mercy and blessing on them, as a favor and honor from Him. So He said;

(Degrees of (higher) grades from Him, and forgiveness and mercy. And Allah is Ever Oft-Forgiving, Most Merciful.). In the Two Sahihs, it is recorded that Abu Sa`id Al-Khudri said that the Messenger of Allah said,

«إِنَّ فِي الْجَنَّةِ مِائَةَ دَرَجَةٍ، أَعَدَّهَا اللهُ لِلْمُجَاهِدِينَ فِي سَبِيلِهِ، مَا بَيْنَ كُلِّ دَرَجَتَيْنِ كَمَا بَيْنَ السَّمَاءِ وَالْأَرْضِ»

(There are a hundred grades in Paradise that Allah has prepared for the Mujahidin in His cause, between each two grades is the distance between heaven and Earth.)

Surah: 4 Ayah: 97, Ayah: 98, Ayah: 99 & Ayah: 100

﴿ إِنَّ ٱلَّذِينَ تَوَفَّىٰهُمُ ٱلْمَلَـٰٓئِكَةُ ظَالِمِىٓ أَنفُسِهِمْ قَالُواْ فِيمَ كُنتُمْ قَالُواْ كُنَّا مُسْتَضْعَفِينَ فِى ٱلْأَرْضِ قَالُوٓاْ أَلَمْ تَكُنْ أَرْضُ ٱللَّهِ وَٰسِعَةً فَتُهَاجِرُواْ فِيهَا فَأُوْلَـٰٓئِكَ مَأْوَىٰهُمْ جَهَنَّمُ وَسَآءَتْ مَصِيرًا ۝ ﴾

97. Verily! As for those whom the angels take (in death) while they are wronging themselves (as they stayed among the disbelievers even though emigration was obligatory for them), they (angels) say (to them): "In what (condition) were you?" They reply: "We were weak and oppressed on earth." They (angels) say: "Was not the earth of Allâh spacious enough for you to emigrate therein?" Such men will find their abode in Hell - What an evil destination!

﴿ إِلَّا ٱلْمُسْتَضْعَفِينَ مِنَ ٱلرِّجَالِ وَٱلنِّسَآءِ وَٱلْوِلْدَٰنِ لَا يَسْتَطِيعُونَ حِيلَةً وَلَا يَهْتَدُونَ سَبِيلًا ۝ ﴾

98. Except the weak ones among men, women and children who cannot devise a plan, nor are they able to direct their way.

﴿ فَأُوْلَـٰٓئِكَ عَسَى ٱللَّهُ أَن يَعْفُوَ عَنْهُمْ وَكَانَ ٱللَّهُ عَفُوًّا غَفُورًا ۝ ﴾

99. These are they whom Allâh is likely to forgive them, and Allâh is Ever Oft Pardoning, Oft-Forgiving.

﴿ ۞ وَمَن يُهَاجِرْ فِى سَبِيلِ ٱللَّهِ يَجِدْ فِى ٱلْأَرْضِ مُرَٰغَمًا كَثِيرًا وَسَعَةً وَمَن يَخْرُجْ مِنْ بَيْتِهِۦ مُهَاجِرًا إِلَى ٱللَّهِ وَرَسُولِهِۦ ثُمَّ يُدْرِكْهُ ٱلْمَوْتُ فَقَدْ وَقَعَ أَجْرُهُۥ عَلَى ٱللَّهِ وَكَانَ ٱللَّهُ غَفُورًا رَّحِيمًا ۝ ﴾

100. He who emigrates (from his home) in the Cause of Allâh, will find on earth many dwelling places and plenty to live by. And whosoever leaves his home as an emigrant unto Allâh and His Messenger, and death overtakes him, his reward is then surely incumbent upon Allâh. And Allâh is Ever Oft-Forgiving, Most Merciful.

Transliteration

97. Inna allatheena tawaffahumu almala-ikatu thalimee anfusihim qaloo feema kuntum qaloo kunna mustadAAafeena fee al-ardi qaloo alam takun ardu Allahi wasiAAatan fatuhajiroo feeha faola-ika ma/wahum jahannamu wasaat maseeran 98. Illa almustadAAafeena mina alrrijali waalnnisa-i waalwildani la yastateeAAoona heelatan wala yahtadoona sabeelan 99. Faola-ika AAasa Allahu an yaAAfuwa AAanhum wakana Allahu AAafuwwan ghafooran 100. Waman yuhajir fee sabeeli Allahi yajid fee al-ardi muraghaman katheeran wasaAAatan waman yakhruj min baytihi muhajiran ila Allahi warasoolihi thumma yudrik-hu almawtu faqad waqaAAa ajruhu AAala Allahi wakana Allahu ghafooran raheeman

Tafsir Ibn Kathir

The Prohibition of Residing Among the Disbelievers While Able to Emigrate

Al-Bukhari recorded that Muhammad bin `Abdur-Rahman, Abu Al-Aswad, said, "The people of Al-Madinah were forced to prepare an army (to fight against the people of Ash-Sham during the Khilafah of Abdullah bin Az-Zubayir at Makkah), and I was enlisted in it. Then I met `Ikrimah, the freed slave of Ibn `Abbas, and informed him (about it), and he forbade me strongly from doing so (i.e., to enlist in that army), and then he said to me, `Ibn `Abbas told me that some Muslims used to go out with the idolators increasing the size of their army against the Messenger of Allah . Then, an arrow would hit one of them and kill him, or he would be struck on his neck (with a sword) and killed, and Allah sent down the Ayah,

(Verily, as for those whom the angels take (in death) while they are wronging themselves)." Ad-Dahhak stated that this Ayah was revealed about some hypocrites who did not join the Messenger of Allah but remained in Makkah and went out with the idolators for the battle of Badr. They were killed among those who were killed. Thus, this honorable Ayah was revealed about those who reside among the idolators, while able to perform Hijrah and unable to practice the faith. Such people will be committing injustice against themselves and falling into a prohibition according to the consensus and also according to this Ayah,

(Verily, as for those whom the angels take (in death) while they are wronging themselves,) by refraining from Hijrah,

(They (angels) say (to them): "In what (condition) were you") meaning, why did you remain here and not perform Hijrah

(They reply: "We were weak and oppressed on the earth.") meaning, we are unable to leave the land or move about in the earth,

(They (angels) say: "Was not the earth of Allah spacious enough for you). Abu Dawud recorded that Samurah bin Jundub said that the Messenger of Allah said,

«مَنْ جَامَعَ الْمُشْرِكَ وَسَكَنَ مَعَهُ فَإِنَّهُ مِثْلُهُ»

(Whoever mingles with the idolator and resides with him, he is just like him.) Allah's statement,

(Except the weak) until the end of the Ayah, is an excuse that Allah gives for this type of people not to emigrate, because they are unable to free themselves from the idolators. And even if they did, they would not know which way to go. This is why Allah said,

(Who cannot devise a plan, nor are they able to direct their way), meaning, they do not find the way to emigrate, as Mujahid, `Ikrimah and As-Suddi stated. Allah's statement,

(These are they whom Allah is likely to forgive them,) means, pardon them for not migrating, and here, `likely' means He shall,

(and Allah is Ever Oft-Pardoning, Oft-Forgiving). Al-Bukhari recorded that Abu Hurayrah said, "While the Messenger of Allah was praying `Isha', he said, `Sami` Allahu Liman Hamidah.' He then said before he prostrated,

«اللَّهُمَّ أَنْجِ عَيَّاشَ بْنَ أَبِي رَبِيعَةَ، اللَّهُمَّ أَنْجِ سَلَمَةَ بْنَ هِشَامٍ، اللَّهُمَّ أَنْجِ الْوَلِيدَ بْنَ الْوَلِيدِ، اللَّهُمَّ أَنْجِ الْمُسْتَضْعَفِينَ مِنَ الْمُؤْمِنِينَ، اللَّهُمَّ اشْدُدْ وَطْأَتَكَ عَلَى مُضَرَ، اللَّهُمَّ اجْعَلْهَا سِنِينَ كَسِنِي يُوسُفَ»

(O Allah! Save `Ayyash bin Abi Rabi`ah. O Allah! Save Salamah bin Hisham. O Allah! Save Al-Walid bin Al-Walid. O Allah! Save the weak Muslims. O Allah! Be very hard on Mudar tribe. O Allah! Afflict them with years (of famine) similar to the (famine) years of the time of Prophet Yusuf.)" Al-Bukhari recorded that Abu An-Nu`man said that Hammad bin Zayd said that Ayyub narrated that Ibn Abi Mulaykah said that Ibn `Abbas commented on the verse,

(Except the weak ones among men), "I and my mother were among those (weak ones) whom Allah excused." Allah's statement,

(He who emigrates in the cause of Allah, will find on earth many dwelling places and plenty to live by.) this encourages the believers to perform Hijrah and abandon the idolators, for wherever the believer emigrates, he will find a safe refuge to resort to. Mujahid said that,

Chapter 4: An-Nisaa (The Women), Verses 024-147

(many dwelling places) means, he will find a way out of what he dislikes. Allah's statement,

(and plenty to live by.) refers to provision. Qatadah also said that,

(...will find on earth many dwelling places and plenty to live by.) means, Allah will take him from misguidance to guidance and from poverty to richness. Allah's statement,

(And whosoever leaves his home as an emigrant unto Allah and His Messenger, and death overtakes him, his reward is then surely, incumbent upon Allah.) means, whoever starts emigrating and dies on the way, he will acquire the reward of those who emigrate for Allah. The Two Sahihs, along with the Musnad and Sunan compilers, recorded that `Umar bin Al-Khattab said that the Messenger of Allah said,

«إِنَّمَا الْأَعْمَالُ بِالنِّيَّاتِ، وَإِنَّمَا لِكُلِّ امْرِىءٍ مَا نَوَى، فَمَنْ كَانَتْ هِجْرَتُهُ إِلَى اللهِ وَرَسُولِهِ، فَهِجْرَتُهُ إِلَى اللهِ وَرَسُولِهِ، وَمَنْ كَانَتْ هِجْرَتُهُ إِلَى دُنْيَا يُصِيبُهَا، أَوِ امْرَأَةٍ يَتَزَوَّجُهَا، فَهِجْرَتُهُ إِلَى مَا هَاجَرَ إِلَيْهِ»

(The reward of deeds depends upon the intentions, and every person will be rewarded according to what he has intended. So, whoever emigrated to Allah and His Messenger, then his emigration is for Allah and His Messenger. And whoever emigrated for worldly benefits or for a woman to marry, his emigration is for what he emigrated for.) This Hadith is general, it applies to Hijrah as well as every other deed. In the Two Sahihs, it is recorded that a man killed ninety-nine people and completed the number one hundred when he killed a worshipper. He then asked a scholar if he has a chance to repent. The scholar said, "What prevents you from repentance" The scholar told the killer to emigrate from his land to another land where Allah is worshipped. When he left his land and started on the migration to the other land, death overtook him on the way. The angels of mercy and the angels of torment disputed about the man, whereas the former said that he went out in repentance, while the latter said that he did not arrive at his destination. They were commanded to measure the distance between the two lands and to whichever land he is closer to, he will be considered part of that land. Allah commanded that the righteous land to move closer and the land of evil to move farther. The angels found that he died closer to the land that he intended to emigrate to by a hand-span, and thus the angels of mercy captured his soul. In another narration, when death came to that man, he moved his chest towards the righteous village that he emigrated to.

Surah: 4 Ayah: 101

﴿ وَإِذَا ضَرَبْتُمْ فِى ٱلْأَرْضِ فَلَيْسَ عَلَيْكُمْ جُنَاحٌ أَن تَقْصُرُواْ مِنَ ٱلصَّلَوٰةِ إِنْ خِفْتُمْ أَن يَفْتِنَكُمُ ٱلَّذِينَ كَفَرُوٓاْ إِنَّ ٱلْكَـٰفِرِينَ كَانُواْ لَكُمْ عَدُوّاً مُّبِيناً ﴾

101. And when you (Muslims) travel in the land, there is no sin on you if you shorten As-Salât (the prayer) if you fear that the disbelievers may put you in trial (attack you etc.), verily, the disbelievers are ever unto you open enemies.

Transliteration

101. Wa-itha darabtum fee al-ardi falaysa AAalaykum junahun an taqsuroo mina alssalati in khiftum an yaftinakumu allatheena kafaroo inna alkafireena kanoo lakum AAaduwwan mubeenan

Tafsir Ibn Kathir

Salat Al-Qasr, Shortening the Prayer

Allah said,

(And when you Darabtum in the land,) meaning if you travel in the land. In another Ayah, Allah said,

(He knows that there will be some among you sick, others Yadribuna (traveling) through the land, seeking of Allah's bounty...) (73:20). Allah's statement,

(there is no sin on you if you shorten the Salah (prayer)) by reducing (the units of the prayer) from four to two. Allah's statement,

(if you fear that the disbelievers may put you in trial (attack you)), refers to the typical type of fear prevalent when this Ayah was revealed. In the beginning of Islam, and after the Hijrah, Muslims used to experience fear during most of their travels. Rather, they restricted their movements to large or short military expeditions. During that era, most areas were areas of combatant enemies of Islam and its people. But when the prevalent circumstances cease, or a new situation is prevalent, decrees of this nature may not be understood, as Allah said;

(And force not your slave girls to prostitution, if they desire chastity). And His saying;

(And your stepdaughters, under your guardianship, born of your wives whom you have gone into) Imam Ahmad recorded that Ya`la bin Umayyah said, "I asked `Umar bin Al-Khattab about the verse:

(there is no sin on you if you shorten the prayer. If you fear that the disbelievers may put you in trial,) e `Allah granted Muslims safety now' `Umar said to me, `I wondered about the same thing and asked the Messenger of Allah about it and he said,

»صَدَقَةٌ تَصَدَّقَ اللّهُ بِهَا عَلَيْكُمْ فَاقْبَلُوا صَدَقَتَهُ«

(A gift that Allah has bestowed on you, so accept His gift)." Muslim and the collectors of Sunan recorded this Hadith. At-Tirmidhi said, "Hasan Sahih". `Ali bin Al-Madini said, "This Hadith is Hasan Sahih from the narration of `Umar, and it is not preserved by any other route besides this one, and its narrators are all known." Abu Bakr Ibn Abi Shaybah recorded that Abu Hanzalah Al-Hadha' said, "I asked Ibn `Umar about the Qasr prayer and he said, `It consists of two Rak`ahs.' I said, what about Allah's statement,

(if you fear that the disbelievers may put you in trial (attack you),) `We are safe now.' He said, `This is the Sunnah of the Messenger of Allah .'". Al-Bukhari recorded that Anas said, "We went out with the Messenger of Allah from Al-Madinah to Makkah; he used to pray two Rak`ahs until we went back to Al-Madinah." When he was asked how long they remained in Makkah, he said, "We remained in Makkah for ten days." This was recorded by the Group. Imam Ahmad recorded that Harithah bin Wahb Al-Khuza`i said, "I prayed behind the Prophet for the Zuhr and `Asr prayers in Mina, when the people were numerous and very safe, and he prayed two Rak`ahs." This was recorded by the Group, with the exception of Ibn Majah. Al-Bukhari's narration of this Hadith reads, "The Prophet led us in the prayer at Mina during the peace period by offering two Rak`ahs. "

Surah: 4 Ayah: 102

﴿ وَإِذَا كُنتَ فِيهِمْ فَأَقَمْتَ لَهُمُ ٱلصَّلَوٰةَ فَلْتَقُمْ طَآئِفَةٌ مِّنْهُم مَّعَكَ وَلْيَأْخُذُوٓاْ أَسْلِحَتَهُمْ فَإِذَا سَجَدُواْ فَلْيَكُونُواْ مِن وَرَآئِكُمْ وَلْتَأْتِ طَآئِفَةٌ أُخْرَىٰ لَمْ يُصَلُّواْ فَلْيُصَلُّواْ مَعَكَ وَلْيَأْخُذُواْ حِذْرَهُمْ وَأَسْلِحَتَهُمْ وَدَّ ٱلَّذِينَ كَفَرُواْ لَوْ تَغْفُلُونَ عَنْ أَسْلِحَتِكُمْ وَأَمْتِعَتِكُمْ فَيَمِيلُونَ عَلَيْكُم مَّيْلَةً وَٰحِدَةً وَلَا جُنَاحَ عَلَيْكُمْ إِن كَانَ بِكُمْ أَذًى مِّن مَّطَرٍ أَوْ كُنتُم مَّرْضَىٰٓ أَن تَضَعُوٓاْ أَسْلِحَتَكُمْ وَخُذُواْ حِذْرَكُمْ إِنَّ ٱللَّهَ أَعَدَّ لِلْكَٰفِرِينَ عَذَابًا مُّهِينًا ﴾

102. When you (O Messenger Muhammad (peace be upon him)) are among them, and lead them in As-Salât (the prayer), let one party of them stand up (in Salât (prayer)) with you taking their arms with them; when they finish their prostrations, let them take their positions in the rear and let the other party come up which have not yet prayed, and let them pray with you taking all the precautions and bearing arms. Those who disbelieve wish, if you were negligent of your arms and your baggage, to attack you in a single rush, but there is no sin on you if you put away your arms because of the inconvenience of rain or because you are ill, but take every precaution for yourselves. Verily, Allâh has prepared a humiliating torment for the disbelievers.

Transliteration

102. Wa-itha kunta feehim faaqamta lahumu alssalata faltaqum ta-ifatun minhum maAAaka walya/khuthoo aslihatahum fa-itha sajadoo falyakoonoo min wara-ikum walta/ti ta-ifatun okhra lam yusalloo falyusalloo maAAaka walya/khuthoo hithrahum waaslihatahum wadda allatheena kafaroo law taghfuloona AAan aslihatikum waamtiAAatikum fayameeloona AAalaykum maylatan wahidatan wala junaha AAalaykum in kana bikum athan min matarin aw kuntum marda an tadaAAoo aslihatakum wakhuthoo hithrakum inna Allaha aAAadda lilkafireena AAathaban muheenan

Tafsir Ibn Kathir

The Description of The Fear Prayer

The Fear prayer has different forms, for the enemy is sometimes in the direction of the Qiblah and sometimes in another direction. The Fear prayer consists sometimes of four Rak`ahs, three Rak`ahs, as for Maghrib, and sometimes two Rak`ah like Fajr and prayer during travel. The Fear prayer is sometimes prayed in congregation, but when the battle is raging, congregational prayer may not be possible. In this case, they pray each by himself, facing the Qiblah or otherwise, riding or on foot. In this situation, they are allowed to walk and fight, all the while performing the acts of the prayer. Some scholars said that in the latter case, they pray only one Rak`ah, for Ibn `Abbas narrated, "By the words of your Prophet, Allah has ordained the prayer of four Rak`ah while residing, two Rak`ah during travel, and one Rak`ah during fear." Muslim, Abu Dawud, An-Nasa'i and Ibn Majah recorded it. This is also the view of Ahmad bin Hanbal. Al-Mundhiri said, "This is the saying of `Ata', Jabir, Al-Hasan, Mujahid, Al-Hakam, Qatadah and Hammad; and Tawus and Ad-Dahhak also prefered it." Abu `Asim Al-`Abadi mentioned that Muhammad bin Nasr Al-Marwazi said the Fajr prayer also becomes one Rak`ah during fear. This is also the opinion of Ibn Hazm. Ishaq bin Rahwayh said, "When a battle is raging, one Rak`ah during which you nod your head is sufficient for you. If you are unable, then one prostration is sufficient, because the prostration is remembrance of Allah."

The Reason behind Revealing this Ayah

Imam Ahmad recorded that Abu `Ayyash Az-Zuraqi said, "We were with the Messenger of Allah in the area of `Usfan (a well known place near Makkah), when the idolators met us under the command of Khalid bin Al-Walid, and they were between us and the Qiblah. The Messenger of Allah led us in Zuhr prayer, and the idolators said, `They were busy with something during which we had a chance to attack them.' They then said, `Next, there will come a prayer (`Asr) that is dearer to them than their children and themselves.' However, Jibril came down with these Ayat between the prayers of Zuhr and `Asr,

(When you (O Messenger Muhammad) are among them, and lead them in Salah (prayer)). When the time for prayer came, the Messenger of Allah commanded Muslims to hold their weapons and he made us stand in two lines behind him. When he bowed, we all bowed behind him. When he raised his head, we all raised our heads. The Prophet then prostrated with the line that was behind him while the rest

Chapter 4: An-Nisaa (The Women), Verses 024-147

stood in guard. When they finished with the prostration and stood up, the rest sat and performed prostration, while those who performed it stood up in guard after the two lines exchanged position. The Prophet then bowed and they all bowed after him, then raised their heads after he raised his head. Then the Prophet performed prostration with the line that was behind him, while the rest stood in guard. When those who made prostration sat, the rest prostrated. The Prophet then performed the Taslim and ended the prayer. The Messenger of Allah performed this prayer twice, once in `Usfan and once in the land of Banu Sulaym.'" This is the narration recorded by Abu Dawud and An-Nasa'i, and it has an authentic chain of narration and many other texts to support it. Al-Bukhari recorded that Ibn `Abbas said, "Once the Prophet led the Fear prayer and the people stood behind him. He said Allahu-Akbar and the people said the same. He bowed and some of them bowed. Then he prostrated and they also prostrated. Then he stood for the second Rak`ah and those who had prayed the first Rak`ah left and guarded their brothers. The second party joined him and performed bowing and prostration with him. All the people were in prayer, but they were guarding one another during the prayer." Imam Ahmad recorded that Jabir bin `Abdullah said that the Messenger of Allah led them in the Fear prayer. A group of them stood before him and a group behind him. The Prophet led those who were behind him with one Rak`ah and two prostrations. They then moved to the position of those who did not pray, while the others stood in their place, and the Messenger of Allah performed one Rak`ah and two prostrations and then said the Salam. Therefore, the Prophet prayed two Rak`ah while they prayed one. An-Nasa'i recorded this Hadith, while Muslim collected other wordings for it. Collectors of the Sahih, Sunan and Musnad collections recorded this in a Hadith from Jabir. Ibn Abi Hatim recorded that Salim said that his father said,

(When you (O Messenger Muhammad) are among them, and lead them in Salah (prayer)) refers to the Fear prayer. The Messenger of Allah led one group and prayed one Rak`ah, while the second group faced the enemy. Then the second group that faced the enemy came and Allah's Messenger led them, praying one Rak`ah, and then said the Salam. Each of the two groups then stood up and prayed one more Rak`ah each (while the other group stood in guard)." The Group collected this Hadith with Ma`mar in its chain of narrators. This Hadith also has many other chains of narration from several Companions, and Al-Hafiz Abu Bakr Ibn Marduwyah collected these various narrations, as did Ibn Jarir. As for the command to hold the weapons during the Fear prayer, a group of scholars said that it is obligatory according to the Ayah. What testifies to this is that Allah said;

(But there is no sin on you if you put away your arms because of the inconvenience of rain or because you are ill, but take every precaution for yourselves) meaning, so that when necessary, you will be able to get to your weapons easily,

(Verily, Allah has prepared a humiliating torment for the disbelievers).

Surah: 4 Ayah: 103 & Ayah: 104

﴿ فَإِذَا قَضَيْتُمُ ٱلصَّلَوٰةَ فَٱذْكُرُواْ ٱللَّهَ قِيَٰمًا وَقُعُودًا وَعَلَىٰ جُنُوبِكُمْ ۚ فَإِذَا ٱطْمَأْنَنتُمْ فَأَقِيمُواْ ٱلصَّلَوٰةَ ۚ إِنَّ ٱلصَّلَوٰةَ كَانَتْ عَلَى ٱلْمُؤْمِنِينَ كِتَٰبًا مَّوْقُوتًا ﴾

103. When you have finished As-Salât (the congregational prayer), remember Allâh standing, sitting down, and (lying down) on your sides, but when you are free from danger, perform As-Salât (Iqâmat-as- Salât). Verily, As-Salât (the prayer) is enjoined on the believers at fixed hours.

﴿ وَلَا تَهِنُواْ فِى ٱبْتِغَآءِ ٱلْقَوْمِ ۖ إِن تَكُونُواْ تَأْلَمُونَ فَإِنَّهُمْ يَأْلَمُونَ كَمَا تَأْلَمُونَ ۖ وَتَرْجُونَ مِنَ ٱللَّهِ مَا لَا يَرْجُونَ ۗ وَكَانَ ٱللَّهُ عَلِيمًا حَكِيمًا ﴾

104. And don't be weak in the pursuit of the enemy; if you are suffering (hardships) then surely, they (too) are suffering (hardships) as you are suffering, but you have a hope from Allâh (for the reward, i.e. Paradise) that for which they hope not; and Allâh is Ever All-Knowing, All-Wise.

Transliteration

103. Fa-itha qadaytumu alssalata faothkuroo Allaha qiyaman waquAAoodan waAAala junoobikum faitha itma/nantum faaqeemoo alssalata inna alssalata kanat AAala almu/mineena kitaban mawqootan   104. Wala tahinoo fee ibtigha-i alqawmi in takoonoo ta/lamoona fa-innahum ya/lamoona kama ta/lamoona watarjoona mina Allahi ma la yarjoona wakana Allahu AAaleeman hakeeman

Tafsir Ibn Kathir

The Order for Ample Remembrance After the Fear Prayer

Allah commands Dhikr after finishing the Fear prayer, in particular, even though such Dhikr is encouraged after finishing other types of prayer in general. In the case of Fear prayer, Dhikr is encouraged even more because the pillars of the prayer are diminished since they move about while performing it, etc., unlike other prayers. Allah said about the Sacred Months,

(so wrong not yourselves therein), even though injustice is prohibited all year long. However, injustice is particularly outlawed during the Sacred Months due to their sanctity and honor. So Allah's statement,

(When you have finished Salah, remember Allah standing, sitting down, and on your sides,) means, in all conditions,

(But when you are free from danger perform the Salah.) when you are safe, tranquil and fear subsides, (perform the Salah) by performing it as you were commanded; fulfilling its obligations, with humbleness, completing the bowing and prostration positions etc. Allah's statement,

(Verily, the Salah is Kitaban on the believers at fixed hours.) means, enjoined, as Ibn `Abbas stated. Ibn `Abbas also said, "The prayer has a fixed time, just as the case with Hajj." Similar is reported from Mujahid, Salim bin `Abdullah, `Ali bin Al-Husayn, Muhammad bin `Ali, Al-Hasan, Muqatil. As-Suddi and `Atiyah Al-`Awfi.

The Encouragement to Pursue the Enemy Despite Injuries

Allah's statement,

(And don't be weak in the pursuit of the enemy;) means, do not weaken your resolve in pursuit of your enemy. Rather, pursue them vigorously, fight them and be wary of them.

(if you are suffering then surely they are suffering as you are suffering,) meaning, just as you suffer from injuries and death, the same happens to the enemy. In another Ayah, Allah said,

(If you suffer a harm, be sure a similar harm has struck the others). Allah then said,

(but you have a hope from Allah that for which they hope not;) meaning, you and they are equal regarding the injuries and pain that you suffer from. However, you hope for Allah's reward, victory and aid, just as He has promised you in His Book and by the words of his Messenger . Surely, Allah's promise is true. On the other hand, your enemies do not have hope for any of this. So, it is you, not they, who should be eager to fight so that you establish the Word of Allah and raise it high. i

(And Allah is Ever All-Knowing, All-Wise.) means, He is most knowledgeable and wise in all what He decides, decrees, wills and acts on concerning various worldly and religious ordainments, and He is worthy of praise in all conditions.

Surah: 4 Ayah: 105, Ayah: 106, Ayah: 107, Ayah: 108 & Ayah: 109

﴿ إِنَّا أَنزَلْنَا إِلَيْكَ ٱلْكِتَٰبَ بِٱلْحَقِّ لِتَحْكُمَ بَيْنَ ٱلنَّاسِ بِمَا أَرَىٰكَ ٱللَّهُ وَلَا تَكُن لِّلْخَآئِنِينَ خَصِيمًا ﴿١٠٥﴾ ﴾

105. Surely, We have sent down to you (O Muhammad) the Book (this Qur'ân) in truth that you might judge between men by that which Allâh has shown you (i.e. has taught you through Divine Revelation), so be not a pleader for the treacherous)

﴿ وَٱسْتَغْفِرِ ٱللَّهَ إِنَّ ٱللَّهَ كَانَ غَفُورًا رَّحِيمًا ﴿١٠٦﴾ ﴾

106. And seek the Forgiveness of Allâh, certainly, Allâh is Ever Oft-Forgiving, Most Merciful.

﴿ وَلَا تُجَٰدِلْ عَنِ ٱلَّذِينَ يَخْتَانُونَ أَنفُسَهُمْ ۚ إِنَّ ٱللَّهَ لَا يُحِبُّ مَن كَانَ خَوَّانًا أَثِيمًا ﴾

107. And argue not on behalf of those who deceive themselves. Verily, Allâh does not like anyone who is a betrayer, sinner.

﴿ يَسْتَخْفُونَ مِنَ ٱلنَّاسِ وَلَا يَسْتَخْفُونَ مِنَ ٱللَّهِ وَهُوَ مَعَهُمْ إِذْ يُبَيِّتُونَ مَا لَا يَرْضَىٰ مِنَ ٱلْقَوْلِ ۚ وَكَانَ ٱللَّهُ بِمَا يَعْمَلُونَ مُحِيطًا ﴾

108. They may hide (their crimes) from men, but they cannot hide (them) from Allâh; for He is with them (by His Knowledge), when they plot by night in words that He does not approve. And Allâh ever encompasses what they do.

﴿ هَٰٓأَنتُمْ هَٰٓؤُلَآءِ جَٰدَلْتُمْ عَنْهُمْ فِى ٱلْحَيَوٰةِ ٱلدُّنْيَا فَمَن يُجَٰدِلُ ٱللَّهَ عَنْهُمْ يَوْمَ ٱلْقِيَٰمَةِ أَم مَّن يَكُونُ عَلَيْهِم وَكِيلًا ﴾

109. Lo! You are those who have argued for them in the life of this world, but who will argue for them on the Day of Resurrection against Allâh, or who will then be their defender?

Transliteration

105. Inna anzalna ilayka alkitaba bialhaqqi litahkuma bayna alnnasi bima araka Allahu wala takun lilkha-ineena khaseeman 106. Waistaghfiri Allaha inna Allaha kana ghafooran raheeman 107. Wala tujadil AAani allatheena yakhtanoona anfusahum inna Allaha la yuhibbu man kana khawwanan atheeman 108. Yastakhfoona mina alnnasi wala yastakhfoona mina Allahi wahuwa maAAahum ith yubayyitoona ma la yarda mina alqawli wakana Allahu bima yaAAmaloona muheetan 109. Haantum haola-i jadaltum AAanhum fee alhayati alddunya faman yujadilu Allaha AAanhum yawma alqiyamati am man yakoonu AAalayhim wakeelan

Tafsir Ibn Kathir

The Necessity of Referring to What Allah has Revealed for Judgement

Allah says to His Messenger, Muhammad ,

(Surely, We have sent down to you the Book in truth) meaning, it truly came from Allah and its narrations and commandments are true. Allah then said,

(that you might judge between men by that which Allah has shown you,) In the Two Sahihs, it is recorded that Zaynab bint Umm Salamah said that Umm Salamah said that the Messenger of Allah heard the noise of disputing people close to the door of his room, and he went out to them saying,

Chapter 4: An-Nisaa (The Women), Verses 024-147

«أَلَا إِنَّمَا أَنَا بَشَرٌ، وَإِنَّمَا أَقْضِي بِنَحْوٍ مِمَّا أَسْمَعُ، وَلَعَلَّ أَحَدَكُمْ أَنْ يَكُونَ أَلْحَنَ بِحُجَّتِهِ مِنْ بَعْضٍ فَأَقْضِيَ لَهُ، فَمَنْ قَضَيْتُ لَهُ بِحَقِّ مُسْلِمٍ، فَإِنَّمَا هِيَ قِطْعَةٌ مِنْ نَارٍ، فَلْيَحْمِلْهَا أَوْ لِيَذَرْهَا»

(Verily, I am only human and I judge based on what I hear. Some of you might be more eloquent in presenting his case than others, so that I judge in his favor. If I judge in one's favor concerning the right of another Muslim, then it is a piece of the Fire. So let one take it or leave it.) Imam Ahmad recorded that Umm Salamah said, "Two men from the Ansar came to the Messenger of Allah with a dispute regarding some old inheritance, but they did not have evidence. The Messenger of Allah said,

«إِنَّكُمْ تَخْتَصِمُونَ إِلَيَّ، وَإِنَّمَا أَنَا بَشَرٌ، وَلَعَلَّ بَعْضَكُمْ أَلْحَنُ بِحُجَّتِهِ مِنْ بَعْضٍ، وَإِنَّمَا أَقْضِي بَيْنَكُمْ عَلَى نَحْوٍ مِمَّا أَسْمَعُ، فَمَنْ قَضَيْتُ لَهُ مِنْ حَقِّ أَخِيهِ شَيْئًا فَلَا يَأْخُذْهُ، فَإِنَّمَا أَقْطَعُ لَهُ قِطْعَةً مِنَ النَّارِ، يَأْتِي بِهَا إِسْطَامًا فِي عُنُقِهِ يَوْمَ الْقِيَامَةِ»

(You bring your disputes to me, but I am only human. Some of you might be more persuasive in their arguments than others. I only judge between you according to what I hear. Therefore, whomever I judge in his favor and give him a part of his brother's right, let him not take it, for it is a part of the Fire that I am giving him and it will be tied around his neck on the Day of Resurrection.) The two men cried and each one of them said, `I forfeit my right to my brother.' The Messenger of Allah said,

«أَمَا إِذْ قُلْتُمَا فَاذْهَبَا فَاقْتَسِمَا، ثُمَّ تَوَخَّيَا الْحَقَّ ثُمَّ اسْتَهِمَا، ثُمَّ لِيُحْلِلْ كُلُّ وَاحِدٍ مِنْكُمَا صَاحِبَهُ»

(Since you said that, then go and divide the inheritance, and try to be just in your division. Then draw lots, and each one of you should forgive his brother thereafter (regardless of who got the best share).)" Allah's statement,

(They may hide (their crimes) from men, but they cannot hide (them) from Allah;) chastises the hypocrites because they hide their evil works from the people so that they will not criticize them. Yet, the hypocrites disclose this evil with Allah, Who has perfect watch over their secrets and knows what is in their hearts. This is why Allah said, (for He is with them (by His knowledge), when they plot by night in words that He does not approve. And Allah ever encompasses what they do) threatening and warning them. Allah then said,

(Lo! You are those who have argued for them in the life of this world,) meaning, suppose these people gain the verdict from the rulers in their favor in this life, since the rulers judge according to what is apparent to them. However, what will their condition be on the Day of Resurrection before Allah, Who knows the secret and what is even more hidden Who will be his advocate on that Day Verily, none will support them that Day. Hence, Allah's statement,

(or who will then be their defender)

Surah: 4 Ayah: 110, Ayah: 111, Ayah: 112 & Ayah: 113

﴿ وَمَن يَعْمَلْ سُوٓءًا أَوْ يَظْلِمْ نَفْسَهُۥ ثُمَّ يَسْتَغْفِرِ ٱللَّهَ يَجِدِ ٱللَّهَ غَفُورًا رَّحِيمًا ﴾

110. And whoever does evil or wrongs himself but afterwards seeks Allâh's Forgiveness, he will find Allâh Oft-Forgiving, Most Merciful.

﴿ وَمَن يَكْسِبْ إِثْمًا فَإِنَّمَا يَكْسِبُهُۥ عَلَىٰ نَفْسِهِۦ ۚ وَكَانَ ٱللَّهُ عَلِيمًا حَكِيمًا ﴾

111. And whoever earns sin, he earns it only against himself. And Allâh is Ever All-Knowing, All-Wise.

﴿ وَمَن يَكْسِبْ خَطِيٓـَٔةً أَوْ إِثْمًا ثُمَّ يَرْمِ بِهِۦ بَرِيٓـًٔا فَقَدِ ٱحْتَمَلَ بُهْتَٰنًا وَإِثْمًا مُّبِينًا ﴾

112. And whoever earns a fault or a sin and then throws it on to someone innocent, he has indeed burdened himself with falsehood and a manifest sin.

﴿ وَلَوْلَا فَضْلُ ٱللَّهِ عَلَيْكَ وَرَحْمَتُهُۥ لَهَمَّت طَّآئِفَةٌ مِّنْهُمْ أَن يُضِلُّوكَ وَمَا يُضِلُّونَ إِلَّآ أَنفُسَهُمْ ۖ وَمَا يَضُرُّونَكَ مِن شَىْءٍ ۚ وَأَنزَلَ ٱللَّهُ عَلَيْكَ ٱلْكِتَٰبَ وَٱلْحِكْمَةَ وَعَلَّمَكَ مَا لَمْ تَكُن تَعْلَمُ ۚ وَكَانَ فَضْلُ ٱللَّهِ عَلَيْكَ عَظِيمًا ﴾

113. Had not the Grace of Allâh and His Mercy been upon you (O Muhammad (peace be upon him)) a party of them would certainly have made a decision to mislead you, but (in fact) they mislead none except their own selves, and no harm can they do to you in the least. Allâh has sent down to you the Book (The Qur'ân), and Al-Hikmah (Islâmic laws, knowledge of legal and illegal things i.e. the Prophet's Sunnah - legal ways), and taught you that which you knew not. And Ever Great is the Grace of Allâh unto you (O Muhammad (peace be upon him))

Chapter 4: An-Nisaa (The Women), Verses 024-147

Transliteration

110. Waman yaAAmal soo-an aw yathlim nafsahu thumma yastaghfiri Allaha yajidi Allaha ghafooran raheeman   111. Waman yaksib ithman fa-innama yaksibuhu AAala nafsihi wakana Allahu AAaleeman hakeeman   112. Waman yaksib khatee-atan aw ithman thumma yarmi bihi baree-an faqadi ihtamala buhtanan waithman mubeenan   113. Walawla fadlu Allahi AAalayka warahmatuhu lahammat ta-ifatun minhum an yudillooka wama yudilloona illa anfusahum wama yadurroonaka min shay-in waanzala Allahu AAalayka alkitaba waalhikmata waAAallamaka ma lam takun taAAlamu wakana fadlu Allahi AAalayka AAatheeman

Tafsir Ibn Kathir

The Encouragement to Seek Allah's Forgiveness, and Warning those who Falsely Accuse Innocent People

Allah emphasizes His generosity and kindness, in that He forgives whoever repents to Him from whatever evil they commit. Allah said,

(And whoever does evil or wrongs himself but afterwards seeks Allah's forgiveness, he will find Allah Oft-Forgiving, Most Merciful.) `Ali bin Abi Talhah said that Ibn `Abbas commented about this Ayah, "Allah informs His servants of His forgiveness, forbearing generosity and expansive mercy. So whoever commits a sin, whether minor or major,

(but afterwards seeks Allah's forgiveness, he will find Allah Oft-Forgiving, Most Merciful.) even if his sins were greater than the heavens, the earth and the mountains." Imam Ahmad recorded that `Ali said, "Whenever I hear anything from the Messenger of Allah, Allah benefits me with whatever He wills of that. Abu Bakr told me, and Abu Bakr has said the truth, that the Messenger of Allah said,

«مَا مِنْ مُسْلِمٍ يُذْنِبُ ذَنْبًا، ثُمَّ يَتَوَضَّأُ فَيُصَلِّي رَكْعَتَيْنِ، ثُمَّ يَسْتَغْفِرُ اللهَ لِذَلِكَ الذَّنْبِ، إِلَّا غَفَرَ لَه»

(No Muslim commits a sin and then performs ablution, prays two Rak`ahs and begs Allah for forgiveness for that sin, but He forgives him.) He then recited these two Ayat,

(And whoever does evil or wrongs himself), and,

(And those who, when they have committed Fahishah or wronged themselves with evil)." Allah's statement,

(And whoever earns sin, he earns it only against himself.) is similar to His statement,

(And no bearer of burdens shall bear the burden of another). So no one will avail anyone else. Rather, every soul, and none else, shall carry its own burden. This is why Allah said,

(And Allah is Ever All-Knowing, All-Wise.) meaning, this occurs due to His knowledge, wisdom, fairness and mercy.

(and taught you that which you knew not.), before this revelation was sent down to you. Similarly, Allah said,

(And thus We have sent to you (O Muhammad) a Ruh (a revelation, and a mercy) of Our command. You knew not what is the Book) until the end of the Surah. Allah said,

(And you were not expecting that the Book (this Qur'an) would be sent down to you, but it is a mercy from your Lord). So Allah said;

(And ever great is the grace of Allah unto you (O Muhammad)).

Surah: 4 Ayah: 114 & Ayah: 115

﴿ ۞ لَّا خَيْرَ فِى كَثِيرٍ مِّن نَّجْوَىٰهُمْ إِلَّا مَنْ أَمَرَ بِصَدَقَةٍ أَوْ مَعْرُوفٍ أَوْ إِصْلَٰحٍ بَيْنَ ٱلنَّاسِ ۚ وَمَن يَفْعَلْ ذَٰلِكَ ٱبْتِغَآءَ مَرْضَاتِ ٱللَّهِ فَسَوْفَ نُؤْتِيهِ أَجْرًا عَظِيمًا ﴾

114. There is no good in most of their secret talks save (in) him who orders Sadaqah (charity in Allâh's Cause), or Ma'rûf (Islâmic Monotheism and all the good and righteous deeds which Allâh has ordained), or conciliation between mankind; and he who does this, seeking the good Pleasure of Allâh, We shall give him a great reward.

﴿ وَمَن يُشَاقِقِ ٱلرَّسُولَ مِنْ بَعْدِ مَا تَبَيَّنَ لَهُ ٱلْهُدَىٰ وَيَتَّبِعْ غَيْرَ سَبِيلِ ٱلْمُؤْمِنِينَ نُوَلِّهِ مَا تَوَلَّىٰ وَنُصْلِهِ جَهَنَّمَ ۖ وَسَآءَتْ مَصِيرًا ﴾

115. And whoever contradicts and opposes the Messenger (Muhammad (peace be upon him)) after the right path has been shown clearly to him, and follows other than the believers' way. We shall keep him in the path he has chosen, and burn him in Hell - what an evil destination!

Transliteration

114. La khayra fee katheerin min najwahum illa man amara bisadaqatin aw maAAroofin aw islahin bayna alnnasi waman yafAAal thalika ibtighaa mardati Allahi fasawfa nu/teehi ajran AAatheeman 115. Waman yushaqiqi alrrasoola min baAAdi ma tabayyana lahu alhuda wayattabiAA ghayra sabeeli almu/mineena nuwallihi ma tawalla wanuslihi jahannama wasaat maseeran

Tafsir Ibn Kathir

Righteous Najwa, Secret Talk

Allah said,

Chapter 4: An-Nisaa (The Women), Verses 024-147

(There is no good in most of their secret talks) meaning, what the people say to each other.

(save him who orders Sadaqah (charity), or goodness, or reconciliation between mankind;) meaning, except for this type of talk. Imam Ahmad recorded that Umm Kulthum bint `Uqbah said that she heard the Messenger of Allah saying,

«لَيْسَ الْكَذَّابُ الَّذِي يُصْلِحُ بَيْنَ النَّاسِ فَيَنْمِي خَيْرًا، أَوْ يَقُولُ خَيْرًا»

(He who brings about reconciliation between people by embellishing good or saying good things, is not a liar.) She also said, "I never heard him allow what the people say (lies) except in three cases: in war, bringing peace between people and the man's speech (invented compliments) to his wife and her speech to her husband." Umm Kulthum bint `Uqbah was among the immigrant women who gave their pledge of allegiance to the Messenger of Allah . The Group also recorded this Hadith, with the exception of Ibn Majah. Imam Ahmad recorded that Abu Ad-Darda' said that the Messenger of Allah said,

«أَلَا أُخْبِرُكُمْ بِأَفْضَلَ مِنْ دَرَجَةِ الصِّيَامِ، وَالصَّلَاةِ، وَالصَّدَقَةِ؟»

(Should I tell you what is better than the grade of fasting, praying and Sadaqah) They said, "Yes, O Allah's Messenger!" He said,

«إِصْلَاحُ ذَاتِ الْبَيْنِ»

(Bringing reconciliation between people.) He also said,

«وَفَسَادُ ذَاتِ الْبَيْنِ هِيَ الْحَالِقَة»

(Spoiling the relationship (between people) is the destroyer.) Abu Dawud and At-Tirmidhi also recorded this Hadith, and At-Tirmidhi said, "Hasan Sahih". Allah said,

(and he who does this, seeking the good pleasure of Allah,) with sincerity and awaiting the reward with Allah, the Exalted and Most Honored,

(We shall give him a great reward.) meaning, an immense, enormous and tremendous reward.

The Punishment for Contradicting and Opposing the Messenger and Following a Path Other than That of the Believers

Allah's statement,

(And whoever contradicts and opposes the Messenger after the right path has been shown clearly to him.) refers to whoever intentionally takes a path other than the path of the Law revealed to the Messenger, after the truth has been made clear, apparent and plain to him. Allah's statement,

(and follows other than the believers' way,) refers to a type of conduct that is closely related to contradicting the Messenger . This contradiction could be in the form of contradicting a text (from the Qur'an or Sunnah) or contradicting what the Ummah of Muhammad has agreed on. The Ummah of Muhammad is immune from error when they all agree on something, a miracle that serves to increase their honor, due to the greatness of their Prophet. There are many authentic Hadiths on this subject. Allah warned against the evil of contradicting the Prophet and his Ummah, when He said, e

(We shall keep him in the path he has chosen, and burn him in Hell --- what an evil destination!) meaning, when one goes on this wicked path, We will punish him by making the evil path appear good in his heart, and will beautify it for him so that he is tempted further. For instance, Allah said,

(Then leave Me Alone with such as belie this Qur'an. We shall punish them gradually from directions they perceive not),

(So when they turned away (from the path of Allah), Allah turned their hearts away), and,

(And We shall leave them in their trespass to wander blindly). Allah made the Fire the destination of such people in the Hereafter. Indeed, the path of those who avoid the right guidance will only lead to the Fire on the Day of Resurrection, as evident by Allah's statements,

((It will be said to the angels): "Assemble those who did wrong, together with their companions (from the devils)), and,

(And the criminals, shall see the Fire and apprehend that they have to fall therein. And they will find no way of escape from there).

Surah: 4 Ayah: 116, Ayah: 117, Ayah: 118, Ayah: 119, Ayah: 120, Ayah: 121 & Ayah: 122

﴿ إِنَّ ٱللَّهَ لَا يَغْفِرُ أَن يُشْرَكَ بِهِۦ وَيَغْفِرُ مَا دُونَ ذَٰلِكَ لِمَن يَشَآءُ وَمَن يُشْرِكْ بِٱللَّهِ فَقَدْ ضَلَّ ضَلَٰلًۢا بَعِيدًا ﴾

116. Verily! Allâh forgives not (the sin of) setting up partners (in worship) with Him, but He forgives whom He wills sins other than that, and whoever sets up partners in worship with Allâh, has indeed strayed far away.

﴿ إِن يَدْعُونَ مِن دُونِهِۦٓ إِلَّآ إِنَٰثًا وَإِن يَدْعُونَ إِلَّا شَيْطَٰنًا مَّرِيدًا ﴾

Chapter 4: An-Nisaa (The Women), Verses 024-147

117. They (all those who worship others than Allâh) invoke nothing but female deities besides Him (Allâh), and they invoke nothing but Shaitân (Satan), a persistent rebel!

﴿ لَعَنَهُ ٱللَّهُ وَقَالَ لَأَتَّخِذَنَّ مِنْ عِبَادِكَ نَصِيبًا مَّفْرُوضًا ۝ ﴾

118. Allâh cursed him. And he (Shaitân (Satan)) said: "I will take an appointed portion of your slaves.

﴿ وَلَأُضِلَّنَّهُمْ وَلَأُمَنِّيَنَّهُمْ وَلَآمُرَنَّهُمْ فَلَيُبَتِّكُنَّ ءَاذَانَ ٱلْأَنْعَٰمِ وَلَآمُرَنَّهُمْ فَلَيُغَيِّرُنَّ خَلْقَ ٱللَّهِ ۚ وَمَن يَتَّخِذِ ٱلشَّيْطَٰنَ وَلِيًّا مِّن دُونِ ٱللَّهِ فَقَدْ خَسِرَ خُسْرَانًا مُّبِينًا ۝ ﴾

119. Verily, I will mislead them, and surely, I will arouse in them false desires; and certainly, I will order them to slit the ears of cattle, and indeed I will order them to change the nature created by Allâh." And whoever takes Shaitân (Satan) as a Walî (protector or helper) instead of Allâh, has surely suffered a manifest loss.

﴿ يَعِدُهُمْ وَيُمَنِّيهِمْ ۖ وَمَا يَعِدُهُمُ ٱلشَّيْطَٰنُ إِلَّا غُرُورًا ۝ ﴾

120. He (Shaitan (Satan)) makes promises to them, and arouses in them false desires; and Shaitan's (Satan) promises are nothing but deceptions.

﴿ أُوْلَٰٓئِكَ مَأْوَىٰهُمْ جَهَنَّمُ وَلَا يَجِدُونَ عَنْهَا مَحِيصًا ۝ ﴾

121. The dwelling of such (people) is Hell, and they will find no way of escape from it.

﴿ وَٱلَّذِينَ ءَامَنُوا۟ وَعَمِلُوا۟ ٱلصَّٰلِحَٰتِ سَنُدْخِلُهُمْ جَنَّٰتٍ تَجْرِى مِن تَحْتِهَا ٱلْأَنْهَٰرُ خَٰلِدِينَ فِيهَآ أَبَدًا ۖ وَعْدَ ٱللَّهِ حَقًّا ۚ وَمَنْ أَصْدَقُ مِنَ ٱللَّهِ قِيلًا ۝ ﴾

122. But those who believe (in the Oneness of Allâh - Islâmic Monotheism) and do deeds of righteousness, We shall admit them to the Gardens under which rivers flow (i.e. in Paradise) to dwell therein forever. Allâh's Promise is the Truth; and whose words can be truer than those of Allâh? (Of course, none).

Transliteration

116. Inna Allaha la yaghfiru an yushraka bihi wayaghfiru ma doona thalika liman yashao waman yushrik biAllahi faqad dalla dalalan baAAeedan 117. In yadAAoona min doonihi illa inathan wa-in yadAAoona illa shaytanan mareedan 118. LaAAanahu Allahu waqala laattakhithanna min AAibadika naseeban mafroodan 119. Walaodillannahum walaomanniyannahum walaamurannahum falayubattikunna athana alanAAami walaamurannahum falayughayyirunna khalqa Allahi waman yattakhithi alshshaytana waliyyan min dooni Allahi faqad khasira khusranan mubeenan 120. YaAAiduhum wayumanneehim wama yaAAiduhumu alshshaytanu illa ghurooran 121.

Ola-ika ma/wahum jahannamu wala yajidoona AAanha maheesan 122. Waallatheena amanoo waAAamiloo alssalihati sanudkhiluhum jannatin tajree min tahtiha alanharu khalideena feeha abadan waAAda Allahi haqqan waman asdaqu mina Allahi qeelan

Tafsir Ibn Kathir

Shirk Shall not be Forgiven, in Reality the Idolators Worship Shaytan

We talked about Allah's statement,

(Verily, Allah forgives not (the sin of) setting up partners (in worship) with Him, but He forgives whom He wills, sins other than that,) before and mentioned the relevant Hadiths in the beginning of this Surah. Allah's statement,

(and whoever sets up partners in worship with Allah, has indeed strayed far away.) means, he will have taken other than the true path, deviated from guidance and righteousness, destroyed himself in this life and the Hereafter, and lost contentment in this life and the Hereafter. Juwaybir said that Ad-Dahhak said about Allah's statement,

(They invoke nothing but female deities besides Him (Allah),) "The idolators claimed that the angels are Allah's daughters, saying, `We only worship them so that they bring us closer to Allah.' So they took the angels as gods, made the shapes of girls and decided, `These (idols) resemble the daughters of Allah (i.e., the angels), Whom we worship.'" This is similar to Allah's statements,

(Have you then considered Al-Lat and Al-`Uzza)

(And they make the angels who themselves are servants of the Most Gracious (Allah) females) and,

(And they have invented a kinship between Him and the Jinn). Allah's statement,

(and they invoke nothing but Shaytan, a persistent rebel!) means, Shaytan has commanded them to do this and made it seem fair and beautiful in their eyes. Consequently, they are worshipping Shaytan in reality, just as Allah said in another Ayah,

(Did I not command you, O Children of Adam, that you should not worship Shaytan) Allah said that, on the Day of Resurrection, the angels shall proclaim about the idolators who worshipped them in this life:

(Nay, but they used to worship the Jinn; most of them were believers in them). Allah's statement,

(Allah cursed him), means, He expelled him and banished him from His mercy and His grace.

(I will take an appointed portion of your servants) means, a fixed and known share. Muqatil bin Hayyan commented, "From every one thousand, nine hundred and ninety-nine will go to the Fire and one to Paradise."

(Verily, I will mislead them) from the true path,

(and surely, I will arouse in them false desires;) tempting them to feign repentance, arousing false hopes in them, encouraging them to delay and procrastinate with righteous deeds, deceiving them.

(and certainly, I will order them to slit the ears of cattle,) meaning, slitting their ears to designate them as Bahirah, Sa'ibah, and a Wasilah, as Qatadah and As-Suddi stated.

(And indeed I will order them to change the nature created by Allah.) means tattooing, according to Al-Hasan bin Abi Al-Hasan Al-Basri. In his Sahih, Muslim recorded the prohibition of tattooing the face, which in one of its wordings states: "May Allah curse whoever does this." It is also recorded in the Sahih that Ibn Mas`ud said, "May Allah curse those who have tattoos and those who do it, who pluck their (facial) hairs and the one who does it for them, and those who make spaces between their teeth for the purpose of beauty, changing what Allah has created." He then said, "Why should not I curse whom the Messenger of Allah has cursed, when the Book of Allah commands it," referring to the Ayah,

(And whatsoever the Messenger gives you, take it; and whatsoever he forbids you, abstain (from it)). Allah's statement,

(And whoever takes Shaytan as a Wali (protector or helper) instead of Allah, has surely suffered a manifest loss.) means, he will have lost this life and the Hereafter. Indeed, this is a type of loss that cannot be compensated or restored. Allah's statement,

(He (Shaytan) makes promises to them, and arouses in them false desires;) explains the true reality. Surely, Shaytan deceitfully promises his supporters and tempts them into believing that they are winners in this and the Hereafter. This is why Allah said,

(and Shaytan's promises are nothing but deceptions.) Allah states that on the Day of Return,

(And Shaytan will say when the matter has been decided: "Verily, Allah promised you a promise of truth. And I too promised you, but I betrayed you. I had no authority over you), until,

(Verily, there is a painful torment for the wrongdoers.) Allah's statement,

(of such (people)) refers to those who like and prefer what Shaytan is promising and assuring them of,

(The dwelling of such (people) is Hell), as their destination and abode on the Day of Resurrection,

(and they will find no way of escape from it.), meaning, they will not be able to avoid, avert, evade or elude the Hellfire.

The Reward of Righteous Believers

Allah then mentions the condition of the content righteous believers and the perfect honor they will earn in the end. Allah said,

(And those who believe and do righteous good deeds,) meaning, their hearts were truthful and their limbs obedient with the righteous acts they were commanded, all the while abandoning the evil they were prohibited from doing.

(We shall admit them to Gardens under which rivers flow (Paradise)) meaning, they will think of where they want these rivers to flow and they will flow there,

(to dwell therein forever), without end or being removed from it.

(Allah's promise is the truth), meaning, this is a true promise from Allah, and verily, Allah's promise shall come to pass. Allah then said,

(and whose words can be truer than those of Allah) meaning, none is more truthful in statement and narration than Allah. There is no deity worthy of worship, or Lord except Him. The Messenger of Allah used to proclaim in his speech,

«إِنَّ أَصْدَقَ الْحَدِيثِ كَلَامُ اللهِ، وَخَيْرَ الْهَدْيِ هَدْيُ مُحَمَّدٍ صلى الله عليه وسلم، وَشَرَّ الْأُمُورِ مُحْدَثَاتُهَا، وَكُلَّ مُحْدَثَةٍ بِدْعَةٌ، وَكُلَّ بِدْعَةٍ ضَلَالَةٌ، وَكُلَّ ضَلَالَةٍ فِي النَّارِ»

(The most truthful speech is Allah's Speech, and the best guidance is the guidance of Muhammad. The worst matters are the newly invented (in religion), every newly invented matter is an innovation, and every innovation is a heresy, and every heresy is in the Fire.)

Surah: 4 Ayah: 123, Ayah: 124, Ayah: 125 & Ayah: 126

﴿ لَيْسَ بِأَمَانِيِّكُمْ وَلَا أَمَانِيِّ أَهْلِ ٱلْكِتَٰبِ مَن يَعْمَلْ سُوٓءًا يُجْزَ بِهِۦ وَلَا يَجِدْ لَهُۥ مِن دُونِ ٱللَّهِ وَلِيًّا وَلَا نَصِيرًا ﴾

123. It will not be in accordance with your desires (Muslims), nor those of the people of the Scripture (Jews and Christians), whosoever works evil, will have the recompense thereof, and he will not find any protector or helper besides Allâh.

﴿ وَمَن يَعْمَلْ مِنَ ٱلصَّٰلِحَٰتِ مِن ذَكَرٍ أَوْ أُنثَىٰ وَهُوَ مُؤْمِنٌ فَأُوْلَٰٓئِكَ يَدْخُلُونَ ٱلْجَنَّةَ وَلَا يُظْلَمُونَ نَقِيرًا ﴾

Chapter 4: An-Nisaa (The Women), Verses 024-147

124. And whoever does righteous good deeds, male or female, and is a (true) believer (in the Oneness of Allâh (Muslim)) such will enter Paradise and not the least injustice, even to the size of a speck on the back of a date-stone, will be done to them.

﴿ وَمَنْ أَحْسَنُ دِينًا مِمَّنْ أَسْلَمَ وَجْهَهُ لِلَّهِ وَهُوَ مُحْسِنٌ وَٱتَّبَعَ مِلَّةَ إِبْرَٰهِيمَ حَنِيفًا وَٱتَّخَذَ ٱللَّهُ إِبْرَٰهِيمَ خَلِيلًا ﴾ ۱۲۵

125. And who can be better in religion than one who submits his face (himself) to Allâh (i.e. follows Allâh's Religion of Islâmic Monotheism); and he is a Muhsin (a good-doer - see V.2:112). And follows the religion of Ibrâhîm (Abraham) Hanîfa (Islâmic Monotheism - to worship none but Allâh Alone). And Allâh did take Ibrâhîm (Abraham) as a Khalil (an intimate friend)!

﴿ وَلِلَّهِ مَا فِى ٱلسَّمَٰوَٰتِ وَمَا فِى ٱلْأَرْضِ وَكَانَ ٱللَّهُ بِكُلِّ شَىْءٍ مُّحِيطًا ﴾ ۱۲٦

126. And to Allâh belongs all that is in the heavens and all that is in the earth. And Allâh is Ever Encompassing all things.

Transliteration

123. Laysa bi-amaniyyikum wala amaniyyi ahli alkitabi man yaAAmal soo-an yujza bihi wala yajid lahu min dooni Allahi waliyyan wala naseeran 124. Waman yaAAmal mina alssalihati min thakarin aw ontha wahuwa mu/minun faola-ika yadkhuloona aljannata wala yuthlamoona naqeeran 125. Waman ahsanu deenan mimman aslama wajhahu lillahi wahuwa muhsinun waittabaAAa millata ibraheema haneefan waittakhatha Allahu ibraheema khaleelan 126. Walillahi ma fee alssamawati wama fee al-ardi wakana Allahu bikulli shay-in muheetan

Tafsir Ibn Kathir

Success is Only Achieved by Performing Righteous Deeds, not Wishful Thinking

Qatadah said, "We were told that the Muslims and the People of the Scriptures mentioned their own virtues to each other. People of the Scriptures said, `Our Prophet came before your Prophet and our Book before your Book. Therefore, we should have more right to Allah than you have.' Muslims said, `Rather, we have more right to Allah than you, our Prophet is the Final Prophet and our Book supersedes all the Books before it.' Allah sent down,

(It will not be in accordance with your desires (Muslims), nor those of the People of the Scripture (Jews and Christians), whosoever works evil, will have the recompense thereof),

(And who can be better in religion than one who submits his face (himself) to Allah; and he is a Muhsin.) Allah then supported the argument of the Muslims against their opponents of the other religions." Similar statements were attributed to As-Suddi,

Masruq, Ad-Dahhak and Abu Salih. Al-`Awfi reported that Ibn `Abbas commented on this Ayah (4:123), "The followers of various religions disputed, the people of the Tawrah said, `Our Book is the best Book and our Prophet (Musa) is the best Prophet.' The people of the Injil said similarly, the people of Islam said, `There is no religion except Islam, our Book has abrogated every other Book, our Prophet is the Final Prophet, and you were commanded to believe in your Books and adhere to our Book.' Allah judged between them, saying,

(It will not be in accordance with your desires, nor those of the People of the Scripture, whosoever works evil, will have the recompense thereof)." This Ayah indicates that the religion is not accepted on account of wishful thinking or mere hopes. Rather, the accepted religion relies on what resides in the heart and which is made truthful through actions. It is not true that when one utters a claim to something, he attains it merely on account of his claim. It is not true that every person who claims to be on the truth is considered as such, merely on account of his words, until his claim gains merit with proof from Allah. Hence Allah's statement,

(It will not be in accordance with your desires, nor those of the People of the Scripture, whosoever works evil, will have the recompense thereof), meaning safety will not be acquired by you or them just by wishful thinking. Rather, the key is in obeying Allah and following what He has legislated through the words of His honorable Messengers. This is why Allah said afterwards,

(whosoever works evil, will have the recompense thereof,) Similarly, Allah said,

(So whosoever does good equal to the weight of an atom, shall see it. And whosoever does evil equal to the weight of an atom, shall see it.) and it was reported that when these Ayat were revealed, they became hard on many Companions. Ibn Abi Hatim recorded that `A'ishah said, "I said, `O Messenger of Allah! I know the hardest Ayah in the Qur'an.' He said, `What is it, O `A'ishah!' I said,

(whoever works evil, will have the recompense thereof,) He said,

«هُوَ مَا يُصِيبُ الْعَبْدَ الْمُؤْمِنَ، حَتَّى النَّكْبَةِ يُنْكَبُهَا»

(That is what strikes the believing servant, even the problems that bother him.)" Ibn Jarir and Abu Dawud also recorded this Hadith. Sa`id bin Mansur recorded that Abu Hurayrah said, "When the Ayah,

(whosoever works evil, will have the recompense thereof,) was revealed, it was hard on Muslims. The Messenger of Allah said to them,

«سَدِّدُوا وَقَارِبُوا، فَإِنَّ فِي كُلِّ مَا يُصَابُ بِهِ الْمُسْلِمُ كَفَّارَةً، حَتَّى الشَّوْكَةِ يُشَاكُهَا، وَالنَّكْبَةِ يُنْكَبُهَا»

Chapter 4: An-Nisaa (The Women), Verses 024-147

(Be steadfast and seek closeness. Everything that afflicts the Muslim, even the thorn that pierces his skin and the hardship he suffers, will be an expiation for him.)" This is the wording collected by Ahmad through Sufyan bin `Uyaynah. Muslim and At-Tirmidhi also recorded it. Allah's statement,

(and he will not find any protector or helper besides Allah,) `Ali bin Abi Talhah reported that Ibn `Abbas said; "Unless he repents and Allah forgives him." Ibn Abi Hatim recorded it. Allah then said,

(And whoever does righteous good deeds, male or female, and is a believer). Allah mentions the recompense for evil actions and that He will surely inflict its punishment on the servant, either in this life, which is better for him, or in the Hereafter, we seek refuge with Allah from this end. We also beg Allah for our well-being in this life and the Hereafter and for His forgiveness, mercy and pardon. Allah then mentions His kindness, generosity and mercy in accepting the good deeds from His servants, whether male or female, with the condition that they embrace the faith. He also stated that He will admit the believers into Paradise and will not withhold any of their righteous deeds, even the weight of a Naqir - speck on the back of a date-stone. Earlier, we discussed the Fatil - the scalish thread in the long slit of a date-stone, and both of these, along with the Qitmir -- the thin membrane over the date-stone were mentioned in the Qur'an. Allah then said,

(And who can be better in religion than one who submits his face to Allah.) meaning, performs the good actions in sincerity for his Lord with faith and awaiting the reward with Allah,

(and he is a Muhsin) following the correct guidance that Allah legislated in the religion of truth which He sent His Messenger with. These are the two conditions, in the absence of which no deed will be accepted from anyone; sincerity and correctness. The work is sincere when it is performed for Allah alone and it becomes correct when it conforms to the Shari`ah. So, the deed becomes outwardly correct with following the Sunnah and inwardly correct with sincerity. When any deed lacks either of these two conditions, the deed becomes null and void. For instance, when one lacks the pillar of sincerity in his work, he becomes a hypocrite who shows off for people. Whoever does not follow the Shari`ah, he becomes an ignorant, wicked person. When one combines both pillars, his actions will be the deeds of the faithful believers whose best deeds are accepted from them and their errors erased. Consequently, Allah said,

(And follows the religion of Ibrahim the Hanif (Monotheist).) referring to Muhammad and his following, until the Day of Resurrection. Allah said,

(Verily, among mankind who have the best claim to Ibrahim are those who followed him, and this Prophet), and,

(Then, We have sent the Revelation to you (saying): "Follow the religion of Ibrahim the Hanif (Monotheist) and he was not of the Mushrikin). The Hanif, intentionally and with knowledge, avoids Shirk, he goes attentively to the truth, allowing no one to hinder him or stop him from it.

Ibrahim is Allah's Khalil

Allah's statement,

(And Allah did take Ibrahim as a Khalil (an intimate friend)!) encourages following Ibrahim Al-Khalil, because he was and still is an Imam whose conduct is followed and imitated. Indeed, Ibrahim reached the ultimate closeness to Allah that the servants seek, for he attained the grade of Khalil, which is the highest grade of love. He acquired all this due to his obedience to His Lord, just as Allah has described him,

(And of Ibrahim, the one who fulfilled),

(And (remember) when the Lord of Ibrahim tried him with (certain) commands, which he fulfilled), and,

(Verily, Ibrahim was an Ummah, obedient to Allah, a Hanif, and he was not one of the Mushrikin). Al-Bukhari recorded that `Amr bin Maymun said that when Mu`adh came back from Yemen, he led them in the Fajr prayer and recited,

(And Allah did take Ibrahim as a Khalil!) One of the men present commented, "Surely, the eye of Ibrahim's mother has been comforted." Ibrahim was called Allah's Khalil due to his Lord's great love towards him, on account of the acts of obedience he performed that Allah loves and prefers. We should mention here that in the Two Sahihs, it is recorded that Abu Sa`id Al-Khudri said that when the Messenger of Allah gave them his last speech, he said,

«أَمَّا بَعْدُ، أَيُّهَا النَّاسُ فَلَوْ كُنْتُ مُتَّخِذًا مِنْ أَهْلِ الْأَرْضِ خَلِيلًا، لَاتَّخَذْتُ أَبَا بَكْرِ ابْنَ أَبِي قُحَافَةَ خَلِيلًا، وَلكِنْ صَاحِبُكُمْ خَلِيلُ الله»

(O people! If I were to take a Khalil from the people of the earth, I would have taken Abu Bakr bin Abi Quhafah as my Khalil. However, your companion (meaning himself) is the Khalil of Allah.) Jundub bin `Abdullah Al-Bajali, `Abdullah bin `Amr bin Al-`As and `Abdullah bin Mas`ud narrated that the Prophet said,

«إِنَّ اللهَ اتَّخَذَنِي خَلِيلًا، كَمَا اتَّخَذَ إِبْرَاهِيمَ خَلِيلًا»

(Allah has chosen me as His Khalil, just as He has chosen Ibrahim as His Khalil.) Allah's statement,

(And to Allah belongs all that is in the heavens and all that is in the earth.) means, everything and everyone are His property, servants and creation, and He has full authority over all of this. There is no one who can avert Allah's decision or question His judgment. He is never asked about what He does due to His might, ability, fairness, wisdom, compassion and mercy. Allah's statement,

Chapter 4: An-Nisaa (The Women), Verses 024-147   131

(And Allah is Ever Encompassing all things.) means, His knowledge encompasses everything and nothing concerning His servants is ever hidden from Him. Nothing, even the weight of an atom, ever escapes His observation in the heavens and earth, nor anything smaller or bigger than that.

Surah: 4 Ayah: 127

﴿ وَيَسْتَفْتُونَكَ فِى ٱلنِّسَآءِ قُلِ ٱللَّهُ يُفْتِيكُمْ فِيهِنَّ وَمَا يُتْلَىٰ عَلَيْكُمْ فِى ٱلْكِتَٰبِ فِى يَتَٰمَى ٱلنِّسَآءِ ٱلَّٰتِى لَا تُؤْتُونَهُنَّ مَا كُتِبَ لَهُنَّ وَتَرْغَبُونَ أَن تَنكِحُوهُنَّ وَٱلْمُسْتَضْعَفِينَ مِنَ ٱلْوِلْدَٰنِ وَأَن تَقُومُوا۟ لِلْيَتَٰمَىٰ بِٱلْقِسْطِ وَمَا تَفْعَلُوا۟ مِنْ خَيْرٍ فَإِنَّ ٱللَّهَ كَانَ بِهِۦ عَلِيمًا ﴿١٢٧﴾ ﴾

127. They ask your legal instruction concerning women, say: Allâh instructs you about them, and about what is recited unto you in the Book concerning the orphan girls whom you give not the prescribed portions (as regards Mahr and inheritance) and yet whom you desire to marry, and (concerning) the children who are weak and oppressed, and that you stand firm for justice to orphans. And whatever good you do, Allâh is Ever All-Aware of it.

Transliteration

127. Wayastaftoonaka fee alnnisa-i quli Allahu yufteekum feehinna wama yutla AAalaykum fee alkitabi fee yatama alnnisa-i allatee la tu/toonahunna ma kutiba lahunna watarghaboona an tankihoohunna waalmustadAAafeena mina alwildani waan taqoomoo lilyatama bialqisti wama tafAAaloo min khayrin fa-inna Allaha kana bihi AAaleeman

Tafsir Ibn Kathir

The Ruling Concerning Female Orphans

Al-Bukhari recorded that `A'ishah said about the Ayah,

(They ask your instruction concerning women. Say, "Allah instructs you about them...) until,

(whom you desire to marry...) "It is about the man who is taking care of a female orphan, being her caretaker and inheritor. Her money is joined with his money to such an extent, that she shares with him even the branch of a date that he has. So he likes (for material gain) to marry her himself, and hates to marry her to another man who would have a share in his money, on account of her share in his money. Therefore, he refuses to let her marry anyone else. So, this Ayah was revealed.'' Muslim also recorded it. Ibn Abi Hatim recorded that `A'ishah said, "The people asked Allah's Messenger (about orphan girls), so Allah revealed,

(They ask your instruction concerning women. Say, "Allah instructs you about them and about what is recited unto you in the Book...") What is meant by Allah's saying, `And about what is recited unto you in the Book' is the former verse which said,

(If you fear that you shall not be able to deal justly with the orphan girls, then marry (other) women of your choice.)" `A'ishah said, "Allah's statement,

(whom you desire to marry...) also refers to the desire of the guardian not to marry an orphan girl under his supervision when she lacks property or beauty. The guardians were forbidden to marry their orphan girls possessing property and beauty without being just to them, as they generally refrain from marrying them (when they are neither beautiful nor wealthy)." The basis of this is recorded in Two Sahihs. Consequently, when a man is the caretaker of a female orphan, he might like to marry her himself. In this case, Allah commands him to give her a suitable dowry that other women of her status get. If he does not want to do that, then let him marry other women, for Allah has made this matter easy for Muslims. Sometimes, the caretaker does not desire to marry the orphan under his care, because she is not attractive to his eye. In this case, Allah forbids the caretaker from preventing the female orphan from marrying another man for fear that her husband would share in the money that is mutually shared between the caretaker and the girl. `Ali bin Abi Talhah said that Ibn `Abbas said, "During the time of Jahiliyyah, the caretaker of a female orphan would cover her with his rope, and when he did that, no man would marry her. If she was beautiful and he desired to marry her, he married her and took control of her wealth. If she was not beautiful, he did not allow her to marry until she died, and when she died he inherited her money. Allah prohibited and outlawed this practice. " He also said about Allah's statement,

(and the children who are weak and oppressed,) that during the time of Jahiliyyah, they used to deny young children and females a share of inheritance. So Allah's statement,

(you give not what they deserve) thus prohibiting this practice and designating a fixed share for each,

(To the male, a portion equal to that of two females..) whether they were young or old, as Sa`id bin Jubayr and others stated. Sa`id bin Jubayr said about Allah's statement,

(and that you stand firm for justice to orphans.) "Just as when she is beautiful and wealthy you would want to marry her and have her for yourself, so when she is not wealthy or beautiful, marry her and have her for yourself." Allah's statement,

r(And whatever good you do, Allah is Ever All-Aware of it.) encourages performing the good deeds and fulfilling the commandments, and states that Allah is knowledgeable of all of this and He will reward for it in the best and most perfect manner.

Chapter 4: An-Nisaa (The Women), Verses 024-147   133

Surah: 4 Ayah: 128, Ayah: 129 & Ayah: 130

﴿ وَإِنِ ٱمْرَأَةٌ خَافَتْ مِنۢ بَعْلِهَا نُشُوزًا أَوْ إِعْرَاضًا فَلَا جُنَاحَ عَلَيْهِمَآ أَن يُصْلِحَا بَيْنَهُمَا صُلْحًا ۚ وَٱلصُّلْحُ خَيْرٌ ۗ وَأُحْضِرَتِ ٱلْأَنفُسُ ٱلشُّحَّ ۚ وَإِن تُحْسِنُوا۟ وَتَتَّقُوا۟ فَإِنَّ ٱللَّهَ كَانَ بِمَا تَعْمَلُونَ خَبِيرًا ۝ ﴾

128. And if a woman fears cruelty or desertion on her husband's part, there is no sin on them both if they make terms of peace between themselves; and making peace is better. And human inner-selves are swayed by greed. But if you do good and keep away from evil, verily, Allâh is Ever Well-Acquainted with what you do.

﴿ وَلَن تَسْتَطِيعُوٓا۟ أَن تَعْدِلُوا۟ بَيْنَ ٱلنِّسَآءِ وَلَوْ حَرَصْتُمْ ۖ فَلَا تَمِيلُوا۟ كُلَّ ٱلْمَيْلِ فَتَذَرُوهَا كَٱلْمُعَلَّقَةِ ۚ وَإِن تُصْلِحُوا۟ وَتَتَّقُوا۟ فَإِنَّ ٱللَّهَ كَانَ غَفُورًا رَّحِيمًا ۝ ﴾

129. You will never be able to do perfect justice between wives even if it is your ardent desire, so do not incline too much to one of them (by giving her more of your time and provision) so as to leave the other hanging (i.e. neither divorced nor married). And if you do justice, and do all that is right and fear Allâh by keeping away from all that is wrong, then Allâh is Ever Oft-Forgiving, Most Merciful.

﴿ وَإِن يَتَفَرَّقَا يُغْنِ ٱللَّهُ كُلًّا مِّن سَعَتِهِۦ ۚ وَكَانَ ٱللَّهُ وَٰسِعًا حَكِيمًا ۝ ﴾

130. But if they separate (by divorce), Allâh will provide abundance for everyone of them from His Bounty. And Allâh is Ever All-Sufficient for His creatures' need, All-Wise.

Transliteration

128. Wa-ini imraatun khafat min baAAliha nushoozan aw iAAradan fala junaha AAalayhima an yusliha baynahuma sulhan waalssulhu khayrun waohdirati al-anfusu alshshuhha wa-in tuhsinoo watattaqoo fa-inna Allaha kana bima taAAmaloona khabeeran 129. Walan tastateeAAoo an taAAdiloo bayna alnnisa-i walaw harastum fala tameeloo kulla almayli fatatharooha kaalmuAAallaqati wa-in tuslihoo watattaqoo fa-inna Allaha kana ghafooran raheeman 130. Wa-in yatafarraqa yughni Allahu kullan min saAAatihi wakana Allahu wasiAAan hakeeman

Tafsir Ibn Kathir

The Ruling Concerning Desertion on the Part of the Husband

Allah states, and thus legislates accordingly, that sometimes, the man inclines away from his wife, sometimes towards her and sometimes he parts with her. In the first case, when the wife fears that her husband is steering away from her or deserting her, she is allowed to forfeit all or part of her rights, such as provisions, clothing, dwelling, and so forth, and the husband is allowed to accept such concessions from her. Hence, there is no harm if she offers such concessions, and if her husband accepts them. This is why Allah said,

(there is no sin on them both if they make terms of peace between themselves;) He then said,

(and making peace is better) than divorce. Allah's statement,

(And human souls are swayed by greed.) means, coming to peaceful terms, even when it involves forfeiting some rights, is better than parting. Abu Dawud At-Tayalisi recorded that Ibn `Abbas said, "Sawdah feared that the Messenger of Allah might divorce her and she said, `O Messenger of Allah! Do not divorce me; give my day to `A'ishah.' And he did, and later on Allah sent down,

(And if a woman fears cruelty or desertion on her husband's part, there is no sin on them both) Ibn `Abbas said, "Whatever (legal agreement) the spouses mutually agree to is allowed.". At-Tirmidhi recorded it and said, "Hasan Gharib". In the Two Sahihs, it is recorded that `A'ishah said that when Sawdah bint Zam`ah became old, she forfeited her day to `A'ishah, and the Prophet used to spend Sawdah's night with `A'ishah. There is a similar narration also collected by Al-Bukhari. Al-Bukhari also recorded that `A'ishah commented;

(And if a woman fears cruelty or desertion on her husband's part), that it refers to, "A man who is married to an old woman, and he does not desire her and wants to divorce her. So she says, `I forfeit my right on you.' So this Ayah was revealed."

Meaning of "Making Peace is Better

Allah said,

(And making peace is better). `Ali bin Abi Talhah related that Ibn `Abbas said that the Ayah refers to, "When the husband gives his wife the choice between staying with him or leaving him, as this is better than the husband preferring other wives to her." However, the apparent wording of the Ayah refers to the settlement where the wife forfeits some of the rights she has over her husband, with the husband agreeing to this concession, and that this settlement is better than divorce. For instance, the Prophet kept Sawdah bint Zam`ah as his wife after she offered to forfeit her day for `A'ishah. By keeping her among his wives, his Ummah may follow this kind of settlement. Since settlement and peace are better with Allah than parting, Allah said,

(and making peace is better). Divorce is not preferred with Allah. The meaning of Allah's statement,

(But if you do good and have Taqwa, verily, Allah is Ever Well-Acquainted with what you do) if you are patient with the wife you dislike and treat her as other wives are treated, then Allah knows what you do and will reward you for it perfectly. Allah's statement,

(You will never be able to do perfect justice between wives even if it is your ardent desire,) means, O people! You will never be able to be perfectly just between wives in every respect. Even when one divides the nights justly between wives, there will still be various degrees concerning love, desire and sexual intimacy, as Ibn `Abbas, `Ubaydah As-Salmani, Mujahid, Al-Hasan Al-Basri and Ad-Dahhak bin Muzahim stated. Imam Ahmad and the collectors of the Sunan recorded that `A'ishah said, "The Messenger of Allah used to treat his wives equally and proclaim,

«اللَّهُمَّ هَذَا قَسْمِي فِيمَا أَمْلِكُ، فَلَا تَلُمْنِي فِيمَا تَمْلِكُ وَلَا أَمْلِكُ»

(O Allah! This is my division in what I own, so do not blame me for what You own and I do not own) referring to his heart. This was the wording that Abu Dawud collected, and its chain of narrators is Sahih. Allah's statement,

(so do not incline too much to one of them) means, when you like one of your wives more than others, do not exaggerate in treating her that way,

(so as to leave the other hanging.) referring to the other wives. Ibn `Abbas, Mujahid, Sa`id bin Jubayr, Al-Hasan, Ad-Dahhak, Ar-Rabi` bin Anas, As-Suddi and Muqatil bin Hayyan said that Mu`allaqah (hanging) means, "She is neither divorced nor married." Abu Dawud At-Tayalisi recorded that Abu Hurayrah said that the Messenger of Allah said,

«مَنْ كَانَتْ لَهُ امْرَأَتَانِ فَمَالَ إِلَى إِحْدَاهُمَا، جَاءَ يَوْمَ الْقِيَامَةِ وَأَحَدُ شِقَّيْهِ سَاقِطٌ»

(Whoever has two wives and inclines to one of them (too much), will come on the Day of Resurrection with one of his sides dragging.) Allah's statement,

(And if you do justice, and do all that is right and have Taqwa, then Allah is Ever Oft-Forgiving, Most Merciful.) The Ayah states: If you do justice and divide equally in what you have power over, while fearing Allah in all conditions, then Allah will forgive you the favoritism that you showed to some of your wives. Allah then said,

(But if they separate (divorce), Allah will provide abundance for everyone of them from His bounty. And Allah is Ever All-Sufficient for His creatures' needs, All-Wise.) This is the third case between husband and wife, in which divorce occurs. Allah states that if the spouses separate by divorce, then Allah will suffice them by giving him a better wife and her a better husband. The meaning of,

(And Allah is Ever All-Sufficient for His creatures' needs, All-Wise.) is: His favor is tremendous, His bounty is enormous and He is All-Wise in all His actions, decisions and commandments.

Surah: 4 Ayah: 131, Ayah: 132, Ayah: 133 & Ayah: 134

﴿ وَلِلَّهِ مَا فِى ٱلسَّمَٰوَٰتِ وَمَا فِى ٱلْأَرْضِ ۗ وَلَقَدْ وَصَّيْنَا ٱلَّذِينَ أُوتُوا۟ ٱلْكِتَٰبَ مِن قَبْلِكُمْ وَإِيَّاكُمْ أَنِ ٱتَّقُوا۟ ٱللَّهَ ۚ وَإِن تَكْفُرُوا۟ فَإِنَّ لِلَّهِ مَا فِى ٱلسَّمَٰوَٰتِ وَمَا فِى ٱلْأَرْضِ ۚ وَكَانَ ٱللَّهُ غَنِيًّا حَمِيدًا ۝ ﴾

131. And to Allâh belongs all that is in the heavens and all that is in the earth. And verily, We have recommended to the people of the Scripture before you, and to you (O Muslims) that you (all) fear Allâh, and keep your duty to Him. But if you disbelieve, then unto Allâh belongs all that is in the heavens and all that is in the earth, and Allâh is Ever Rich (Free of all wants), Worthy of all praise.

﴿ وَلِلَّهِ مَا فِى ٱلسَّمَٰوَٰتِ وَمَا فِى ٱلْأَرْضِ ۚ وَكَفَىٰ بِٱللَّهِ وَكِيلًا ۝ ﴾

132. And to Allâh belongs all that is in the heavens and all that is in the earth. And Allâh is Ever All-Sufficient as a Disposer of affairs.

﴿ إِن يَشَأْ يُذْهِبْكُمْ أَيُّهَا ٱلنَّاسُ وَيَأْتِ بِـَٔاخَرِينَ ۚ وَكَانَ ٱللَّهُ عَلَىٰ ذَٰلِكَ قَدِيرًا ۝ ﴾

133. If He wills, He can take you away, O people, and bring others. And Allâh is Ever All-Potent over that.

﴿ مَّن كَانَ يُرِيدُ ثَوَابَ ٱلدُّنْيَا فَعِندَ ٱللَّهِ ثَوَابُ ٱلدُّنْيَا وَٱلْـَٔاخِرَةِ ۚ وَكَانَ ٱللَّهُ سَمِيعًۢا بَصِيرًا ۝ ﴾

134. Whoever desires a reward in this life of the world, then with Allâh (Alone and none else) is the reward of this worldly life and of the Hereafter. And Allâh is Ever All-Hearer, All-Seer.

Transliteration

131. Walillahi ma fee alssamawati wama fee al-ardi walaqad wassayna allatheena ootoo alkitaba min qablikum wa-iyyakum ani ittaqoo Allaha wa-in takfuroo fa-inna lillahi ma fee alssamawati wama fee alardi wakana Allahu ghaniyyan hameedan   132. Walillahi ma fee alssamawati wama fee al-ardi wakafa biAllahi wakeelan   133. In yasha/ yuthhibkum ayyuha alnnasu waya/ti bi-akhareena wakana Allahu AAala thalika qadeeran   134. Man kana yureedu thawaba aldddunya faAAinda Allahi thawabu alddunya waal-akhirati wakana Allahu sameeAAan baseeran

Tafsir Ibn Kathir

The Necessity of Taqwa of Allah

Allah states that He is the Owner of the heavens and earth and that He is the Supreme Authority over them. Hence Allah's statement,

(And verily, We have recommended to the People of the Scripture before you, and to you) meaning, We have recommended to you what We recommended to the People of Scriptures; Taqwa of Allah, by worshipping Him Alone without partners. Allah then said,

(But if you disbelieve, then unto Allah belongs all that is in the heavens and all that is in the earth). In another Ayah, Allah said that Musa said to his people,

("If you disbelieve, you and all on the earth together, then verily, Allah is Rich (free of any need), Owner of all praise."). Allah said,

(So they disbelieved and turned away. But Allah was not in need (of them). And Allah is Rich (free of any need), Worthy of all praise) meaning, He is far too Rich than to need His servants, and worthy of all praise in all His decisions and commandments. The meaning of Allah's statement,

(And to Allah belongs all that is in the heavens and all that is in the earth. And Allah is Ever All-Sufficient as a Disposer of affairs.) He has perfect watch over every soul, knowing what it deserves, He is the Watcher, and Witness of all things. Allah's statement,

(If He wills, He can take you away, O people, and bring others. And Allah is Ever All-Potent over that.) means, He is able to take you away and replace you with other people if you disobey Him. In a similar Ayah, Allah said,

(And if you turn away, He will exchange you for some other people and they will not be your likes) Allah's statement,

(Whoever desires the rewards of this life, then with Allah is the reward of this worldly life and of the Hereafter.) means, O those whose ultimate desire is this life, know that Allah owns the rewards of this life and the Hereafter. Therefore, if you ask Allah for both, He will enrich you, award you and suffice for you. As Allah said,

(But of mankind there are some who say: "Our Lord! Give us in this world!" and for such there will be no portion in the Hereafter. And of them there are some who say: "Our Lord! Give us in this world that which is good and in the Hereafter that which is good, and save us from the torment of the Fire!" For them there will be alloted a share for what they have earned),

(Whosoever desires (by his deeds) the reward of the Hereafter, We give him increase in his reward), and

(Whoever desires the quick-passing (transitory enjoyment of this world), We readily grant him what We will for whom We like) until,

(See how We prefer one above another (in this world)). So Allah said here,

(And Allah is Ever All-Hearer, All-Seer.)

Surah: 4 Ayah: 135

$$\text{﴿ يَـٰٓأَيُّهَا ٱلَّذِينَ ءَامَنُوا۟ كُونُوا۟ قَوَّٰمِينَ بِٱلْقِسْطِ شُهَدَآءَ لِلَّهِ وَلَوْ عَلَىٰٓ أَنفُسِكُمْ أَوِ ٱلْوَٰلِدَيْنِ وَٱلْأَقْرَبِينَ ۚ إِن يَكُنْ غَنِيًّا أَوْ فَقِيرًا فَٱللَّهُ أَوْلَىٰ بِهِمَا ۖ فَلَا تَتَّبِعُوا۟ ٱلْهَوَىٰٓ أَن تَعْدِلُوا۟ ۚ وَإِن تَلْوُۥٓا۟ أَوْ تُعْرِضُوا۟ فَإِنَّ ٱللَّهَ كَانَ بِمَا تَعْمَلُونَ خَبِيرًا ﴾}$$

135. O you who believe! Stand out firmly for justice, as witnesses to Allâh, even though it be against yourselves, or your parents, or your kin, be he rich or poor, Allâh is a Better Protector to both (than you). So follow not the lusts (of your hearts), lest you avoid justice; and if you distort your witness or refuse to give it, verily, Allâh is Ever Well-Acquainted with what you do.

Transliteration

135. Ya ayyuha allatheena amanoo koonoo qawwameena bialqisti shuhadaa lillahi walaw AAala anfusikum awi alwalidayni waal-aqrabeena in yakun ghaniyyan aw faqeeran faAllahu awla bihima fala tattabiAAoo alhawa an taAAdiloo wa-in talwoo aw tuAAridoo fa-inna Allaha kana bima taAAmaloona khabeeran

Tafsir Ibn Kathir

Commanding Justice and Conveying the Witness for Allah

Allah commands His believing servants to stand up for justice and fairness and not to deviate from it, right or left. They should not fear the blame of anyone or allow anyone to prevent them from doing something for the sake of Allah. They are also required to help, support and aid each other for Allah's sake. Allah's statement,

(as witnesses to Allah) is similar to His statement,

(And establish the testimony for Allah). Testimony should be delivered precisely, for the sake of Allah, thus making the testimony correct, truly just, and free of alterations, changes or deletions. This is why Allah said,

(even though it be against yourselves,) meaning, give correct testimony, and say the truth when you are asked about it, even if harm will effect you as a consequence. Indeed, Allah shall make a way out and give relief for those who obey Him in every matter. Allah's statement,

(or your parents, or your kin,) means, even if you have to testify against your parents and kin, do not compromise for their sake. Rather, give the correct and just witness even if they are harmed in the process, for the truth presides above everyone and is preferred to everyone. Allah's statement,

Chapter 4: An-Nisaa (The Women), Verses 024-147   139

(be he rich or poor, Allah is a better Protector to both.) means, do not favor someone (in your testimony) because he is rich, or feel pity for him because he is poor, for Allah is their caretaker, a better Protector of them than you, and has better knowledge of what is good for them. Allah's statement,

(So follow not the lusts, lest you may avoid justice;) means, let not desire, lust or the hatred you have against others, lure you into injustice in your affairs. Rather, stand for justice in all situations. Allah said;

(And let not the enmity and hatred of others make you avoid justice. Be just: that is nearer to piety) when the Prophet sent `Abdullah bin Rawahah to collect the tax on the fruits and produce of the Jews of Khaybar, they offered him a bribe so that he would go easy on them. He said; "By Allah! I have come to you from the dearest of the creation to me (Muhammad), and you are more hated by me than an equivelent number of apes and swine. However, my love for him (the Prophet) and hatred for you shall not prevent me from being just with you." On that, they said, "This (justice) is the basis which the heavens and earth were created. " We will mention this Hadith later in Surat Al-Ma'idah (chapter 5) Allah willing. Allah's statement afterwards,

(and if you Talwu or Tu`ridu) means, "Distort your testimony and change it", according to Mujahid and several others among the Salaf. Talwu, includes distortion and intentional lying. For instance, Allah said,

(And verily, among them is a party who Yalwuna (distort) the Book with their tongues (as they read)). Tu`ridu, includes hiding and withholding the testimony. Allah said,

(Who hides it, surely, his heart is sinful) The Prophet said,

«خَيْرُ الشُّهَدَاءِ الَّذِي يَأْتِي بِشَهَادَتِهِ قَبْلَ أَنْ يُسْأَلَهَا»

(The best witness is he who discloses his testimony before being asked to do so.) Allah then warned,

(Verily, Allah is Ever Well-Acquainted with what you do.) and will reward or punish you accordingly.

Surah: 4 Ayah: 136

﴿ يَـٰٓأَيُّهَا ٱلَّذِينَ ءَامَنُوٓاْ ءَامِنُواْ بِٱللَّهِ وَرَسُولِهِۦ وَٱلۡكِتَـٰبِ ٱلَّذِى نَزَّلَ عَلَىٰ رَسُولِهِۦ وَٱلۡكِتَـٰبِ ٱلَّذِىٓ أَنزَلَ مِن قَبۡلُ ۚ وَمَن يَكۡفُرۡ بِٱللَّهِ وَمَلَـٰٓئِكَتِهِۦ وَكُتُبِهِۦ وَرُسُلِهِۦ وَٱلۡيَوۡمِ ٱلۡأٓخِرِ فَقَدۡ ضَلَّ ضَلَـٰلَۢا بَعِيدًا ﴿١٣٦﴾ ﴾

136. O you who believe! Believe in Allâh, and His Messenger (Muhammad (peace be upon him)) and the Book (the Qur'ân) which He has sent down to His Messenger, and the Scripture which He sent down to those before (him); and whosoever

disbelieves in Allâh, His Angels, His Books, His Messengers, and the Last Day, then indeed he has strayed far away.

Transliteration

136. Ya ayyuha allatheena amanoo aminoo biAllahi warasoolihi waalkitabi allathee nazzala AAala rasoolihi waalkitabi allathee anzala min qablu waman yakfur biAllahi wamala-ikatihi wakutubihi warusulihi waalyawmi al-akhiri faqad dalla dalalan baAAeedan

Tafsir Ibn Kathir

The Order to Have Faith after Believing

Allah commands His faithful servants to adhere to all the elements of faith, its branches, pillars and cornerstones. This is not stated as mere redundancy, but from the view of completing faith and the continual maintenance of it. For instance, the believer proclaims in every prayer,

(Guide us to the straight way.) which means, make us aware of the straight path and increase us in guidance and strengthen us on it. In this Ayah (4:136), Allah commands the believers to believe in Him and in His Messenger, just as He said elsewhere,

(O you who believe! Have Taqwa of Allah, and believe in His Messenger,). Allah's statement,

(and the Book which He has sent down to His Messenger,) refers to the Qur'an, while,

(and the Scripture which He sent down to those before (him);) refers to the previously revealed divine Books. Allah then said,

(and whosoever disbelieves in Allah, His Angels, His Books, His Messengers, and the Last Day, then indeed he has strayed far away.) meaning, he will have deviated from the correct guidance and strayed far away from its path.

Surah: 4 Ayah: 137, Ayah: 138, Ayah: 139 & Ayah: 140

﴿ إِنَّ ٱلَّذِينَ ءَامَنُواْ ثُمَّ كَفَرُواْ ثُمَّ ءَامَنُواْ ثُمَّ كَفَرُواْ ثُمَّ ٱزْدَادُواْ كُفْرًا لَّمْ يَكُنِ ٱللَّهُ لِيَغْفِرَ لَهُمْ وَلَا لِيَهْدِيَهُمْ سَبِيلًا ﴿١٣٧﴾

137. Verily, those who believe, then disbelieve, then believe (again), and (again) disbelieve, and go on increasing in disbelief; Allâh will not forgive them, nor guide them on the (Right) Way.

﴿ بَشِّرِ ٱلْمُنَٰفِقِينَ بِأَنَّ لَهُمْ عَذَابًا أَلِيمًا ﴿١٣٨﴾ ﴾

138. Give to the hypocrites the tidings that there is for them a painful torment.

Chapter 4: An-Nisaa (The Women), Verses 024-147   141

﴿ ٱلَّذِينَ يَتَّخِذُونَ ٱلْكَٰفِرِينَ أَوْلِيَآءَ مِن دُونِ ٱلْمُؤْمِنِينَ ۚ أَيَبْتَغُونَ عِندَهُمُ ٱلْعِزَّةَ فَإِنَّ ٱلْعِزَّةَ لِلَّهِ جَمِيعًا ﴾ ﴿١٣٩﴾

139. Those who take disbelievers for Auliyâ' (protectors or helpers or friends) instead of believers, do they seek honor, power and glory with them? Verily, then to Allâh belongs all honor, power and glory.

﴿ وَقَدْ نَزَّلَ عَلَيْكُمْ فِى ٱلْكِتَٰبِ أَنْ إِذَا سَمِعْتُمْ ءَايَٰتِ ٱللَّهِ يُكْفَرُ بِهَا وَيُسْتَهْزَأُ بِهَا فَلَا تَقْعُدُواْ مَعَهُمْ حَتَّىٰ يَخُوضُواْ فِى حَدِيثٍ غَيْرِهِۦۤ ۚ إِنَّكُمْ إِذًا مِّثْلُهُمْ ۗ إِنَّ ٱللَّهَ جَامِعُ ٱلْمُنَٰفِقِينَ وَٱلْكَٰفِرِينَ فِى جَهَنَّمَ جَمِيعًا ﴾ ﴿١٤٠﴾

140. And it has already been revealed to you in the Book (this Qur'ân) that when you hear the Verses of Allâh being denied and mocked at, then sit not with them, until they engage in a talk other than that; (but if you stayed with them) certainly in that case you would be like them. Surely, Allâh will collect the hypocrites and disbelievers all together in Hell.

Transliteration

137. Inna allatheena amanoo thumma kafaroo thumma amanoo thumma kafaroo thumma izdadoo kufran lam yakuni Allahu liyaghfira lahum wala liyahdiyahum sabeelan   138. Bashshiri almunafiqeena bi-anna lahum AAathaban aleeman   139. Allatheena yattakhithoona alkafireena awliyaa min dooni almu/mineena ayabtaghoona AAindahumu alAAizzata fa-inna alAAizzata lillahi jameeAAan   140. Waqad nazzala AAalaykum fee alkitabi an itha samiAAtum ayati Allahi yukfaru biha wayustahzao biha fala taqAAudoo maAAahum hatta yakhoodoo fee hadeethin ghayrihi innakum ithan mithluhum inna Allaha jamiAAu almunafiqeena waalkafireena fee jahannama jameeAAan

Tafsir Ibn Kathir

Characteristics of the Hypocrites and Their Destination

Allah states that whoever embraces the faith, reverts from it, embraces it again, reverts from it and remains on disbelief and increases in it until death, then he will never have a chance to gain accepted repentance after death. Nor will Allah forgive him, or deliver him from his plight to the path of correct guidance. This is why Allah said,

(Allah will not forgive them, nor guide them on the (right) way). Ibn Abi Hatim recorded that his father said that Ahmad bin `Abdah related that Hafs bin Jami' said that Samak said that `Ikrimah reported that Ibn `Abbas commented;

(and go on increasing in disbelief), "They remain on disbelief until they die." Mujahid said similarly. Allah then said,

(Give to the hypocrites the tidings that there is for them a painful torment.) Hence, the hypocrites have this characteristic, for they believe, then disbelieve, and this is why their hearts become sealed. Allah describes the hypocrites as taking the disbelievers as friends instead of the believers, meaning they are the disbelievers' supporters in reality, for they give them their loyalty and friendship in secret. They also say to disbelievers when they are alone with them, "We are with you, we only mock the believers by pretending to follow their religion." Allah said, while chastising them for being friends with the disbelievers,

(do they seek honor, with them) Allah then states that honor, power and glory is for Him Alone without partners, and for those whom Allah grants such qualities to. Allah said,

(Whosoever desires honor, then to Allah belong all honor), and,

(But honor belongs to Allah, and to His Messenger, and to the believers, but the hypocrites know not). The statement that honor is Allah's Alone, is meant to encourage the servants to adhere to their servitude to Allah and to be among His faithful servants who will gain victory in this life and when the Witnesses stand up to testify on the Day of Resurection. Allah's statement,

(And it has already been revealed to you in the Book that when you hear the verses of Allah being denied and mocked at, then sit not with them, until they engage in talk other than that; certainly in that case you would be like them.) The Ayah means, if you still commit this prohibition after being aware of its prohibition, sitting with them where Allah's Ayat are rejected, mocked at and denied, and you sanction such conduct, then you have participated with them in what they are doing. So Allah said,

((But if you stayed with them) certainly in that case you would be like them.) concerning the burden they will earn. What has already been revealed in the Book -- as the Ayah says -- is the Ayah in Surat Al-An`am (6), which was revealed in Makkah,

(And when you see those who engage in false conversation about Our verses (of the Qur'an) by mocking at them, stay away from them). Muqatil bin Hayyan said that this Ayah (4:140) abrogated the Ayah in Surat Al-An`am, referring to the part that says here,

((But if you stayed with them) certainly in that case you would be like them), and Allah's statement in Al-An`am,

(Those who fear Allah, keep their duty to Him and avoid evil, are not responsible for them (the disbelievers) in any case, but (their duty) is to remind them, that they may have Taqwa). Allah's statement,

(Surely, Allah will collect the hypocrites and disbelievers all together in Hell.) means, just as the hypocrites participate in the Kufr of disbelievers, Allah will join them all together to reside in the Fire for eternity, dwelling in torment, punishment, enchained, restrained and in drinking boiling water.

Chapter 4: An-Nisaa (The Women), Verses 024-147

Surah: 4 Ayah: 141

﴿ ٱلَّذِينَ يَتَرَبَّصُونَ بِكُمْ فَإِن كَانَ لَكُمْ فَتْحٌ مِّنَ ٱللَّهِ قَالُوٓاْ أَلَمْ نَكُن مَّعَكُمْ وَإِن كَانَ لِلْكَٰفِرِينَ نَصِيبٌ قَالُوٓاْ أَلَمْ نَسْتَحْوِذْ عَلَيْكُمْ وَنَمْنَعْكُم مِّنَ ٱلْمُؤْمِنِينَ ۚ فَٱللَّهُ يَحْكُمُ بَيْنَكُمْ يَوْمَ ٱلْقِيَٰمَةِ ۗ وَلَن يَجْعَلَ ٱللَّهُ لِلْكَٰفِرِينَ عَلَى ٱلْمُؤْمِنِينَ سَبِيلًا ﴾

141. Those (hypocrites) who wait and watch about you; if you gain a victory from Allâh, they say: "Were we not with you?" but if the disbelievers gain a success, they say (to them): "Did we not gain mastery over you and did we not protect you from the believers?" Allâh will judge between you (all) on the Day of Resurrection. And never will Allâh grant to the disbelievers a way (to triumph) over the believers.

Transliteration

141. Allatheena yatarabbasoona bikum fa-in kana lakum fathun mina Allahi qaloo alam nakun maAAakum wa-in kana lilkafireena naseebun qaloo alam nastahwith AAalaykum wanamnaAAkum mina almu/mineena faAllahu yahkumu baynakum yawma alqiyamati walan yajAAala Allahu lilkafireena AAala almu/mineena sabeelan

Tafsir Ibn Kathir

Hypocrites Wait and Watch what Happens to Muslims

Allah states that the hypocrites watch and await the harm that occurs to the believers, awaiting the time when the Muslim circumstances and religion are dissolved and the state of Kufr takes over.

(if you gain a victory from Allah) triumph, aid and booty,

(they say, "Were we not with you") trying to come closer to the believers with this statement. However,

(But if the disbelievers gain a success,) by gaining victory over the believers sometimes, just as occurred during Uhud, for surely, the Messengers are tested, but the final victory is theirs.

(they say (to them), "Did we not gain mastery over you and did we not protect you from the believers") meaning, did we not help you in secret and try our best to confuse the believers and weaken their resolve, until you gained victory over them This statement of the hypocrites is an attempt to strengthen relations with the disbelievers, because they pretend to be friends with both parties so that they will be safe from their harm, due to their weak faith and lack of certainty. Allah said,

(Allah will judge between you (all) on the Day of Resurrection) meaning, by what He knows about you, O hypocrites. Therefore, do not be deceived by being shaded under the protection of Islamic Law in this life, which is such only out of Allah's wisdom. Surely, on the Day of Resurrection, your pretending shall not benefit you, because on that Day, the secrets of the souls will be disclosed and the contents of the hearts will be collected. Allah said,

(And never will Allah grant to the disbelievers a way (to triumph) over the believers). `Abdur-Razzaq recorded that Yasi` Al-Kindi said, "A man came to `Ali bin Abi Talib and said, `What about this Ayah,

(And never will Allah grant to the disbelievers a way (to triumph) over the believers.) `Ali said, `Come closer, come closer. Allah will judge between you on the Day of Resurrection, and He will not grant victory for the disbelievers over the believers.' " Ibn Jurayj recorded that `Ata' Al-Khurasani said that Ibn `Abbas said that,

(And never will Allah grant to the disbelievers a way (to triumph) over the believers.) "Will occur on the Day of Resurrection." As-Suddi recorded that Abu Malik Al-Ashja`i said that it occurs on the Day of Resurrection. As-Suddi said that "way" means, proof. It is possible that the meaning of, `and never will Allah grant to the disbelievers a way (to triumph) over the believers', is in this life by being unable to exterminate the believers completely, although they sometimes gain victory over some Muslims. However, the Final Triumph will be for the believers in this life and the Hereafter. Allah said,

(Verily, We will indeed make victorious Our Messengers and those who believe in the worldly life) This provides a rebuttal to the wishes of the hypocrites for the destruction of the believers, and their loyalty to the disbelievers, fearing for themselves if they are victorious.

Surah: 4 Ayah: 142 & Ayah: 143

﴿ إِنَّ ٱلْمُنَـٰفِقِينَ يُخَـٰدِعُونَ ٱللَّهَ وَهُوَ خَـٰدِعُهُمْ وَإِذَا قَامُوٓاْ إِلَى ٱلصَّلَوٰةِ قَامُواْ كُسَالَىٰ يُرَآءُونَ ٱلنَّاسَ وَلَا يَذْكُرُونَ ٱللَّهَ إِلَّا قَلِيلًا ۝ ﴾

142. Verily, the hypocrites seek to deceive Allâh, but it is He Who deceives them. And when they stand up for As-Salât (the prayer), they stand with laziness and to be seen of men, and they do not remember Allâh but little.

﴿ مُّذَبْذَبِينَ بَيْنَ ذَٰلِكَ لَآ إِلَىٰ هَـٰٓؤُلَآءِ وَلَآ إِلَىٰ هَـٰٓؤُلَآءِ ۚ وَمَن يُضْلِلِ ٱللَّهُ فَلَن تَجِدَ لَهُۥ سَبِيلًا ۝ ﴾

143. (They are) swaying between this and that, belonging neither to these nor to those; and he whom Allâh sends astray, you will not find for him a way (to the truth - Islâm).

Transliteration

142. Inna almunafiqeena yukhadiAAoona Allaha wahuwa khadiAAuhum wa-itha qamoo ila alssalati qamoo kusala yuraoona alnnasa wala yathkuroona Allaha illa

Chapter 4: An-Nisaa (The Women), Verses 024-147

qaleelan   143. Muthabthabeena bayna thalika la ila haola-i wala ila haola-i waman yudlili Allahu falan tajida lahu sabeelan

Tafsir Ibn Kathir

The Hypocrites Try to Deceive Allah and Sway Between Believers and Disbelievers

In the beginning of Surat Al-Baqarah (2), we mentioned Allah's statement,

(They (think to) deceive Allah and those who believe). Here, Allah states,

(Verily, the hypocrites seek to deceive Allah, but it is He Who deceives them.) There is no doubt that Allah can never be deceived, for He has perfect knowledge of the secrets and what the hearts conceal. However, the hypocrites, due to their ignorance, scarce knowledge and weak minds, think that since they were successful in deceiving people, using Islamic Law as a cover of safety for themselves, they will acquire the same status with Allah on the Day of Resurrection and deceive Him too. Allah states that on that Day, the hypocrites will swear to Him that they were on the path of righteousness and correctness thinking that such statement will benefit them with Allah. For instance, Allah said,

(On the Day when Allah will resurrect them all together; then they will swear to Him as they swear to you) Allah's statement,

(but it is He Who deceives them) means, He lures them further into injustice and misguidance. He also prevents them from reaching the truth in this life and on the Day of Resurrection. Allah said,

(On the Day when the hypocrites - men and women - will say to the believers: "Wait for us! Let us get something from your light!" It will be said: "Go back to your rear! Then seek a light!") until,

(And worst indeed is that destination). A Hadith states;

«مَنْ سَمَّعَ سَمَّعَ اللهُ بِهِ، وَمَنْ رَاءَى رَاءَى اللهُ بِهِ»

(Whoever wants to be heard of, Allah will make him heard of, and whoever wants to be seen, Allah will show him.) Allah's statement,

(And when they stand up for Salah, they stand with laziness). This is the characteristic of the hypocrites with the most honored, best and righteous act of worship, the prayer. When they stand for prayer, they stand in laziness because they neither truly intend to perform it nor do they believe in it, have humility in it, or understand it. This is the description of their outward attitude! As for their hearts, Allah said,

(to be seen of men) meaning, they do not have sincerity when worshipping Allah. Rather, they show off to people so that they gain closeness to them. They are often absent from the prayers that they can hide away from, such as the `Isha' prayer and the Dawn prayer that are prayed in darkness. In the Two Sahihs, it is recorded that the Messenger of Allah said,

«أَثْقَلُ الصَّلَاةِ عَلَى الْمُنَافِقِينَ صَلَاةُ الْعِشَاءِ وَصَلَاةُ الْفَجْرِ، وَلَوْ يَعْلَمُونَ مَا فِيهِمَا لَأَتَوْهُمَا وَلَوْ حَبْوًا، وَلَقَدْ هَمَمْتُ أَنْ آمُرَ بِالصَّلَاةِ فَتُقَامُ، ثُمَّ آمُرَ رَجُلًا فَيُصَلِّيَ بِالنَّاسِ، ثُمَّ أَنْطَلِقَ مَعِيَ بِرِجَالٍ مَعَهُمْ حُزَمٌ مِنْ حَطَبٍ، إِلَى قَوْمٍ لَا يَشْهَدُونَ الصَّلَاةَ، فَأُحَرِّقَ عَلَيْهِمْ بُيُوتَهُمْ بِالنَّارِ»

(The heaviest prayers on the hypocrites are the `Isha' and Dawn prayers. If they know their rewards, they will attend them even if they have to crawl. I was about to order someone to pronounce the Adhan for the prayer, then order someone to lead the prayer for the people, then order some men to collect fire-wood (fuel); then I would burn the houses around men who did not attend the (compulsory congregational) prayer.) In another narration, the Prophet said,

«وَالَّذِي نَفْسِي بِيَدِهِ، لَوْ عَلِمَ أَحَدُهُمْ أَنَّهُ يَجِدُ عَرْقًا سَمِينًا أَوْ مِرْمَاتَيْنِ حَسَنَتَيْنِ، لَشَهِدَ الصَّلَاةَ، وَلَوْلَا مَا فِي الْبُيُوتِ مِنَ النِّسَاءِ وَالذُّرِّيَّةِ لَحَرَّقْتُ عَلَيْهِمْ بُيُوتَهُمْ بِالنَّارِ»

(By Him, in Whose Hand my soul is, if anyone of them had known that he would get a bone covered with good meat or two (small) pieces of meat between two ribs, he would have turned up for the prayer, and had it not been that the houses have women and children in them, I would burn their homes around them.) Allah's statement,

(And they do not remember Allah but little) means, during the prayer they do not feel humbleness or pay attention to what they are reciting. Rather, during their prayer, they are inattentive, jesting and avoid the good that they are meant to receive from prayer. Imam Malik reported that Al-`Ala' bin `Abdur-Rahman said that Anas bin Malik said that the Messenger of Allah said,

«تِلْكَ صَلَاةُ الْمُنَافِقِ، تِلْكَ صَلَاةُ الْمُنَافِقِ، تِلْكَ صَلَاةُ الْمُنَافِقِ، يَجْلِسُ يَرْقُبُ الشَّمْسَ، حَتَّى إِذَا كَانَتْ بَيْنَ قَرْنَيِ الشَّيْطَانِ، قَامَ فَنَقَرَ أَرْبَعًا، لَا يَذْكُرُ اللَّهَ فِيهَا إِلَّا قَلِيلًا»

(This is the prayer of the hypocrite, this is the prayer of the hypocrite, this is the prayer of the hypocrite. He sits watching the sun until when it goes down between the two horns of the devil, he stands up pecks out four Rak`ahs (for `Asr) without remembering Allah during them except little.) Muslim, At-Tirmidhi and An-Nasa'i also recorded it. At-Tirmidhi said "Hasan Sahih". Allah's statement,

((They are) swaying between this and that, belonging neither to these) means that the hypocrites are swaying between faith and disbelief. So they are neither with believers inwardly or outwardly nor with disbelievers inwardly or outwardly. Rather, they are with the believers outwardly and with the disbelievers inwardly. Some of them would suffer fits of doubt, leaning towards these sometimes and towards those sometimes,

(Whenever it flashes for them, they walk therein, and when darkness covers them, they stand still). Mujahid said;

((They are) swaying between this and that, belonging neither to these) "The Companions of Muhammad ,

(nor to those): the Jews." Ibn Jarir recorded that Ibn `Umar said that the Prophet said,

«مَثَلُ الْمُنَافِقِ كَمَثَلِ الشَّاةِ الْعَائِرَةِ بَيْنَ الْغَنَمَيْنِ، تَعِيرُ إلى هَذِهِ مَرَّةً، وَإلَى هَذِهِ مَرَّةً، وَلَا تَدْرِي أَيَّتَهُمَا تَتْبَع»

(The example of the hypocrite is the example of the sheep wandering between two herds, sometimes she goes to one of them, and sometimes the other, confused over whom she should follow.) Muslim also recorded it. This is why Allah said afterwards,

(and he whom Allah sends astray, you will not find for him a way.) meaning, whomever He leads astray from the guidance,

(For him you will find no Wali (guiding friend) to lead him (to the right path)) because,

(Whomsoever Allah sends astray, none can guide him). So the hypocrites whom Allah has led astray from the paths of safety will never find a guide to direct them, nor someone to save them. There is none who can resist Allah's decision, and He is not asked about what He does, while they all will be asked.

Surah: 4 Ayah: 144, Ayah: 145, Ayah: 146 & Ayah: 147

﴿ يَٰٓأَيُّهَا ٱلَّذِينَ ءَامَنُوا۟ لَا تَتَّخِذُوا۟ ٱلْكَٰفِرِينَ أَوْلِيَآءَ مِن دُونِ ٱلْمُؤْمِنِينَ أَتُرِيدُونَ أَن تَجْعَلُوا۟ لِلَّهِ عَلَيْكُمْ سُلْطَٰنًا مُّبِينًا ﴾

144. O you who believe! Take not for Auliyâ' (protectors or helpers or friends) disbelievers instead of believers. Do you wish to offer Allâh a manifest proof against yourselves?

﴿إِنَّ ٱلْمُنَـٰفِقِينَ فِى ٱلدَّرْكِ ٱلْأَسْفَلِ مِنَ ٱلنَّارِ وَلَن تَجِدَ لَهُمْ نَصِيرًا﴾

145. Verily, the hypocrites will be in the lowest depth (grade) of the Fire; no helper will you find for them.

﴿إِلَّا ٱلَّذِينَ تَابُوا۟ وَأَصْلَحُوا۟ وَٱعْتَصَمُوا۟ بِٱللَّهِ وَأَخْلَصُوا۟ دِينَهُمْ لِلَّهِ فَأُو۟لَـٰٓئِكَ مَعَ ٱلْمُؤْمِنِينَ وَسَوْفَ يُؤْتِ ٱللَّهُ ٱلْمُؤْمِنِينَ أَجْرًا عَظِيمًا﴾

146. Except those who repent (from hypocrisy), do righteous good deeds, hold fast to Allâh, and purify their religion for Allâh (by worshipping none but Allâh, and do good for Allâh's sake only, not to show-off), then they will be with the believers. And Allâh will grant the believers a great reward.

﴿مَّا يَفْعَلُ ٱللَّهُ بِعَذَابِكُمْ إِن شَكَرْتُمْ وَءَامَنتُمْ وَكَانَ ٱللَّهُ شَاكِرًا عَلِيمًا﴾

147. Why should Allâh punish you if you have thanked (Him) and have believed in Him. And Allâh is Ever All-Appreciative (of good), All-Knowing.

Transliteration

144. Ya ayyuha allatheena amanoo la tattakhithoo alkafireena awliyaa min dooni almu/mineena atureedoona an tajAAaloo lillahi AAalaykum sultanan mubeenan 145. Inna almunafiqeena fee alddarki al-asfali mina alnnari walan tajida lahum naseeran 146. Illa allatheena taboo waaslahoo waiAAtasamoo biAllahi waakhlasoo deenahum lillahi faola-ika maAAa almu/mineena wasawfa yu/ti Allahu almu/mineena ajran AAatheeman 147. Ma yafAAalu Allahu biAAathabikum in shakartum waamantum wakana Allahu shakiran AAaleeman

Tafsir Ibn Kathir

The Prohibition of Wilayah with the Disbelievers

Allah forbids His believing servants from taking the disbelievers as friends instead of the believers. This includes being friends and associates of the disbelievers, advising them, being intimate with them and exposing the secrets of the believers to them. In another Ayah, Allah said,

(Let not the believers take the disbelievers as friends instead of the believers, and whoever does that, will never be helped by Allah in any way, except if you indeed fear a danger from them. And Allah warns you against Himself). meaning, He warns you against His punishment if you fall into what He has prohibited. This is why Allah said here,

Chapter 4: An-Nisaa (The Women), Verses 024-147

(Do you wish to offer Allah a manifest Sultan against yourselves) meaning, proof against you that warrants receiving His torment. Ibn Abi Hatim narrated that Ibn `Abbas commented;

(manifest Sultan), "The word Sultan in the Qur'an means proof. " There is an authentic chain of narration for this statement, which is also the saying of Mujahid, `Ikrimah, Sa`id bin Jubayr, Muhammad bin Ka`b Al-Qurazi, Ad-Dahhak, As-Suddi and An-Nadr bin `Arabi.

The Hypocrites and the Friends of Disbelievers are in the Lowest Depth of the Fire, Unless they Repent

Allah then states that,

(Verily, the hypocrites will be in the lowest depths of the Fire;) on the Day of Resurrection due to their tremendous Kufr. Al-Walibi (`Ali bin Abi Talhah) said that Ibn `Abbas said,

(in the lowest depths (grade) of the Fire;) means, in the bottom of the Fire. Other scholars said that the Fire has ever lower depths just as Paradise had ever higher grades. Ibn Jarir recorded that `Abdullah bin Mas`ud said that,

(Verily, the hypocrites will be in the lowest depths (grade) of the Fire), "Inside coffins of Fire that surround them, for they are closed and sealed in them." Ibn Abi Hatim recorded that when Ibn Mas`ud was asked about the hypocrites, he said, "They will be placed in coffins made of fire and they will be closed in them in the lowest depth of the Fire."

(no helper will you find for them.) to save them from their misery and painful torment. Allah then states that whoever among the hypocrites repents in this life, Allah will accept his repentance and sorrow, if his repentance were sincere and he then follows it by performing righteous deeds, all the while depending on his Lord. Allah said, a

(Except those who repent (from hypocrisy), do righteous good deeds, depend on Allah, and purify their religion for Allah) replacing showing off with sincerity, so that their good deeds will benefit them, even if they were minute.

(then they will be with the believers.) on the Day of Resurrection,

(And Allah will grant to the believers a great reward.) Allah then states that He is too Rich to need anyone and that He only punishes the servants because of their sins,

(Why should Allah punish you if you have thanked (Him) and have believed in Him.) by correcting your actions and having faith in Allah and His Messenger ,

(And Allah is Ever All-Appreciative (of good), All-Knowing.) Allah appreciates those who appreciate Him, and has knowledge of those whose hearts believe in Him, and He will give them perfect reward.

www.ingramcontent.com/pod-product-compliance
Lightning Source LLC
Chambersburg PA
CBHW081112080526
44587CB00021B/3555